# CHURCH

The Human Story of God

# CHURCH

## The Human Story of God

*Edward Schillebeeckx*

CROSSROAD • NEW YORK

1994

The Crossroad Publishing Company
370 Lexington Avenue, New York, NY 10017

Translated by John Bowden from the Dutch
*Mensen als verhaal van God*, published 1989 by Uitgeverij H.Nelissen, Baarn,
reprinted with corrections 1990.

© Uitgeverij H.Nelissen 1989

Translation © 1990 by The Crossroad Publishing Company

Printed in the United States of America

*Library of Congress Cataloging-in-Publication Data*

Schillebeeckx, Edward, 1914–
   [Mensen als verhaal van God. English]
   Church : the human story of God / by Edward Schillebeeckx ;
[translated by John Bowden from the Dutch].
     p.  cm.
   Translation of : Mensen als verhaal van God.
   Includes bibliographical references and index.
   ISBN 0-8245-1050-X; 0-8245-1372-X (pbk.)
   1. Church.  2. Catholic Church—Doctrines.  I. Title.
BX1746.S2913    1990
262—dc20
                                       90-36343
                                          CIP

'Human beings are the evidence for the existence of God'
(Heinrich Böll)

'As I brought Israel out of Egypt, so I brought the Philistines
from Caphtor, and Aram from Kir' (Amos 9.7)

# Contents

*Chapter 4*

# Towards Democratic Rule of the Church as a Community of God 187

# Foreword

A small boy is said once to have remarked, 'People are the words with which God tells his story.' His remark is the theme of this book.

This book is about the life of men and women and their bond with God as God has become visible above all in Jesus of Nazareth, confessed as the Christ by the Christian churches – which are increasingly aware that they live in a secular world amidst other religions.

The book was originally intended to be an *ecclesiological third part* of the trilogy I announced some time ago. It was to be the completion of *Jesus* (1974, English translation 1979) and *Christ* (1977, English translation 1980). And so it is, but not from the perspective that I originally planned.

For much has changed since the decade between 1970 and 1980, above all in the Roman Catholic church. Delight in belonging to this church, a delight which increased greatly during the Second Vatican Council and the years immediately following, has been sorely tested over the last decade. After a good deal of study and editorial work, this situation compelled me to make quite considerable changes to my original plan for this book. I came to the conclusion that it was better to investigate the heart of the gospel and the Christian religion, its distinctive and unique features, than in a period of church polarization to be directly concerned with what are really secondary, domestic church problems relating to the very content of the gospel faith and the question of what Christians should be doing in this world. For is it not by the heart of the gospel message that any ecclesiology, too, can and must be measured?

I am aware that if this view of the heart of the gospel and Christianity (which is never generally available, though we can certainly point to it) is not given an appropriate institutional form in structures guaranteeed by church law, which breathe and provide room to breathe (and all the indications are that for the moment this is not the case), edifying theology and loyal theological criticism within the church, including theological criticism, remain barren. Those engaged in this activity must then stand by powerless and watch the exclusion of their legitimate but modest influence on church events and on the possibility of a new church movement in keeping with the gospel, of which we and many others boldly dreamed in the 1960s. During the 1970s and above all during the 1980s, precisely those elements in Vatican II which were 'new' in comparison to the post-Tridentine life of the church and its ecclesiology have not been given any consistent institutional structures by the official church. On the contrary, some church structures prescribed by the new Codex are quite alien to the deepest intentions of Vatican II.

Moreover, sociologically speaking, regardless of whether one is inclined towards or against the institution, it is an undeniable fact that in a world church, from the moment when the freedom and values of the gospel are no longer protected and supported by institutional structures, above all the so-called ordinary believers find themselves at a loss; they are struck dumb, and with them a great many pastors and theologians. It was the conciliar assembly of the church itself which on a large scale, after sensitive concessions to a minority which was powerful in church politics but theologically one-sided (fixated on Trent and Vatican I), promised its believers, and explicitly also the theologians among them, Christian freedom within the open space of the binding gospel of Jesus Christ. And when this Christian freedom recognized by the council was not subsequently guaranteed and protected by church law, this promise became an empty gesture, without any evangelical influence on our history. Then the breath of the council was cut off and its spirit, the Holy Spirit, was extinguished. Then, by virtue of various concerns (which were often matters of church politics), church hierarchies achieved an uncontrolled power over men and women of God, 'God's people on the way', who had been put under tutelage.

Nevertheless, even in such painful circumstances, the theologian continues to work on consistently, also for the sake of ecumenism. Here he or she is encouraged by much of what is growing throughout the grassroots of the church as a result of Vatican II: an unprecedented and authentic flourishing of the gospel. No one can take this hope from me, and a great many other theologians feel encouraged by it. For never before have women and men, the so-called laity, been so committed to the work of the local church for the church and the world as a whole. This tough perseverance in pure Christian trust at the same time directs us to other choices in our theological investigation. For while this hope is indeed based on a church directed towards God, a community 'of God', this church is a church of men and women bound to God which also has a critical presence in solidarity with men and women 'in the world', with their problems, great and small, and their 'secular', authentically human and inhuman history. What many believers are abandoning is the 'supernaturalist' church which is alien to the world, the church of the period between Trent and the Second Vatican Council. They are leaving this church, a triumphalistic, legalistic and clerical church, which claims down to details to be the irrefutable instrument of God's will, but which distorts the truth in this statement by its (tacit) denial of all the often very ambiguous historical mediations in its statements and actions as a church: as if the church were a spotless gift from heaven, beyond all criticism, quite apart from its situation in the world. Here some people think that for example they can and must identify all official actions of the church with God's superabundant grace, above criticism although not always comprehensible to men and women. But have we not heard in the New Testament book of Revelation the constant rebuke to the seven churches of the ecumene: 'I have against you...'? Did we not hear the same warning from Vatican II, '*Ecclesia semper purificanda*', the church must constantly purify itself? These very texts express a real love of the church: authentic belief, as we experience this from the gospel, and not an oppressive love which is concerned only with maintaining an institution which has grown up through history.

All this has produced a completely different book from my PC-pen than I had planned ten years ago. In it I want to offer what through my own reflection I have made my own as a liberating theology from and thanks to the great Christian tradition. I offer it as nurture for the faith of those who are at work in the base communities, to those who suffer and love there. I hope that among my readers there will be some of those in authority in the church, who will also listen to the confession of faith of a theologian who all his life did nothing but seek what God can mean for men and women, tentatively and stammeringly. To get to know that, one has to go and stand alongside these men and women: their lives, they themselves, are the story of God in our midst. Thus the stories of the Old and New Testaments resound in the lives of men and women today. That happens again and again, down the centuries. In this way we are listening to the gospel of yesterday, today and tomorrow.

Of course I have been influenced by criticisms that the first two volumes of this trilogy have been hard to read. Like all researchers, theologians, too, often talk in jargon. We get involved, and find so many facets to polish and clarify theologically that our language becomes too compact and therefore difficult. But I have also paid attention to my readers, and so I have spent a good deal of time making this third part readable. That, along with the handicaps of my own old age, which are already beginning, is another reason why this book has taken so long in coming.

But in no way do I want to give up the deep and solid attention that is called for in the theological investigation of the mystery of the reciprocal relationship between the living God and the men and women who live in and through him – God's story in human history – in favour of a fluent but in that case perhaps also a superficial reading of this work.

So I hope that the book will be useful to many people. As far as I am concerned, it is a Christian confession of faith of a consistently rational theologian, who is conscious of standing in the great Catholic tradition on the basis of which he may be able to, indeed has to, say something – *as an offer* – to his fellow men and women.

*Nijmegen, on the Feast of St Dominic,*
*8 August 1989*                                   Edward Schillebeeckx OP

# A Guide to the Book

In the 'universal' Christian council of 1442, held in Florence-Ferrara, the council fathers arrived at a declaration which is in a way understandable for that time, but is bewildering to us today:

> The holy church of Rome firmly believes, confesses and proclaims that no one – not just the heathen but also the Jews, heretics and schismatics – outside the Catholic church can have a part in eternal life, but that they will go to the hell fire 'that is prepared for the devil and his angels' (Matt.25.41) unless they allow themselves to be received into the church before their life's end.[1]

Few Catholics would still endorse this solemn judgment, although for centuries Catholics have warmly confessed this exclusivism and acted accordingly, even with armed force.

Not so much since, but at any rate at the Second Vatican Council, by contrast and in just as official a way as before (apart from later conservative developments), we hear a very different voice:

> Those who through no fault of their own do not know the Gospel of Christ or his church, but who nevertheless seek God with a sincere heart, and, moved by grace, try in their actions to do his will as they know it through the dictates of their conscience – those too may achieve eternal salvation.[2]

Centuries of human tragedy lie between these two official church-historical statements which, at least literally, are diametrically opposed – although there are always theologians who are able to reconcile the two statements in the abstract in an unhistorical way with some so-called hermeneutical acrobatics. We must certainly note that even Vatican II does not make it clear what 'seek God' really means. Is it being explicitly in search of God, or giving a glass of water from one's own almost empty water flask to someone in great need who is gasping for breath (Matt.25.31-46)?

In this book I am certainly not going to outline the history of the old adage 'no salvation outside the church'. Enough theologically responsible literature can be found on that. I am just putting the two church-theological statements side by side above all as a challenge to all those who are fond of deliberately calling themselves 'obedient believers' and who thus (whether intentionally or not) disqualify their Christian or Catholic fellow-believers. I myself believe that the church has and indeed needs a _magisterial_, i.e. teaching, function and that believers need to take account of this. But in that case account must also be taken in our attitude as believers of the historical facts that I have just indicated in the teaching authority in the church – and I have chosen one instance from many – if we are not to lapse into idolatry as the absolutizing of the relative.

Present-day people live in quite a different time, with a different sense of life, with other pictures of human beings and the world. They move in an open world with contacts not only with all the world religions but also with people who by their own statement (and we must take this statement seriously) live, without any religion, an ordinary secular or secularized life and who moreover are hardly distinguishable from Christians, dedicating themselves in all kinds of ways to the individual and social humanity of men and women. In this situation the earlier exclusivist attitude in both society and church, the insistent determination to be right, is difficult for us to understand. But in the past all parties interpreted their sense of being right in the same way.

Being human is just a process of historical growth. It took a gradual process of maturing in the human consciousness and above all historical facts like wars of religion, wars between Christians, the persecution of Jews, Christians and Muslims, attacks on human rights, the events of the Enlightenment and the French Revolution to make people look at their attitude to life in a different way. No binding truth can underlie inhuman tyranny and strife. Much that was once generally taken for granted has come to grief on this.

It is difficult for us to pass judgment on people living in a pre-critical time. Nor shall I do that. But that does not relieve us now of our post-critical responsibility, especially in a time in which we have gone through the shame, criticism and scorn of the ages and in a converted 'second innocence' can once again walk with God in the garden as with a familiar Friend.

I do not want to turn the old adage round completely and compose another to set against it: _extra mundum nulla salus_, outside the world there is no salvation (but see below). Former one-sidedness is not removed by modern accents which are perhaps just as one-sided. Are we better than former generations? 'Our modern world' which thinks that the time of churches and religions is past has perhaps brought more disaster to humankind in barely two centuries of secularization than the seventeen so-called 'dark' church centuries before it. I once heard that more people are living at present than have ever died. If that is true (and I do not know that it is), I have to point out that now, at least in our present world, a small portion of humankind, especially 'the powerful of this world', is doing fundamental injustice to the majority of humankind and oppressing it more than ever. The present and the past should not throw stones at one another!

Nevertheless, or more precisely on the basis of the past and the present, in this book I want to put the church 'in its place' and at the same time give it 'the place which is its due'. The church never exists for its own sake, although it has often forgotten this (as have many religions). For that very reason, in this 'ecclesiological' book I shall not be saying too much directly about the church. We need a bit of *negative ecclesiology*, church theology in a minor key, in order to do away with the centuries-long ecclesiocentrism of the empirical phenomenon of 'Christian religion': for the sake of God, for the sake of Jesus the Christ and for the sake of humankind. And these three – God, Jesus Christ and humankind – are one in the sense that they may never be set over against one another or made into rivals.

Even sin hurts God only in his creatures: in men and women and also in the world of creatures, in animals and plants, in their and our natural environment, in our society, in our hearts, our inwardness and our solidarity with our fellow human beings. To hurt and damage this world is, from a theological perspective, a sin against the Creator of heaven and earth, against the one whom, under whatever name, many people call God: the Mystery that has a passion for the 'whole-ness' of nature however much this name is dishonoured and defiled by the behaviour of those who in many different religions believe in God.

# CHAPTER 1

# World History and Salvation History, History of Revelation and History of Suffering

## 1. Introduction: who or what brings human beings salvation and liberation?

In the beginning of modern times, to be precise in 1492, Giovanni Pico della Mirandola announced in an almost prophetic way the coming modern age in which human beings would take their fate into their own hands through science and technology. He did so in a modern rewriting of the creation story from the book of Genesis. He wrote:

> God creates pleasure in man as a being that has no clearly discernible image. God put him in the midst of the world and said to him: We have given you no particular dwelling, no face of your own, no special gift of one kind or another, O Adam (= man), so that you can have and possess any dwelling you like, any face you like and all the gifts that you could desire, also in accordance with your will and your own opinion. The nature of other beings is determined by the laws laid down by us and they are kept within bounds by these laws. However, you (man) are not restrained by any boundary that you may not pass, but you shall determine your own nature yourself, in accordance with your own free will, and I have put your fate in your own hands. We have created you as neither a heavenly nor an earthly being, as neither mortal nor immortal; rather, as your own self, wholly free and working as a sculptor and poet for your own honour, you shall give yourself that form in which you want to live.[1]

With this quotation from the eve of modern times, even before the rise of modern science and technology, this philosopher of culture clarified the anthropological condition for the possibility of these modern sciences and technology: man becomes the creative subject of all that happens in a cosmically conditioned but religiously and cosmically 'disenchanted world'.

However, after so many centuries of science and technology, during the last decades to our detriment and shame, we have had to learn how this arbitrary, unrestrained self-fulfilment in the West has failed to bring men and women either personal or socio-political salvation. Moreover, we have learned that our unrestrained economic expansion, based on a nineteenth-century myth of progress, has brushed aside men and women from other parts of the world[2] and also threatens our natural environment to such a degree that humankind as a whole is endangered by it. At present the project of the total liberation of human beings by human beings seems to be the greatest threat to all humankind. Nowadays 'Western modernity' is again calling in a special way for salvation and liberation: for redemption precisely from those dark powers which modern men and women have themselves called to life. The demonic in our culture and society has adopted a different name and content from the one it had in the world of antiquity and the Middle Ages, but it is no less real and just as threatening. Here I am in no way criticizing science, technology and industrialization, but rather those in whose hands these powers lie and who prefer to use these powers for their own personal, national and continental profit – and so much the worse for those who do not have the good fortune to live in a prosperous country or for those who at best are tolerated in it as immigrant workers.

We may take it to be an irony of history that the cultural forces that we have introduced since the seventeenth century as the historical liberators of humankind, namely science and technology, which were to free us from all that religion had not been able to free humankind – hunger, poverty, tyranny, war and historical fate – have at present not only further increased this hunger and poverty and brought to life the possibility of a nuclear war but – in human hands – form the greatest threat to our future. 'Knowledge is power' was already a saying of Francis Bacon. But our control of nature has led to the beginnings of an attack on the basic principles of life; our unrestrained economic growth threatens our human survival; the spiral of nuclear rearmament grows increasingly higher above our heads; control over and manipulation of genetic and psychological structures evoke threatening pictures of the future in human hands. It is not that science or technology are wrong; the problem lies with human beings themselves and the way in which they deal with science and technology, their estimation of science and technology. What are we doing with accurate knowledge? If we absolutize the means and garb these in a new modern sacrality and impregnability, then rather than representing liberation, they become a threat to human beings and society.

The sciences themselves are a child of their time, and down to their own internal autonomy, rightly acquired in a battle against patronizing religious traditions, they reflect the sicknesses, the relativity and the blindspots of their time. Therefore science is no more a purely objective form of knowledge than other forms of knowledge; moreover it does not have any credentials on the basis of which it may at least legitimately perform this dominant role that it in fact possesses in our Western society as a monopoly, and does so at the expense of many other forms of non-scientific cognitive approaches to reality. The applied sciences, too, are an instrument of the human will, and as a result they are also caught in the web in which the human will can be entangled. Knowledge is power, but power in the hands of an unliberated freedom, of the lust for power, personal or collective egotism and personal security, is essentially the road to ruin.

It is a fact that science and technology have not made human beings holier or wiser. Certainly they have made them more knowledgeable, and in itself this is a good thing. Science and technology can work wonders if they are put to the service of other people's freedom and finally to that of human solidarity generally. But in reality the sciences function as the instrument of human power, of rule over nature, power over society, power over human beings, both female and male. Science is the key to the military might of nations; science is the secret of their economic and social prosperity, in fact often to the detriment of others. Faith in verifiable knowledge and technical know-how as the only instrument for overcoming human disaster is a dominant factor in our present-day cultural world, regardless of whether we look to the north or the south, the west or the east.

Already from the seventeenth century, but above all since the eighteenth century, science seemed to announce the end of all historical religions: this was heedlessly thought to be a phase of childish ignorance in human history. Now that we are approaching the year 2000, it is precisely science and technology which, if the question of human salvation still makes any sense at all, presses 'the religious question' on us more urgently than ever. Scientific theories are now in search of the fundamental condition of the possibility of science itself, and this lies outside or beyond all the sciences. It is not the sciences and technology which make us anxious, but their non-scientific and absolute claims to offer salvation. We arrive at the insight that human, scientific and technological creativity contains the possibility of self-destruction. Science and technology, the once celebrated liberators of humankind, have subjected human beings to a new kind of socially and historically oppressive fate.

There is deep historical irony here when we see how the East is succumbing to the charms of Western science and technology to ensure its material prosperity, while the West is looking to the East for its lost inwardness. Does our human creativity itself threaten the meaning of our history? Is 'the guardian of creation' (Gen.2.15; 1.28) also its betrayer? Or is a finite being ever to be understood and liberated on its own terms? Does not the relationship to 'the transcendent' (he? she? it?) which men and women experience and live out belong with the unfathomable ground of our human creativity and therefore with the deepest and ultimate inspiration of all humanism?

One of the tasks of theology is to safeguard belief in and this hope for a liberating, saving power which loves men and women and which will overcome this evil. Theology therefore opposes any kind of doom thinking, though theologians, like everyone else, are at the same time convinced that we live in a bewildering mixture of meaning and meaninglessness.

However, if religion is allowed to speak an irreplaceable word of its own here, it will need to be a religion which is 'related to the world', a religion which on the basis of belief in a liberating God is concerned for humankind and its humanity in a social and historical context. Is there another humanism which is not cruel and is more universal than the love of God for humankind: of a God concerned for humankind, who wants 'people of God' who are also themselves concerned for humankind? At all events, this is the deepest impulse which comes from is called the Jewish and Christian experiential tradition, despite its empirical manifestations, which often contradict these, its own impulses.

If religions and churches want to continue to proclaim this 'eschatological utopia', they must first acknowledge that they have often hidden, spat upon and even mutilated the face of God's humanity and his care for all his creatures, down to the least of them. Where it is not God himself, but religion, science or some worldly power that is made absolute, not only human beings but also the 'image of God' are sullied: the *ecce homo* on the cross, and on the many crosses which have been erected and continue to be erected, and also the *ecce natura* as the polluted world of creation – in animals and plants and the basic elements of life.

So in this introductory chapter I want first to locate the non-ideological, theological place of religions and churches in our human history, as the ground-plan for this whole book.

# 2. 'No salvation outside the world'

## I    The experience of radical contrast in our human history

I now want to radicalize what I have previously, indeed repeatedly, called important human experiences, namely negative experiences of contrast: they form a basic human experience which as such I regard as being a pre-religious experience and thus a basic experience accessible to all human beings, namely that of a 'no' to the world as it is. This has nothing to do with dualism or opposition between a good world and a bad world in the Hellenistic sense (though we should also reconsider this dualism on the basis of the deeper human experiences of the time). In any case, we have to do with this world of ours, and that worries us. What we experience as reality, what we also see and hear of this reality daily through television and other mass media, is evidently not 'in order'; there is something fundamentally wrong. This reality is full of contradictions. So the human experience of suffering and evil, of oppression and unhappiness, is the basis and source of a fundamental 'no' that men and women say to their actual situation of being-in-this-world. This experience is also more certain, more evident than any verifiable or falsifiable 'knowledge' that philosophy and the sciences can offer us. Indignation (which is certainly not a scientific term) seems to be a basic experience of our life in this world. So, too, is our world, unless we go through it blindly: keen only on consumption, bustle and oblivion... or power.

Without doubt there is also much goodness and beauty, much to be enjoyed in this world. There even seems to be more joy and song among the oppressed than among the oppressors. But all these fragments of goodness, beauty and meaning are constantly contradicted and crushed by evil and hatred, by suffering, whether blatant or dull, by the misuse of power and terror. This contradiction, which is so characteristic of our world, seems to balance out evil and good. Cynics also see it that way. For those who are not cynics, this attitude is anything but a sign of decadence, which no longer finds anything worth living or dying for. Despite all their wretchedness, human beings are too proud to regard evil as being on an equal footing with good.

In the meantime, however, in our world there is that constantly enigmatic mixture of good and evil, of meaning and meaninglessness. We do not know from history which will get the upper hand, nor whether, on the basis of what actually happens, there will even be a last word. History as such can come to grief.

Nevertheless, a positive element in this fundamental experience of contrast, the second element in this basic experience, is this human indignation, which cannot be made light of. There are ethics here, and perhaps even more. (I myself see here what in the Catholic tradition of faith has been called 'natural theology', although that was set in a rather different context.) This human inability to give in to the situation offers an illuminating perspective. It discloses an openness to another situation which has the right to our affirmative 'yes'. One can call it a consensus with 'the unknown', the content of which cannot even be defined in a positive way: a better, other world, which in fact does not yet exist anywhere. Or, to put it in yet another way, the mere assumption of the possibility of improving our world: openness to the unknown and the better.

The fundamental human 'no' to evil therefore discloses an unfulfilled and thus 'open yes' which is as intractable as the human 'no', indeed even stronger, because the 'open yes' is the basis of that opposition and makes it possible. Moreover, from time to time, there are fragmentary but real experiences of meaning and happiness on both a smaller and a larger scale, which constantly keep nurturing, establishing and sustaining the 'open yes'. Both believers and agnostics come together in this experience. That is also a rational basis for solidarity between all people and for common commitment to a better world with a human face.

Those who believe in God fill out the one two-sided basic experience in religious terms. The 'open yes' then takes on a more precise direction. Its origin is not so much, or at least not directly, the transcendence of the divine (which is inexpressible and anonymous and cannot be put into words) as (at least for Christians) the recognizable human face of this transcendence which has appeared among us in the man Jesus, confessed as Christ and Son of God. So for Christians the fundamental muttering of humanity turns into a well-founded hope. Something of a sigh of mercy, of compassion, is hidden in the deepest depths of reality... and in it believers hear the name of God. That is how the Christian story goes. For Christians, the experience of contrast, with its inherent opposition to injustice and its perspective on something better, becomes that in which the unity of history comes about *as God's gift.*

## II  The process of liberation in human history as the medium and material of divine revelation

Facts only become history within a framework of meaning, in a tradition of interpreted facts. This is the first level of meaning: human liberation is achieved and also experienced. Within a religious experiential tradition of belief in God, that element of human liberation is interpreted on a second level of meaning: in relation to God. Believers then confess that God has brought redemption in and through human beings. The secular event becomes the material of the 'word of God'. In this sense revelation has a sacramental structure.[3]

The religious significance of a worldly process presupposes a human significance: in other words, salvation history is a happening which liberates men and women. Revelation presupposes a process meaningful to men and women, an event that already has relevance for them and liberates them, without direct reference to God, *etsi Deus non daretur*. What is decisive is the good action which brings liberation, without which religious nomenclature becomes thin, a meaningless facade and a redundant superstructure. No one can stand above the parties in the struggle for good and against evil, any more than God can reveal his own being in just any arbitrary human event. Only in a secular history in which men and women are liberated for true humanity can God reveal his own being. There are also many histories of suffering and disaster in secular history; God cannot reveal himself in them except... as a veto or as judgment.

Believers see the face of God in the history of human liberation. Unbelievers do not, but at the level of human liberation (the material of God's revelation) that process can be discussed by both believers and unbelievers in a common language. Here understanding and indeed collaboration are possible. So the deciding factor is not the explicit confirmation or denial of God, but the answer to the question, 'Which side do you choose in the struggle between good and evil, between oppressors and oppressed?'

The significance of the newness of the explicit name 'God' as the heart and source of any movement of salvation will emerge later. But the fact is before us large as life: belief in God does not in fact make Christians any more human than the rest. Anyone who begins to speak of God too early in this context arouses the suspicion of talking about an antiquated image of God, about the God of a former picture of the world and society, the God of a handful of rich people, to the detriment of the oppressed and those who have to live on the periphery of society. The real deciding factor is: are we as Christians (perhaps in the whole of our historically and socially privileged situation) in solidarity with the oppressed and the isolated, or are we on the side of the powerful and the oppressors? In the preferential love of men and women for the poor there is an implicit confirmation of what Christians call God's free being: unconditional love; love without a condition. A few examples may clarify this structure of the Jewish-Christian revelation.

It is still clear to us from the book of Exodus what secular historical event forms the basis of the Jewish exodus confession (Deut.26.5-9). The confession runs as follows:

> And you shall make response before the Lord your God, 'A wandering Aramean was my father; and he went into Egypt and sojourned there, few in number; and there he became a nation great, mighty, and populous. And the Egyptians treated us harshly, and afflicted us, and laid upon us hard bondage. Then we cried to the Lord the God of our fathers, and the Lord heard our voice, and saw our affliction, our toil, and our oppression; and the Lord brought us out of Egypt with a mighty hand and an outstretched arm, with great terror, with signs and wonders; and he brought us into this place and gave us this land, a land flowing with milk and honey.'

The historical background to this confession is as follows. Moses 'saw an Egyptian beating a Hebrew, one of his brothers' (Ex.2.11c). He was a 'witness to their forced labour' (Ex.2.11b). Moses looks round, intervenes and kills the Egyptian. This fact becomes known and Moses goes underground. Eventually, in solidarity with Moses, some Semitic tribes also rebel. They liberate themselves from the hands of the Egyptians: a human process of liberation takes place.

Above all in the tradition of Deuteronomy, this secular event is 're-read' by those who believe in YHWH, the Lord; it is interpreted as 'salvation history'. In other words, believers in God arrive at the experiential insight that the Lord saved the people from Egypt. Here the structure of saving event and revelation event becomes clear. Here we can see that talking in the language of faith about the actions of God in history has an experiential basis in a very particular human activity in the world and in history. For there is no other basis for human talk about God's transcendence than our 'contingency', i.e. our limitations – our changeable, precarious human history. Religious language with its own spirituality draws its material from the experience of our human creaturely limitations as a possible (never compulsory) 'disclosure' of deeper dimensions which can nevertheless be experienced.

In the case of Jesus, too, we must first look for a human, historical event which liberated men and women, which brought them to themselves and opened them up to their fellow human beings. For precisely all this was the medium through which believers began to recognize God's face. Without Jesus' human career the whole of christology becomes an ideological superstructure. Without 'human meaning' in the life of Jesus, all religious meaning in his life becomes incredible. Only the human meaning of a historical process can become the material of 'supernatural' or religious meaning, of revelation. On the other hand, unless we also take into account the positive relationship of Jesus to God, above all his 'Abba' relationship, this human process of liberation that is Jesus never leads to a liberating christology. A split then develops between christology and ethics, between Christ-mysticism and ethical commitment, whether personal or political. For Christians there is no Jesus without the church's confession of Christ, just as there is no church confession of Christ without the appearance of the historical Jesus of Nazareth which brought liberation to men and women.

Although we cannot reach Jesus in his fullness unless we also take into account his unique and distinctive relationship to God, that does not mean that Jesus is the only living way to God. Even Jesus does not just reveal God, but also conceals him, where he appears in non-godly, creaturely humanity. And so as a human being he is a historical, contingent or limited being who cannot in any way represent the full riches of God – that is, unless we deny the reality of his humanity (which runs counter to the consensus of the church, expressed in the Council of Chalcedon). So there can be no talk of a Christian religious imperialism on the basis of the gospel. The prophetic complaint 'You are a hidden God' (Isa.45.15) also applies to Jesus, and the Gospels make him say this on the cross. But anyone who does not also take into account the religious relationship of Jesus to this hidden God is trying to understand the historical Jesus either on the basis of pre-existing metaphysical concepts or on the basis of pre-existing social and political frameworks of interpretation (both of which are alien to the gospel). In both cases the contingent or creaturely limited, historical figure of Jesus is distorted.

Here we are confronted on the one hand with the difficult, almost paradoxical, idea of Jesus' particular, indescribably special relationship to God, and on the other with the fact that as a historical phenomenon he is a 'contingent', limited process that cannot shut off or deny other ways to God and thus also cannot appropriate ethics exclusively to itself. This last point also means that we cannot reduce theology to a christology: there are questions and also religious problems which fall outside the field of christology. This is very important for the ecumene of religions. But I shall not be discussing this until Chapter 3. In this introductory chapter I am simply drawing attention to the point. It will be gradually clarified in the course of my exposition, as also will be its consequences for theology as a whole.

### III   The difference between the history of salvation and the history of revelation

I have just said that only a history which brings about human liberation can be experienced as salvation history. However, in the stricter sense, salvation history is not yet the history of revelation... although! I must now clarify this, but first I must remove a misunderstanding that I have caused in a number of previous publications.

I said above that before there can be any question of an interpretation of faith, particular human events take place in so-called 'secular history' which in and of themselves – i.e. still without an explicit reference to some transcendent God – are experienced by men and women as positive: as meaningful events which bring about human liberation. For Christians, human history, to the degree that it liberates men and women for true and good humanity in deep respect for one another, is God's saving history, and is so independently of our awareness of this gracious structure of salvation, but not without the occurence of intentional human liberation. Sometimes theologians give the impression that an 'ontological, unconscious' dimension is brought to 'consciousness' by revelation, on the presupposition that Christian salvation is realized only in the human consciousness. But in that case a veiled, purely 'ontological' relationship (specifically, to God) is simply being translated into categories of consciousness. What is involved is, rather, the religious significance of conscious human action which liberates, heals and establishes communication. The interpretation of faith seeks to make clear what it means in terms of God's promises of salvation to speak of our everyday 'secular' world and society, to the degree that men and women are liberated in it and become themselves, freed from themselves to be free for others. For 'the human' is the medium of the possible revelation of God.

But because God is God, not an ingredient of our world and therefore also not an ingredient of our structuring of the world, he cannot be shut up or limited by any form of human liberation movement. Certainly God is the source and the heart of all truly human movements of liberation and salvation, but he does not coincide with any particular historical liberation event, not even with the liberating exodus event of the Jewish people or the redemptive appearance of Jesus which creates space and liberates men and women. The name of God, for Christians symbolized in the name Jesus Christ, can be misused not only by oppressors but also by liberators. This is the proviso that follows from the 'divine way' in which God is a liberating God. That will also have consequences for the relationship between the history of salvation and the history of revelation which I shall now go on to discuss.

Belief in God is impossible without belief in human beings. In their symbol of faith, which is old and constantly remains new, although it always has to be interpreted, Christians express a living experience which has matured over the centuries in the following way: 'I believe in God: creator of heaven and earth, and in Jesus: the Christ, his only Son, our Lord.' This twofold belief, on the one hand in the unconditional love of the Creator for everything and everyone that he calls to life, and on the other hand in this man, Jesus of Nazareth, is so paradoxical that it is possible only in the power of the Spirit of God, which also dwelt in Jesus: 'I believe in the Holy Spirit'. The subject of this belief is the church community, which at the same time is also the substance of that faith (but with the subtle omission of 'believe *in*'): 'I believe the apostolic and catholic church'.

Belief in God as the ground and source of our world and the history of human liberation in the midst of all kinds of chance, determination and indeterminacy, is not a belief in the existence of God in the way in which people 'believe' in the existence of a distant galaxy in the universe. It is belief in God as salvation of and for human beings whom he brought to life in this world. It is a belief in God's absolute saving presence among men and women in their history. That means that no matter in what circumstances we find ourselves, whether through blind chance, determinism or our own fault, there is no situation in which God cannot come near to us and in which we would not be able to find him. Those who believe in God can still create meaning even in situations where we really experience meaninglessness. That is not to say that whatever circumstances we find ourselves in are 'the will of God'. Talk of the will of God is in fact often blasphemy: the absolutizing of a *status quo*, of blind chance or one's own view by projecting them on to God.

We cannot reduce the active saving presence of God to our awareness or our experience of this presence, which challenges us to make sense. Nor can we reduce salvation from God to the particular places of salvation that we call religions. Salvation history cannot be reduced to the history of religions or to the history of Judaism and Christianity. For the whole of secular history is itself already under the guidance of the liberating God of creation. Moreover the first place where salvation or disaster comes about is our so-called 'secular history', of which God is the liberating creator, but also the verdict on the history of disaster brought about by men and women.

Of course God's absolute saving presence as such is only an offer and a gift; by that very fact it is still not a presence that is assented to or received. No one will ever be saved against his or her will. As experienced reality, salvation is always accepted or appropriated salvation. And a degree of awareness always goes with this appropriation. Although you cannot identify salvation with the awareness of salvation, you cannot separate the two of them either. In classical theology it is the content of awareness rather than the reality of salvation which predominates.

There salvation is seen directly as being realized through God's word, received in faith, bound to the church's proclamation, confessed in a sacramental praxis.

Faith, sacrament and church are indeed the three essential ingredients of all religions. But here salvation becomes synonymous with religion, and that is a misapprehension of the experienced reality of salvation in the world. Talk about religions and churches involves second-order statements; it is not about the direct, not yet 'heard', first realization of well-being and salvation, redemption and liberation. The world and human history in which God wills to bring about salvation are the basis of the whole reality of faith; it is there that salvation is achieved in the first instance... or salvation is rejected and disaster is brought about. In this sense it is true that *extra mundum nulla salus*, there is no salvation outside the human world. The world of creation, our history within the environment of nature, is the sphere of God's saving action in and through human mediation. The history of the religions is only one segment of a broader history; the religions are the place where men and women become explicitly aware of God's saving actions in history.

Moreover it is within this worldly history that religions came into being as movements in which interpretative experience is achieved in relation to the salvation that God is actively bringing about in this world. How else could religions come into being? Not as something which falls down from heaven! The exclusivistic coupling of salvation with religion and church, in place of the recognition of the deeper basis of salvation – the coupling of salvation with the human world – often resulted in an intellectualistic, idealistic, sacramentalistic and neo-Platonic/hierarchical view of God's system of salvation; at the same time it also led to a one-sided concentration of salvation on inwardness. Moreover this version is an obstacle both to the Christian ecumene as the ecumene of all religions and ultimately to the ecumene of all humankind. Thus salvation history is not the same thing as the history of revelation; in the latter, salvation history becomes a conscious and literate experience of faith. Without general salvation history, a special history of revelation like that in Israel and Jesus is impossible.

Salvation from God comes about first of all in the worldly reality of history, and not primarily in the consciousness of believers who are aware of it. The cognitive sense of this is, of course, itself a separate gift, the significance of which we may not underestimate. But where good is furthered and evil is challenged in the human interest, then through this historical practice the being of God – God as salvation for men and women, the ground for universal hope – is also established and men and women also appropriate God's salvation – in and through acts of love.

Human history, the social life of human beings, is the place where the cause of salvation or disaster is decided on.

As such, God and his initiative of salvation are a reality independent of human consciousness, and independent of our expression of God in experience. But our expression of God and his saving initiative is dependent both on that divine initiative and on the historical context in which human beings express him. Moreover our images of God and conceptions of salvation are bound up with a changing social and historical context. As conceptions and images they are closely bound up with a constantly moving history (as also becomes clear from the history of iconography in connection with representations of the figure of Christ).

## IV Religions and churches as the sacrament of salvation in the world

So religions and churches are not salvation, but a 'sacrament' of the salvation that God brings about in the world he has created: through men and women in a very particular context. Precisely because people do not put the church in its place and at the same time give it the place it is due, forgetting the basic process of the salvation that is brought about in the world, churches often become sectarian, clerical and apolitical – and, as a result, in fact become very political in a disguised way. Religions and churches are of the order of 'the sign': a sacrament of salvation. They are the explicit identification of that salvation. Churches are the places where salvation from God is thematized or put into words, confessed explicitly, proclaimed prophetically and celebrated liturgically. So there is an unbreakable connection between the world and religion. At the same time, there is a necessary identity between the disclosure and the veiling of God. Anyone who looks only at unveiling can in fact forget God, silence and even kill God.

Religions and churches are the *anamnesis*, i.e. the living recollection among us, of this universal, 'tacit' but effective will to salvation and the absolute saving presence of God in our world history. By their religious word, their sacrament or ritual and living praxis, religions – synagogues and pagodas, mosques and churches – prevent the universal presence of salvation from being forgotten. But if a religion or church is then by definition referring to world events and what happens in them, the churches understand themselves wrongly (*a*) if they do not see that they are related to the whole world process as it can be experienced, and (*b*) if they think that in their practical and also interpretative relationship to this world process they can dispense with specifically religious forms:

confession, word and sacrament. The condition on which church talk about God becomes possible is thus the real appearance of God in the world process, and the veiling of this presence in our world makes religious and church talk necessary.

The churches live by the salvation that God brings about in the world. Religions – Hinduism, Buddhism, Israel, Jesus, Islam and so on – are a segment of our human history and are incomprehensible without this 'secular' history. The religious symbols of the religions 'mediate' the veiled presence of God to the consciousness of believers. For even to religious people God remains the hidden God – the one who is veiled, even in the man Jesus of Nazareth. There is therefore a 'divine proviso' in respect of both the phenomenon of the 'world' and the phenomenon of the 'church'.

Church and religion are the grateful welcome to what is as it were the anonymous, concealed and modest coming of God into the world. Confession and word, sacrament and praxis of faith, action which heals and opens up communication, following Jesus, do not make experience of the world superfluous, while events in the so-called outside world in turn necessitate talking in the language of faith and Christian praxis. Precisely for that reason, historical and indeed social and political praxis in the world cannot be separated from the action of the church in proclamation, pastoral work and the sacraments. Anyone who severs this connection damages the internal structure of religion and being the church.

Confessional talk of religious people and their leaders is therefore never autonomous, but a gracious answer to that which precedes all talk of believers: God's creative action in history in and through men and women for human salvation. There are people, believers within a particular tradition of experience, who express this action of God, turn it into words: only in this way can we speak of the 'Word of God', and then we do so rightly. God himself is the already existing source of all our talk of God. We owe our confessional talk about God to God who himself addresses us. Therefore churches are also communities which speak *to* God: praying communities of faith and not just one action group or another, however praiseworthy such groups may be. Their praxis is the realization of the story that they tell, above all in the liturgy.

Moreover it may be said to be characteristic that Jesus, who in a unique way, in words and actions, gave a tangible face to this universal will of the creator God for salvation, was condemned to the cross by a secular, profane judgment. In this sense a historical, secular and political process is the central point of reference for the Christian churches, an event which the churches can rightly celebrate liturgically; for they are the celebratory sacrament of the salvation which God brings about in the world.

## 3. Experiences of revelation: in the secular and religious sense

### Introduction

Many Christians still always see an unbridgeable gap and contrast between Christian belief, as obedience or subjection of believers to God's revelation, and human experiences. They are convinced that the obedience of faith is and must be independent of human experiences. Their position is that faith as participation in the gratuitous and absolute divine Mystery cannot be 'mediated' by any human experience. In that case revelation is talk of God, the 'word of God', which is proclaimed to human beings straight from heaven. But that raises the critical question how 'revelation' can be perceived and thus meaningfully affirmed by men and women, especially without human experience.

## I   The cognitive structure of human experiences

### A. *Experience and the tradition of experience*

Experience always presupposes that something – a happening in nature and history, a human encounter, and so on – can be experienced. On the other hand, the experience of an event also presupposes a framework of interpretation which also determines what we experience.

Learning by experience is a process which takes place when a new concrete experience is connected with the knowledge and experience that we have already acquired. This has a reciprocal effect: the whole of the experience we have already had becomes an interpretative framework or a 'horizon of experience' within which we interpret new experiences, while at the same time this pre-existing framework is laid open to criticism by these new experiences: it is supplemented, corrected or sometimes even radically contradicted. At all events, as the result of new experiences, what we have already experienced earlier is seen in a new context and thus in a different way.[4] Our experiences are always within a pre-existing framework of interpretation. And in the end this is none other than the cumulative personal and collective experience of the past, in other words, a tradition of experience. As the totality into which the particular present experience is taken up, this interpretative framework gives meaning to that experience: and as a result it becomes an experience of meaning. Of course this interpretative framework in its turn came into being in the same way as our present experiences. The earlier, even more limited, cumulative experience at that time functioned as an interpretative framework or a horizon of experience within which experiences that were then new – and which are now part of our interpretative framework – were taken up critically, or at least selectively. The interpretative framework is thus itself built up of events and facts which people had already experienced previously.

Experience and its interpretative framework – we can now say experience and tradition (= the tradition of experience) – cannot therefore be directly contrasted; nor, however, can they be seen as factors which confirm each other. Things happen and new experiences arise for which it is difficult to find an appropriate place within the totality of our growing tradition of experience: they seem to be alien elements in our familiar horizon of experience. Such refractory elements can, in the first instance, shift or bend the framework of experience to some degree. Only when all attempts at providing a new context fail are we confronted with the critical question of a kind of Copernican shift in our pre-existing interpretative framework which provides meaning for us – at least if we want to be honest with ourselves.[5] Similar situations can also be found in the natural sciences.[6] Particular experiences or a series of specific new experiences thus influence the pre-existing framework of interpretation and at particular moments can cause a fundamental crisis for an interpretative framework. A fundamental reorientation then becomes necessary.

The meaningful illumination of all particular experiences by a specific tradition of experience, as an interpretative framework or a horizon of experience, has a positive side: it makes it possible to understand new, particular experiences. On the other hand it has a negative aspect: it limits our understanding, makes the interpretation of new experiences selective, and *a priori* already directs coming new interpretations of experience.[7] But both aspects indicate our human condition: outside this perspectivism, any attempt at understanding is human arrogance; it is quite impossible.

## B. *Concealed elements in our experiences: experience and ideology*

From what has just been said, it emerges that conscious human experience is not a blank sheet, unwritten on. Experience (and we shall see in due course that this also applies to revelation) never takes place in a psychological and socio-historical vacuum. The cognitive implication of experiences was analysed above: experience expresses reality within a concrete tradition of experience. But the structure of our experiences is much more complex. Some aspects of this complicated structure must be discussed briefly here, before we can talk about 'revelation' in a non-ideological sense.

## 1. The ideological use of language

The human consciousness which experiences is in the first instance a capacity to express something that we experience. This expression of reality takes place in language, supported by images and concepts, connotations and emotions which already have a long history and thus are also already given in the socio-historical group in which we live. They also have social and economic implications, not to mention the codes that control a language, which are unconscious (though they can be analysed). The concrete use of language already contains particular world-views, images of human beings and the world; language is itself the first world project in which a person is brought up and begins to live a conscious human life. We approach reality through the language we have learned. The 'linguistic' expressions and forms in which experiences are put into words derive from the repertoire of human imagination, and (despite human constants) this is in turn dependent on experiences in history, which themselves in turn have to do with each person's individual situation and with collective, socio-cultural and socio-emotive contexts of life in a quite particular culture. However, there can be no affirmation of the truth (or of lies) without any articulation in language. An analysis of experiences, even of so-called 'experiences of meaning', cannot therefore by-pass the human cognitive activity which expresses itself in language, and all the implications of the concrete use of language, which are also ideological. There are distances between reality, experience and language, which are always almost immeasurable, though they are real. The experiences expressed 'in alienation', especially in language, thus have to be analysed critically if experience is in fact to exercise its own authority and not a supposed authority, a delusion.

## 2. Suspicion about suppressed use of language

As we have learned from the 'masters of suspicion' – Feuerbach, Marx, Freud, Nietzsche and others – the human experiential consciousness is not only the capacity to express reality cognitively but also a capacity, on the basis of unconscious wishes, to express something which, when it is expressed, in fact obscures what really should have been expressed. In psychological or social terms, what should have been expressed is repressed or distorted ideologically. If an experience is to be competent,

i.e. to have authority, it must also be investigated rationally and critically
for the possibility of this suppression.

### 3. The danger of an appeal to our talk of 'direct experiences'

The manifold appeal through language to 'direct experiences' also
calls for critical analysis. For experiences are also 'mediated' socially
and economically. For example, the objective form of society in which
we live in the West does not only exist outside us but also reacts on our
inwardness and there becomes a distinctive form of consciousness.[8]
Because experiences are also mediated socially and economically,
experience is only competent, authoritative and a guide to men and
women where it takes critical account of the conditions in which it came
into being.[9] On the other hand there is no reason to claim that an
analysis of the specific history of the origin of experiences as such already
involves criticism or denial of their validity and revelation of truth. The
knowledge of a historical process of development, and the criticism
of logical connection, validity and truth, are methodologically two
problems which must be kept completely separate. The knowledge of
this process of the development of experiences and outlines of meaning
can certainly help criticism to eliminate immunizing elements.[10]

### 4. Language and the specific social position of the speaker

The previous position, according to which human experiences are
also mediated socially and politically, can remain very abstract as such.
An accurate analysis of the precise contemporary situation is necessary
so that new experiences can manifest their original authority. It has
emerged from such analyses, carried out with precision, that on the one
hand, particularly in the West, our concrete social and economic culture
is intrinsically determined by the 'bourgeois ideology' which, from the
time of the Enlightenment, has brought our society under the influence
of utilitarian individualism (exchange value as the dominant value),[11]
while on the other hand, in the East, society is above all characterized
by an anti-history of a more historical-materialistic dialectic which also
colours all experiences there. What is generally striking in our society
is the ease with which we speak of 'human beings' or 'humankind', of
universality, whereas when we analyse this it emerges that we mean
either the bourgeois subject who is in fact already emancipated socially,
or the Communist comrade ('what is Communist is human, and what
is human is communist'). If one analyses basic human experiences, as
in humanistic psychology, without awareness of these implications,[12]
one may claim to discover a hierarchy of ethical values in basic human

experiences (and so far this is correct); however, these are then called universal human values, whereas on closer analysis for the most part they are the reflection of the basic values respected by a bourgeois, economically emancipated society, in which those who are marginalized socially and economically cannot recognize themselves at all. At present, moreover, technological rationality is being increasingly fused with the rationality of the powers in East and West (the so-called First and Second Worlds, and also within sectors of the Third World), with the result that the great contrasts in the world are turning into a contrast between the rich of the North and the poor of the South. All this is of fundamental importance for a human (and indeed a believing) praxis within the horizon of world experiences.

## 5. Language and the use of models

Experiences are not just interpretative. For not only do interpreted experiences use pre-existing images and concepts to express what is perceived (as I have already said); in addition they work with models and theories created by human beings themselves. In this way as many phenomena of experience as possible are understood as simply and as clearly as possible in scientific terms.[13] Statements of experience, as an expression of experiences, are therefore not merely articulations on the basis of particular so-called direct experiences, but also a bit of human theory or modelling which also colours the real content of experience. Therefore dogmatizing, whether on the basis of direct experience or of models, is to be rejected.

## 6. Elements of projection in language

Within the experiential human consciousness, moreover, there is an active relationship between the sub-conscious (personal and collective) and reflective consciousness. This connection also gives a projective structure to the human consciousness that experiences. Within all *perception* of meaning we also project and symbolize. The symbolizing activity which takes place above all in experiences of transcendence does not occur primarily at the level of conscious reflection, but at the threshold of the transition from sub-consciousness to consciousness. Apart from their own value, as the visualizing of a transcendent reality, symbols, as the metaphorical expression of a particular experience, connect explicit consciousness to the stream of the whole of our sub-conscious world. Since Jung, that the powers of the human unconscious are also active in the interpretative expressions above all of religious experience has been difficult to deny. But this in no way implies *per se* that what is experienced is nothing but the subconscious activity of the human spirit which produces its effects in our explicit consciousness. So we may not pass a negative judgment on the aspect of projection in all experiences which perceive meaning, to the detriment of the possible significance of these experiences in embracing reality.

Here, moreover, we are right to make a distinction between 'archetypal symbols' and 'cultural symbols' (or 'historical master images'),[14] however much the two overlap. Symbols, like kingdom of God, Black power, the flag, and so on, are powerful ideas which also produce a future. In themselves these symbols (of transcendence) are religiously neutral; they are undetermined and undirected and therefore can also become the 'vehicle' or medium of authentic experiences of 'revelation'. The presence of influence from the subconscious level of the human spirit on the affirmative awareness of truth does not say anything as such for or against an authentic experience of transcendence. The other side of this is at the same time that the real significance of experiences of transcendence can never be explained on the basis of their psychological implications for the unconscious, however real these may in fact be.

*7. Non-religious elements in the use of religious language*

Finally, particular experiences are never isolated acts; they are taken up into the stream of a person's total psychical life, of which they are an ingredient and in which they lie embedded. In this respect all psychological experiences (including religious experiences) find their place against the background of a dark and to a large extent also unconscious psychological stream. Expressions like 'a purely religious experience' are therefore simply an abstraction. Any religious experience also contains 'non-religious' elements. Thus a religious experience that is mixed up with 'non-religious' elements is not yet in itself pseudo-religious, as is sometimes asserted. (I shall go on to talk specifically about the 'religious' aspects of our experience later; here I am only concerned with the complexity of all human experiences.)

## Conclusion

From this brief locating of the complex structure of human experiences it already emerges that 'experience' is in no way a one-dimensional phenomenon. Moreover, the now developed insight into this complex structure and the growing sense of the mutability and actual changes in society and culture have given rise to a 'new form of consciousness' that has not without reason been called *Dauerreflexion*:[15] all that has been handed down (the legacy of earlier experiences, our own tradition of experience) is subjected to critical questioning on the basis of new experiences, while this old tradition of experience can also subject our so-called new experiences to criticism.

Therefore experience takes place in a dialectical process: in an interplay of perception (within a framework of interpretation or reading) with thinking and of thinking with perception. Experience has authority only in reflection on experience; experience is more than feelings, something we live through. Moreover, although reason perhaps does not stand at the beginning of experience, competent experience includes reason, critical rationality.[16] Thinking makes experience possible, and experience makes new thinking necessary. Our thought remains empty unless it constantly falls back on living experiences, which in turn can be irrational without reflective reasoning. The authority of experience is ultimately a competence, arising *out of* earlier experiences, and is open to new experiences.[17]

With critical reflection, human experiences, as a revelation of reality, or of what is not thought or not produced by human beings, in fact have authority and validity; they have a cognitive critical and liberating power in the long-lasting search of humanity for truth and goodness, justice and happiness. Freedom is a condition of our experiences achieving this, as is the provision of space within institutions; for institutional violence and a one-track civilization – for example, one that is purely technological and scientific – can also make people poor in experience and manipulate all experiences. Of course the new still has no priority over the old as such. Therefore a 'discerning of the spirits' is necessary, also through critical recollections and new experiences; it belongs to what is called experiential competence or the authority of experiences.

Those (whether as individuals or as a group) who have had an authoritative experience themselves become witnesses by virtue of that fact; they tell what has happened to them. Along with reflection, this story also opens up a legitimate new possibility of life to others; it sets something in motion. So experiential competence become operative in the story of the experience which has been had, and its life-renewing power. Experiential competence – and here the Old and New Testament are models – therefore has a narrative structure;[18] it is a testifying life-story.

## II  Experiences of revelation in everyday-human, secular language

### A. 'That was – or 'You were' – a revelation to me'

Already in everyday human speech we sometimes hear someone say 'That was a revelation for me'. Not all experiences seem to be of such a kind that we exclaim in surprise, 'That was a real revelation!' For many experiences take place within so-called run-of-the-mill life; they pass by us without a murmur, like mayflies. But within this stream of more anonymous and somewhat more explicit average experiences, events sometimes come to the fore of which we say, 'that was a revelation for me'. By that we mean that something surprising took place, something that broke through the experiences of everyday routine, and on closer inspection (for experience is also 'reason' and interpretation) that seemed to be 'news', news in which we nevertheless recognize the deepest of ourselves. Here the new at the same time seemed to be the 'old familiar' which had not yet been expressed; were that not the case, we would not be able to be brought back to ourselves by such facts of revelation. It is as if this experience put the right word in our mouths, a word which we had never been able to find previously: a word which reveals and communicates reality to us. *In* such an experience, what we ourselves had never thought of and never produced occurs to us as a gift.

In experiences which we call experiences of revelation, the possibility of the new is thus disclosed to us: things can be different! Here a space is opened up in which we can see reality differently: a possibility of a new view of the world and of events and within that at the same time an offer of new, different, alternative action. It is also possible to look at the world in a different way from that which is customary in ordinary experiences of life. All this means that 'experiences of revelation' bring us, through a disintegration of our everyday identity, to a new reinterpretation of our own identity which makes us happy, brings us salvation, or makes us whole. It could be said that in any human experience of revelation we may recognize something of a surprising transition, a 'pasch': from an initially everyday, uncritical integration, through disintegration, to a new reintegration with a different orientation. Any 'experience of revelation' includes conversion, amendment of life, reorientation.

In such a secular event of revelation we recognize two aspects which cannot be separated: (*a*) this experience says something about the subjective form of someone's own reaction to an event. In this sense revelations always take place in the present: experiences take place now.

In the story of a past event or in a process of facts experienced here and now, individuals experience something that addresses them in a very personal way and that makes them discover the innermost depths of themselves, of their standpoint in the world, in a completely new way. Because experiences of revelation always take place in the present, here and now, they occur in the personal response of those who experience a particular experience as a 'revelation'. (*b*) But revelation is not the private property of the person who perceives an event as a revelation for herself. Although there are also experiences in which individuals discover a deeper meaning for themselves for purely subjective or arbitrary reasons, without good reason, a particular experience is only appropriately called revelation when in an event of experience – of nature or history, in contact with other people or 'in the world' – something shows itself which provokes this response and no other, though what shows itself is not capable of compelling the subject to only this response. For what shows itself objectively in this experience does so in a veiled form, which always allows of other interpretations. Moreover it shows itself to human freedom in such a way that it can be affirmed or denied, or more precisely, in such a way that some people do not even regard it as an 'experience of revelation'. But through a subjective affirmation – which takes place in the experience itself – this human freedom stands under the norm of what makes itself known in this experience as it were from outside a person and outside his or her own thought, to and most deeply in this person. What has not been thought of nor produced by human beings of course evokes such experiences only in those who know how to listen disinterestedly, in trust. This comes, as it were in a direct psychological succession, to be freely affirmed as the most personal act from the deepest active centre in a person, who thus experiences 'revelation'. It comes over individuals, and yet it is their own act. This experience makes us both think and act. So human experience with its varied range of changing 'density of revelation' (see below) is the great mediating process on the long way of men and women in search of truth and goodness, of justice and happiness, in gift and in freedom.

## B. *The changing density of revelation in human experiences*

Even in inter-personal relations we notice that human beings do not express or reveal themselves fully in all their actions. Some everyday actions betray little of what those involved really are and what they expect or want from their lives. Moreover in these experiences the person with his or her deepest aspirations and inspirations does not become transparent. But within the totality of someone's active life there are also particular actions which we can call revelations of his or her deepest personality and which are experienced as such by others. The more everyday actions do not have the same 'revelatory' power or value; they have this only in connection with, and with reference to, those particular actions with which they ultimately form a single whole. In the particularly striking actions, the less obvious actions, and finally the anonymous actions of an individual, his or her life as a whole is a 'revelation' of what this individual is at the deepest level, although the observer will need benevolent openness and disinterested accommodation to be able to perceive that person's life as it really is, in experience and interpretation. So in respect of the density of revelation one may speak of a hierarchy of experiences: of a hierarchy of truths in our human experiences within the social and historical context of these experiences.

## III   Religious experiences of revelation

### A. *The religious use of human categories of experience*

Though always in a modest and restrained way, human categories of experience are used by religious people to give some account of experiences of what they call God's active concern with humankind and, in Christian belief, God's special concern for the life of Israel and, in a decisive way, for the life of Jesus. The normal human expression 'That was a revelation for me' here retains its human structure, but takes on a religious depth.

Religious experiences display the same structure as our other human experiences: they are clearly related to human experiences of revelation and presuppose them. They do not form a separate world of revelation, but express a dimension of depth in these human experiences. One has religious experiences in and with particular human experiences, though with the illumination and help of a particular religious tradition in which people stand and which is thus influential as an interpretative framework which provides meaning. Our so-called secular experiences also have this necessary structure of experience and tradition of experience (see above); this is in no way peculiar to religious experiences. Religious experiences or experiences of faith take place in a dialectical process, like all experiences. On the one hand the content of faith – itself already a reflective expression of a collective experience of a group of religious people – determines the religious, Christian content of particular human experiences; on the other hand, it is not the content of faith in itself (for example as proclaimed by the churches) which directly brings anyone to a Christian experience of faith. By the guidance and illumination of the content of faith presented to us by Christian churches, which comes from the great Christian tradition of faith, people here and now, in and with present-day authentically human experiences, have a personal *Christian* experience, an experience in which salvation from God in Jesus is perceived here and now.[19] The church's story, and above all the praxis of the churches in the light of the gospel, is the condition for the possibility for others to experience the Christian faith. But only in human experiences here and now do people arrive at a personal Christian experience of faith in which 'revelation' is perceived and affirmed.

People have *Christian* experiences in and through *human* experiences with men and women in our world history, within the natural environment in which we live, but always in the light of the faith-content of the Christian tradition of experience. Authentic, living faith thus comes 'from hearing', but it nevertheless comes about only in a personal experience. Only if the living story of a particular religious tradition is told and put into practice in a specific community can men and women today have Christian experiences from and in and with their present-day human experiences: identifying themselves with that story and this praxis – or distancing themselves from it.[20] In that story individuals with all their human experiences in the world can at the same time discover themselves and realize their own identity. Something then 'clicks' between the Christian tradition of experience and present-day experiences in life – or with some people it does not click, and so they ignore the Christian tradition of faith.[21]

Of course the liturgical worship of the church community of faith is the place where God is praised, thanked and celebrated for the Christian content of salvation, and also the place where the content of faith is narrated. But – above all in a so-called 'secularized' world – we may not narrow down situations which can lead to the experience of faith to the proclamation of the word and liturgical worship, which are themselves already reflective expressions of experiences of salvation in the world. As I have already said, the liturgy of the church and the proclamation of the word themselves presuppose the origin of religious experiences with and in human experiences (for example, the first liberating encounter of a group of people with the man Jesus of Nazareth), and these in turn presuppose a fundamental experience of symbols in and with our human, creaturely world. Without a fundamental experience of creation, no renewal or reorientation of liturgical style nor any 'direct' proclamation of 'church doctrine' can give us a deepened Christian experience which is an authentic experience of presence and not simply an experience of our own subjective reactions to what is happening liturgically in the churches or a purely intellectual affirmation of a teaching that is presented to us. We cannot suddenly experience God in the church's liturgy if we never perceive God outside the church in our everyday experiences of our fellow human beings and the world (although no one should deny the possibility that some people may come to ask religious questions specifically as the result of a surprising contact with a living and meaningful church liturgy and as a result then begin to perceive the 'outside world' in a different way).

Because men and women come to religion through experiences of their fellow human beings and the world, this mediation through the world at the same time explains the difference between the various religions. Moreover, the rise of a multiplicity of religions can be explained from this same source from which religion as such comes into being: the multiplicity of human experiences of human beings and the world within particular divergent human traditions of experience. Talking about God on the basis of human experiences is essential bound up with making it possible to discuss worldly experiences in religious terms. And despite a universal basic human pattern (one which can never be 'abstracted' but always has specific content), human experiences always have a social and historical, indeed also a geographical, colouring. All that also produces variations in the universal human religious theme.

It also follows from this that the environment in which Christian belief thrives and can be handed down is not only the living community of faith or the church but also the world, everyday human experience in the concrete history in which men and women are involved.

In this respect, the essential feature of the Christian revelation is that on the basis of the experience of an encounter with Jesus his followers claim that in this man, in his life and message, in his action and the way in which he died, in his whole person as a human being, God's purposes with men and women and in them God's 'own character' have become revelation, have been brought to human consciousness in the highest degree: according to this experience of faith Jesus is the place where in a decisive way God has revealed himself as salvation of and for men and women. Christians experience Jesus as the supreme density of divine revelation in a whole history of experiences of revelation. In this religious history of revelation human experience has its own indispensable place; but as in every 'experience of revelation', including secular experiences, here revelation is not the fruit of experience but experience is the fruit of revelation. So this event of revelation says something about the self-understanding of particular people. At the same time, in expressing their experience, believers do not just want to say something about themselves, in other words about their experience of renewal of life and new self-understanding, i.e. how *they* see Jesus. In the first place they want to say something about *Jesus himself*: that he is the supreme expression of God, and that precisely for that reason they have experienced salvation in him and continue to do so. By its own, inner direction the statement of faith is thus in no way the foundation of revelation; rather, the revelation itself by its own power attracts the response of faith and forms its own basis. Certainly good reasons can also be given here for demonstrating to some degree that it is not human beings who make their God speak, but that God makes himself known, in and through human experiences, as the one who transcends all precisely described experiences, and makes known how he does so.

However, faith cannot live only by way of experience. Faith is never consummated in a pure fullness of experience. It also contains reflection put into words, the formation of concepts and interpretation, the beginnings of which are given along with the experience itself. Experiences must also be assimilated rationally; this is also part of the nature of experiences of and through men and women. Thus ultimately experiences of faith develop into propositions of faith, statements in which, for example, the Christian tradition of experience is to some degree formulated. Religious experiences are translated into the language of faith, into statements of faith, and now and then even into dogmas; they are ultimately also thematized in well-ordered theological views – in a constantly diminishing certainty of faith and increasing human risk.

## B. Revelation in religious experiences: 'divine revelation'

'Revelation' can be understood at two different levels of language. On the one hand revelation is essentially that which cannot be named, the inexpressible which lies beyond all conceptual knowledge and is the basis of the experience of faith – the praxis of faith and the thought of faith. On the other hand revelation is also that which cannot be named, as caught in some reflection: the manifestation of the foundation of faith which cannot be thought of put into concepts, as it were 'grasped'.[22] At its deepest, revelation is the non-reflective, pre-theoretical givenness – or more correctly, the self-giving – of that which is always already the basis of the process of faith, that which is constitutive for faith and makes it possible. At the level of reflection an attempt is made to express revelation (in the first, fundamental sense) as the foundation of faith, even though this never seems adequate. The ground of faith cannot itself be grounded (by human reasoning). But it can be *named*, to a certain degree. For the naming and reflection never bring the inexpressible Whence and Whither of faith completely 'within our grasp', map it out or put it into words. That revelation is the foundation of experiences of faith means that faith owes neither itself nor its distinctive content to itself. It is a gift and at the same time a human choice, both in one.

In an event which can be perceived by men and women – i.e. for Christians the life of Jesus –, revelation, as a foundation, can nevertheless be heard in our history. Thus revelation also becomes a category, indeed one might say a describable expression, of aspects of unfathomable depths of human experience that can be put into understandable words. Thus in the end it is men and women themselves who express this divine revelation: they narrate what they themselves have not projected or produced. But on the other hand, meaning is perceived only in the giving of meaning. Here too there can be no question of a dualism, in the sense of 'revelation here', 'response of faith there'. So there can be no revelation without faith and no faith without revelation (though from a human perspective there can in fact be 'faith' without revelation!).

## 4. Experiences subjected to the criticism of stories of suffering

I   Resistance: the truth and authority of suffering and oppressed men and women

Although there are many experiences of meaning in any human life, nevertheless it is above all experiences of meaninglessness, of injustice and of innocent suffering that have a revelatory significance *par excellence*. It is a fact that both everyday experiences and experiences in scientific experiments owe much to 'resistance': to experiences of resistance and the intractability of the reality in which we live. Men and women live by guesses and mistakes, by projects and constructions, and therefore by trial and error; their plans can constantly be thwarted by the opposition of reality, which does not always lend itself to rational human anticipation. Where reality offers resistance to human plans and thus imperceptibly supports and directs them, we are in contact with a reality which is independent of us. As has already been said above, we see that through the alienation and disintegration of our achievements and our plans, truth comes nearer to us. So the principle for the interpretation of reality is not what we take for granted, but 'the stumbling block' of a reality which resists us.[23] The authority of experiences therefore culminates in human stories of suffering: stories of suffering over misfortune and failure, the suffering of pain, the suffering of evil and injustice, the suffering of and in love, sorrow or guilt. Here lie the great elements of the revelation of reality in and through finite human experiences. For experiences which do not accommodate themselves to the subject who experiences them, perhaps even to a whole environment and society, really do help us forward. The deepest experiences which direct and support our life are, therefore, experiences of conversion, crucifying experiences which lead us to *metanoia*, lead us to change our mind, our action, our being. Such experiences break off, but do so in order to lead to a new integration.

As I have said, experiences always take place within a horizon of experience, within a searchlight. The searchlight of the Christian tradition of experience does not just have as its content a concern for human liberation and thus an emancipatory significance; it does not want semi-emancipation, which has no eye for the suffering of men and women that has already taken place in history, or the suffering of 'other' groups alien to us.

Earlier forms of ethics, and indeed some contemporary ethics, began and still begin from natural law. They presuppose that 'order' is already given and that from this comes the command not to infringe this order. Here there is a degree of optimism about the interpretative power of 'universal' human reason. It is often forgotten that this abstract universal reason (celebrated by the Enlightenment) is itself also entangled in personal and social sinfulness and the lust for domination. For experience teaches us that even moral reason needs liberation. If we look more closely, we see that the specific starting point for ethics is not so much 'order', which may not be disturbed, as our indignation at human beings in concrete history who are everywhere injured: at the disorder both in the human heart and in society and its institutions. The actual threat and attack on the *humanum* – that which is worthy of human beings – which is desired but can never be defined positively leads to indignation and is therefore a specifically ethical challenge and an ethical imperative, embedded in very specific negative experiences of contrast, of human misfortune and unhappiness, here and now.

In this view, what is ethically good will emerge only from a praxis of liberation and reconciliation. Both believers and non-believers have this protesting experience of contrast. In an autonomous ethic, an ethic without faith in God, there is clearly a kind of utopia which is desperately revered, but which at least will never become an accomplice in the injustice and lack of freedom which are spreading so widely over our world. Of course no single religious tradition can be reduced to its ethics. It can even be said of the Christian tradition that the specific character of the ethic of Christians (in comparison with some other religions) is that they do not have a distinctive ethic, and thus are open to the *humanum* which is sought by all men and women, here and now, again and again. This autonomy was already being defended by Thomas of Aquino.[24] We do not need God as the direct foundation of our ethical action. A morality with an autonomous foundation is concerned with the human dignity of each individual, *etsi Deus non daretur*. And here collective historical humanity itself primarily has its own responsible claim to make.

Nevertheless, we cannot get rid of God from ethical life in this way!


## II   Liberating 'autonomous ethics' within a context of faith

Although religion can never be reduced to ethics, on the other hand there is an intrinsic connection between faith and ethics. Christians see the autonomous morality of humankind specifically in the context of a praxis in accord with the kingdom of God, on which they have set their hope. The spirituality of Christian ethics, which as ethics really does not 'add' anything to an 'autonomous morality' focussed on human beings and their worth, lies at the theologal level: in a warm relationship with God; life in faith, hope and love, which is celebrated in the liturgy, is meditated upon critically but with faith in contemplation, and practised in the everyday life of Christians.

Ethics which is thus rooted in faith in God (despite and in its relative autonomy and its cultural historicity) is supported by a realistic hope in a God who acts in our history to free human beings and their society. This ethic which is directly founded on human worth, which is autonomous, but in the end nevertheless anchored in God, finds its foundation in the acceptance of human beings by God (*iustificatio*) and therefore in the complete liberation of men and women by God. The old principle of 'acting in accordance with human reason ' therefore also appears here; it retains its power and validity, but is given another context: *between* the impulse of belief in God (liberation faith, faith in God, manifested in concern for fellow men and women, in solidarity with each one of them) and ethical action lies the mediation and the criterion of 'moral reason', which also preserves our action as believers from religious fanaticism. However, from the Christian perspective the starting point of this ethic is not (unliberated) universal 'moral reason' (which often works to the detriment of 'the little ones') but belief in God which leads to the historical enterprise of the praxis of human liberation and provokes reflection. Practical moral reason with its demand for rationality is subject to the stimulating criticism of the human history of innocent suffering and injustice, of stories of suffering to which no rational place can be given.[25] It is precisely the Christian gospel which lives by the critical recollection of the human history of suffering: it recalls the message and the praxis of Jesus, who was concerned for the poor and the oppressed and therefore also himself experienced suffering and a painful death. On both a narrower and a wider ethical scale, for believers ethical life is the recognizable content of salvation, the historically consistent manifestation or making transparent of the approaching kingdom of God in fragments of our human history. The religious, or faith, is not the ethical. However, that faith does not manifest itself only in prayer, liturgy and ritual, but also in human ethics, as that side of God-centred life which liberates men and women and makes them happy, and at the same time the visible touchstone of the authenticity of faith, prayer and celebration which, once detached from it, can begin to live a life of their own in an uncommitted way, without personal and political ethical implications. What is decisive is the praxis of the kingdom of God in solidarity with all men and women, and precisely in that and as a result of it, in a partisan choice for the poor and the oppressed, against oppression by the powerful and by structures which hurt people.

Ethics is a form of self-obligation: men and women autonomously impose a norm on themselves. That is a gain in human insight, above all since and thanks to Kant. But without the spirituality of the person who believes in God, or theologal life, purely human ethics often makes excessive demands on people. Ethics without God-centred spirituality often becomes 'graceless', in both senses of the word. In that case there is ethics without the element of love which brings happiness, in which love of God and human love are one and the same indivisible basic attitude or virtue. From a Christian perspective, love for our fellow human beings is at the same time a 'divine virtue', a reflection of God's love for humankind in specific human action. Without spirituality or the perspective of faith in God, ethics is often graceless: intent on vengeance and retribution, where Christians speak of mercy and reconciliation. Although ethics is possible before all religious confessions of faith, ethical competence nevertheless presupposes God's grace and thus theologal life as a living response to this grace. This last ultimately gives us a moral capacity, to the death. The important thing is a human freedom which is ethically effective, not a bourgeois freedom – my freedom, if need be at the expense of other people's freedom! The Christian freedom of the gospel is a freedom in solidarity, in which the freedom of one person is not a threat to another, as often was and still is the case with liberal, bourgeois freedoms, and also with communist freedoms. Freedom in the light of the gospel can only be liberated freedom, freedom redeemed from egoism and power, freedom which rests on the fact that all are accepted by God, even before they begin to act. Our God is a God who accepts men and women beyond the bounds of their ethical capacity and action and regardless of the deficiencies in their particular human state. God is therefore a God of liberation, forgiveness and reconciliation, without which any ethic, whether personal or social and political, can be fatally graceless, often fanatical, and a dishonour to men and women.

Ethics needs a God who is more than ethics. The more we are silent about, indeed hush up, this God who is 'above ethics', the ultimate source and horizon of all ethics, the more we human beings deliver ourselves over to idols or self-made gods, to a faith which does not result in life but in the torture and death of many people. Precisely because God competes with our idols and thus is a 'jealous God', he shows himself to be a 'God of men and women': our God whose honour never comes in conflict with our human worth, but on the contrary upholds it and sustains it.

Sometimes people ask whether we need God for this human work of humanization and liberation. Do not, they say, for example agnostics and unbelievers do the same thing, and sometimes even do it better?

This is a serious question, but the question to be asked in return is: Need what God? And moreover, what do you mean by 'need'? Certainly not God as a stop-gap (the one who fills in in cases of failure or misfortune)? Certainly not a God who imposes his will and law on men and women as a tyrannical potentate, as though not human worth but God were the *direct* foundation of ethical obligation (even for God)? Certainly not a God to whom human beings can appeal when their ethical arguments fall short, so that in order to fill this gap they refer to 'the will of God'? God cannot allow himself to be misused in this way! In their ethics and above all in their particular ethos, believers from many religions have all too often misused the name of God, and in so doing marred human beings, their human worth and happiness; they have enslaved and dishonoured them, and laid burdens on them – on men and particularly on women – which have nothing to do with the will of God. In that case it is better today not to think that there is a 'God' than to adhere to an inhuman God who enslaves men and women, and thus to appeal to radicalism. This is in no way the nineteenth-century belief in progress (as people sometimes whisper, or even state officially) nor the pressure of a permissive society. What is at stake is the nature of the God of Christians: his honour and ours, being allowed to be a human person, thanks to God's good creation. Older religions which have incorporated an 'inhuman God' into their confessions (e.g. one who calls for human sacrifices) have all quickly died out; they cannot stand up to the human (and thank God also religious) pride in 'being allowed to be a human being', despite all human misery. But religions which do not worship an inhuman God in their confession, but only one who is concerned for humanity, can also become incredible because of the concrete form of their proclamation: in so doing they marginalize many believers from their community of faith. These turn their backs, often with honest regret in their hearts, on their church but not on their religious experiential tradition. True happiness also knows the cross and can resist abuse, even from fellow believers and their leaders. But 'the cross' is not cherished in this way , nor is it given by God as an essential part of redemption, in the sense that human beings, not God, prepared the cross for Jesus – though God did not allow himself to be checkmated by this. We certainly do not need any divine grandfather who generously smiles on and makes light of our faults and our cowardice. We need to be serious about humanity and therefore 'need' a God who is pure gratuitousness: unmerited, liberally given grace. For nothing!

For the Christian experiential tradition, only a 'God of life', not a God of life and death; only a living God – a God of living and dead, who still know a future in him – can be worshipped, revered and celebrated by men and women; not a God who diminishes men and women and hurts them or keeps them under and deprives them of their joys. Moreover this God alone has a prophetic liberating power – critical of human beings and society – which through the spirituality of the theologal life of believers and their praise of God, reveals itself in life according to the gospel, both in personal life and in an ethos with a mystical foundation which also brings political liberation.

## 5. Old biblical and present-day Christian experiences of faith

Human beings are subjects of faith, but they are also cultural – cultural beings. So the specific culture in which believers live, that *on which* Christian faith is in fact modelled, is at the same time the culture *through which* this faith is assimilated in a living way and finally that *in which* it is experienced concretely by men and women living here and now. Because of this social and cultural mediation of faith, during fundamental shifts in social and cultural patterns, and the categories of experience and thought that go with them, believers have difficulty with already existing cultural forms of transmitted belief. This belief must be adjusted to the new situation, if it is still to be recognizable to contemporary men and women as Christian belief in the gospel. A historical break with cultural forms of faith can then sometimes be the only possible form of confidence in the gospel, the contemporary presentation of the Christian tradition of faith. Thus it becomes clear that believing today (to put it

schematically) always moves between 'two poles': the Christian tradition of revelation (the tradition of faith, experience and interpretation
in Jewish-Christian worship) and the situation in which believers live
here and now.


## I   Tradition and situation: a definition of concepts

On the one hand the Christian tradition is a tradition of meaning. In
fact, within all the great and above all the classical religious traditions
of humanity[26] there is a force which discloses meaning: through all the
rises and falls of these traditions their history is a cumulative disclosure
of meaning and truth down the ages (apart from possible ideological
misuse). That is the way in which all these traditions understand
themselves. Moreover in these great traditions meaning-and-truth is
expressed precisely as an authentic possibility of life which can be
actualized or become a reality which is alive even now in changed
circumstances in the world and the church. The tradition of faith opens
up a horizon of possible experience for us, too, now.

   On the other hand this tradition of faith is a tradition of religious
meaning with renewing, liberating or redemptive power. The tradition
of faith which discloses meaning is at the same time a call to a well-
defined practical way of life. Whatever the specific name given to the
liberation in which divergent human and religious traditions can also
be involved, these traditions confess salvation and liberation for men
and women through their own disclosure of meaning, truth about life
as human beings. In the end we have here the convergence of two stories,
the story of the gospel tradition of faith and the story of our personal
and social life which in the best instances has itself as it were become
'gospel': a fifth or umpteenth gospel.

   So primarily such great traditions are not concerned with a theoretical
disclosure of meaning but with a way of life, a praxis, and thus with
witness: a narrative revelation of meaning which even in the Old and
New Testaments is constantly accompanied at least by an incipient
theological reflection.

   On the basis of these two facets – a tradition of faith which discloses
meaning *and* does so with liberating power – faith, which also leads to
theology, is an undertaking which on the one hand is interpretative and
on the other hand, as a theory of faith, is related to a particular praxis
of liberation or redemption, of healing men and women and bringing
them to fullness. So the interpretation of faith and theology cannot be
reduced to a purely theoretical interpretation of the Christian past.

There is a dialectical relationship between the present, the past and the future still to be made, a relationship between praxis and theory.

The term I use for what stands over against tradition is situation, in a general sense: the cultural, social and existential context of men and women to whom the gospel is proclaimed here and now; the concrete situation in which the tradition of faith is handed on by Christians to new generations: to contemporary people, living in a modern culture with its good things and its bad, with its new insights and its own particular sensitivities, but also its own blindspots, one-sidednesses and prejudices. So 'situation' is not an unequivocal concept; it covers divergent realities which, moreover, time and again call for an appropriate analysis. Situation is thus a complex totality of contingencies which can partly be analysed but are never completely clear. So no theory can cover the situation as a whole; here all totalitarian theories fall short.

In a more specific sense I use the word situation to describe the present 'Christian situation', i.e. the answer or variety of answers to the question how Christians stand *qua* Christians in this modern society and culture and how far they should take over modern categories of experience and thought. In a conformist way? To legitimize them? Critically? Or rejecting them all without further ado as being of the devil? In other words, what is to be their praxis and understanding of faith here and now? In what way are they to follow Jesus or perhaps diverge from his way of life? Identity with (or perhaps deviation from) the Christian tradition of faith is already given *in* the specific action of believers. In this sense the situation is itself already a bit of 'new' Christian tradition, a new chapter in the story of the Christian experiential tradition, though this may be (as always) in an orthodox or a somewhat divergent direction. That is already to say that the subject of the interpretation of faith is not really the theologian but the Christian communities of faith themselves – the church in its broad spectrum and its cultural distribution over many centres. Here theology is merely a help to the community of faith. Academic theology then tries to integrate the new experiences, the new praxis and the reflections of local communities into the totality of the 'church's recollection' and into the great reserves of the experiences and faith of the whole church down the ages. Theology thus at the same time prevents these new experiences from remaining sporadic or ultimately causing disintegration. Thus academic theology 'mediates' to the base the rich experiential traditions in the churches down the ages, and prevents the base from being cognitively isolated. Theology itself is enriched by the new experiences and reflections from theology which grows in and from the life of the communities of faith.

## II   Encounter between different cultures and traditions of faith

The subject of our closer attention now is the interrelationship between
the Christian past and the Christian present.

I have chosen the term 'interrelationship' deliberately: it is vague
enough to cover the broad spread between clear identity on the one
hand (it clicks) and unmistakable non-identity on the other (it clashes):
from correlation to conflict and confrontation, from complete identification to partial recognition and finally to non-recognition. Here we
have very delicate problems in which both the Scylla of fundamentalism
and the Charybdis of modernism have to be avoided.[27] For there is a
danger on the one hand that church leaders bind believers to particular
forms of faith where God leaves them free; and on the other hand that
the interpretation of faith in fact given by believers and their theologians
distorts the authenticity of the gospel.

On the one hand the fundamental tendency and power of 'the gospel'
is transcendent and universal, and in this sense 'trans-cultural'; by that
I mean only not bound to one culture, not that there is a substance of
faith which is timeless and in that sense transcultural. On the other
hand, precisely this universal message, open to all cultures and a
challenge to all men and women, can be found concretely only in the
forms of particular cultures (Jewish, Jewish-Hellenistic, Hellenistic;
later the culture of late antiquity, Carolingian culture, Celtic, Roman-
esque, contemporary African, Asian and Latin American culture, and
so on), never neat, above or outside any culture, and therefore never in
an 'abstract substance of faith', stripped down and free of any culture.
So there is a constant dialectic between the universality of the gospel,
through which it challenges every culture critically and transcends it,
and its nevertheless constant appearance in particular cultures. Only
in concrete particularity can the gospel be the revelation of the universality of salvation from God, because men and women are cultural
beings with their own particular cultures and can only be reached as
human beings in them. In this sense not only all forms of theology but
also the biblical and magisterial expressions of faith are contextual and
cultural, while they nevertheless seek to express the universal message
of the gospel. So there is the constantly young, abiding 'offer of
revelation', but on each occasion this is acclimatized in a particular
culture, while that offer can never be found in an unhistorical and supra-
cultural form. What we have is a historical identity of what remains,
precisely *in* what gets forgotten and passes away because of its contingency. Here we have the problem of the interpretation of faith, and this
problem cannot be argued away with any amount of authoritative
statements.

What is important here is the insight that 'the situation' is no longer purely the channel in which the transmitted faith flows to meet us. The situation, the context of faith, is itself also theologically relevant. For according to my analysis above, the whole of history stands under God's liberating and redemptive will. The interpretation of faith is not concerned with the adaptation of a normative Bible and an authoritative tradition of faith to a 'theologically free' situation, but rather with the encounter of different cultural forms of the same understanding of faith and the practices that go with it: that of the Bible with all the forms of Christian understanding of the faith which came later, within diverging periods of culture within one cultural tradition and within divergent cultures. What we have here is a theoretical *and* practical, mutually critical encounter between faith cultures and therefore between different faith traditions, an encounter (or better, a long series of encounters) which allows us here and now (with all the limitations of the encounter) to catch sight of the 'offer of revelation', the Christian gospel, that we can never catch hold of and never objectify. In the interrelationship between the two poles there is therefore never any question of an obvious correlation, not even in the sense that one could call one pole (past Christian tradition of faith) the only source, while the other pole (the situation now and then) is not the source but, for example, only the area of dissemination. The contingent situation of the past is already present *in* the Christian tradition, twisting it, and in our contemporary situation God is as creative in liberation as he was before: he has not ceased to be 'the biblical God' in the meantime. I have already said above that we cannot simply set 'experience' and 'tradition' abruptly over against each other, because the tradition is the experiential horizon of all new experiences. So if we may speak of two poles, these poles lie in the past cultural forms and the present cultural forms which have to be sought today for the one gospel, which is itself the real source of both the earlier and the contemporary cultural form and expression of the faith. Of no single period of the tradition of faith, not even that of the Bible, may the cultural forms and historical context be absolutized. But this certainly does not mean that these historical and socio-cultural mediations are worthless for faith or to be neglected. On the contrary, they have a very positive function, for all their relativity, since they are the only possible vehicles for the meaning of the offer of revelation to which an answer is given in faith, precisely because the gospel, which is not bound to one culture, can nevertheless be seen and found *in* the special features of particular, culturally limited structures of understanding (only there and precisely there). Anyone who claims that the historical mediations are theologically irrelevant because of their relative specialization, so that they relate only to the particular situation, is depriving the concrete history of Jesus of its specific importance for our history today. The Christian constants are expressed *in* many historical mediations which change down the ages, and are not as it were 'abstracted' from these concrete events.

At this point I must interrupt my argument in order to remove a misunderstanding that has arisen. Louis Dupré[28] accuses me of having failed in *Jesus* to do justice to the importance of what I there call the 'offer of revelation' in favour of our interpretation of faith (and the 'interpretaments' mentioned there). He says that I attach too much weight to them. In his view there is an interpretation which precedes any human interpretation in faith and is already given with the offer of revelation; and this then itself forms the basis of our further interpretations of faith. On the other hand, in her reaction to my farewell speech Ellen van Wolde[29] says precisely the opposite, namely that I am still attaching too much importance to the 'offer of revelation', which in my view is concealing a transcultural, supratemporal substance of faith. I think that neither of these critics has understood me properly on one point and in so doing they neutralize each other's objections. On the one hand it is clear to me that the offer of revelation is not an empty cipher: it has a meaningful content, thought this can never be grasped or objectified. And this means that the offer-from-God of course provides its own *direction* of interpretation, as the normative basis of our non-arbitrary interpretations of faith. If Dupré means that, then I am completely at one with him, but not if he means more than that. It only means that, regardless of the degree to which experience and interpretation form one whole in the expression of reality, experience is not to be reduced to interpretation. In this sense there are pre-linguistic aspects in the unitary complex of experience and interpretation, but that element of experience is never expressed without interpretation. On the other hand I go along with van Wolde when she says that the object of faith can never be given outside the 'object-subject' relationship. Of course. But in that case the relationship to the object must also be taken seriously within this relationship, and within the relationship as a whole is not a product of the subject. Without an 'objective' content to the offer of meaning (though this can never be 'objectified'), all faith interpretations would be pure projections and would be reaching for something that has never been nor ever will be.[30] However, the divine offer of meaning, or the divine challenge to human beings to provide meaning, cannot be put into human words directly, nor does it coincide directly with the meaning given by men and women.

From what has been said (before this short excursus) it emerges that faith in God's revelation always has a starting point in this world of ours: there are historical mediations. The mediation of revelation varies, depending on place, society and period, but it nevertheless comes within the interpretation of faith which is presented on each occasion. Thus any possible understanding of faith takes place on the basis of and through the medium of the human understanding of reality – distinctive to a particular culture in which the gospel is proclaimed and heard. This understanding of reality is historical and cultural; thus it is there only as one culturally determined, limited and special understanding of reality (despite a universal human element that is present in it, itself above all a logical and largely unconscious basic structure). Therefore the question of Christian identity through the changing centuries can be answered only by a comparison of differing cultural forms of the Christian experience of faith, interpretation of faith, and praxis of faith, as an answer to God's offer of revelation in Jesus. The only difference between the past Christian tradition and the new Christian traditions that we shall have to hand down and make lies in the fact that we can make comparisons with the past after the event; that past has as it were already behind it the risk of the interpretation of faith to be made in its own time. By contrast, we still have it ahead, and are in the middle of the process of interpretation, with all the uncertain dangers of success and failure, of guesses and mistakes, and ultimately of orthodoxy or 'heresy' (with its own content of truth which has got out of joint).


The problem of the interpretation and transmission of faith is thus: how do we build a bridge between the past tradition of faith and our existence as Christians in new situations? In the last resort the Christian message is preached *now*, no longer to the old citizens of Corinth, Ephesus and Thessalonica; it is preached to men and women who are our contemporaries, with their own understanding of themselves and the world, living in an almost post-modern social and economic social system and labour system, with their own, albeit uncertain, political plans. Moreover, believing now means bringing the Christian tradition of faith and experience to life and making it understandable in the present, in other, different historical situations and with other categories of thought and experience. This calls for a mutually critical and nevertheless continuous relationship between the past Christian tradition and our understanding of faith in our contemporary socio-historical and existential situation and our present-day praxis – in such a way that our presentation of the gospel today does not damage the identity of the liberating tradition of the gospel which discloses meaning and truth; in other words, by preserving its dynamics and orthodoxy.

As a result of all this, the living interpretation of faith, expressed schematically, comes about in two phases, which together form one dialectical whole.

First, any believing attitude must be capable of expression with reference to the Christian tradition of faith. This means that believing is also an interpretation of faith. (I shall not enter here into the technical possibilities, difficulties and 'methodological dispute' in contemporary hermeneutics, which I hope to work out technically in another book.)

Secondly, the attitude of any believer must also be capable of being justified with reference to an analysis and interpretation of the present situation in which we live. (This makes any interpretation and praxis of faith, *in* its intention of being universal, at the same time nevertheless contextual.) Otherwise there would be a short-circuit between categories of experience and thought from the past and those from the present.

However, these two stages of the one process of interpretation form a dialectical whole. For we only understand the Christian tradition from questions which are addressed to us from the present situation; the understanding of our past already implies an interpretation of the present. And conversely, our Christian critical understanding of the present is itself also influenced historically by the Christian tradition.

This constant looking in two directions by the believer means that the process of interpretation in faith will consist in bringing the earlier phases of the tradition of faith as we understand them into relationship with our analysis of the contemporary situation, in the twofold sense analysed above: the situation both in the general cultural and in the specifically Christian sense.


## III    Present-day society and culture comes within the understanding of revelation

From the analyses given in this first chapter we have already understood that experiencing-and-understanding revelation is also a constitutive element in the process of revelation itself. Precisely here, perhaps paradoxically, revelation can also be handed down to others. For the personal and collective experience in faith of decisive salvation in Jesus which his first followers had could be communicated to contemporaries and to later generations because these first followers described their experiences by means of their socially shared system of communication (a semiotic system, one conveying meaning). This was initially in the Jewish language, later in the Greek language, in the understanding of reality characteristic of Asia Minor, and so on. In each instance we have a culture-specific appropriation of the message of the gospel: living contact between the gospel and the changing, culturally-shaped understanding of reality by believers in a particular cultural period. Think, for example, of the Christian message as this is translated by the authentic letters of Paul and the same message again translated into the cultural climate of the understanding of reality in Asia Minor at that time in the letters to the Christians of Colossae and Ephesus! The continuity and the difference here become quite clear. Because each time a different semiotic cultural system (or one conveying meaning) is involved, a history of socio-cultural historical mediations comes into being: specifically, a history of Christian believing in a variety of tongues and languages. Moreover, the distinctiveness of these historical mediations, then and now, begins to play a greater role in this conception of what the interpretation of faith and thus the specific form of Christian faith is than Christians were formerly aware, though they did the same thing spontaneously and often without reflection in an instinctive Christian way.


If all this is the case, then it already emerges that for us the identity in the meaning of the gospel cannot primarily lie at the level of the Bible and the past tradition of faith, at least as such, and therefore cannot be found in a material repetition of that past (in any kind of 'fundamentalism', whether in conservative or in progressive forms). Far less, however, can it be found at the level of the situation, then and now, *as such* (whether in a biblicist or a modernist direction). This identity of meaning can only be found in the fluctuating 'middle field', in a swinging to and fro between tradition and situation, and thus at the level of the corresponding relationship between the original message (tradition, which also includes the situation of the time) and the situation, then and now, which is different each time. The fundamental identity of meaning between the successive periods of Christian understanding of the offer of revelation is not to be found in corresponding terms (e.g. a parallel between the situation of the Bible and our situation, on the basis of which one could then, for instance, use Jesus' cleansing of the temple to justify the action of squatters in Amsterdam) but on corresponding relationships between all the terms involved (message and situation, then and now). Moreover there is a fundamental unity and identity: this has no relation to the terms of the factors involved, but to the relationship between all these terms. The following diagram may clarify it to some extent:

the given articulation or relationship

$$\frac{\text{Jesus' message}}{\substack{\text{the socio-historical} \\ \text{context of Jesus}}} = \frac{\text{the New Testament message}}{\substack{\text{the socio-historical} \\ \text{context of the NT}}}$$

is reproduced, for example, in the relationship:

$$\frac{\text{patristic understanding of faith}}{\text{the socio-historical context then}} = \frac{\substack{\text{mediaeval understanding of} \\ \text{faith}}}{\text{the socio-historical context then}}$$

and this relationship, given and reproduced, must ultimately be reproduced once more in the following relationship or articulation:

$$= \frac{\text{the present understanding of faith in the year 1990}}{\text{our socio-historical and existential context in the year 1990}}$$

The identity of relationship between these articulations of nevertheless completely different terms bears the Christian identity of meaning. The equal proportion of relationships down through the Christian tradition of faith is a norm, an orientation and an inspiration; it is the model on the basis of which now, loyal to the gospel, we can nevertheless also make its message comprehensible here and now.

So we never have a direct view of the Christian identity of meaning; moreover it can never be laid down once and for all. But this does not mean that it is arbitrary. Christian identity, which is one and the same, is never complete identity, but proportional identity. In their differing interpretations of the one gospel, particular historical and cultural mediations sometimes contradict one another, in the sense that they cannot all be harmonized on the same level. But that one level is a fiction. The unity is a unity in depth in which some things stand out. Therefore we cannot look at what is called 'the development of dogma' (the life of the Christian tradition in various cultures or at different periods of the same culture) in the same way as the Scholastics or neo-Scholastics, nor even as in the more sophisticated approach of Newman, namely as a permanent explicitation of a substance of faith which was always already implicit, an explicitation from the implicit to the explicit; from the Bible in roughly a straight line to the present day. For although the offer of revelation with its non-objectifiable meaning and content is indeed present from the beginning, this meaning as assignable and expressed is to be found only in the believing interpretations of men and women in a particular social and cultural context. The periodical twists in the cultural understanding of reality rule out a purely explicative process. Something else is involved. What we have is, rather, the process of a constantly new inculturation of a gospel which is not bound to one culture, but which is not given in the Bible, either, apart from a limited, particular cultural form.

A consequence of this is that earlier expressions of faith, even dogmas, are on the one hand irrevocable and irreversible: they cannot be done away with, since within a particular social and cultural system of reference they have time and again expressed and sought to safeguard the mystery of Jesus Christ and thus ultimately the mystery of God in a way which is sometimes more and sometimes less successful for that time. But on the other hand, in their cultural and historical forms they can become irrelevant and indeed meaningless for later generations if they are simply repeated as they stand, because earlier generations expressed their deepest convictions about Christian faith within another semantic field, in another system of communication and through a different perspective on reality. If we think of the solemn statement of the council of Florence-Ferrara with which I began this book, for the council fathers of the time this statement really meant (in retrospect) that *for them* Jesus Christ was the only access and living way to God; they could not imagine anything else for their own belief. That is correct. But essentially bound up with this was their mistake in failing to see God's work of salvation outside Christianity so that they scorned anything that was not Christian. At an even deeper level, the mistake lay in confusing a personal experiential conviction with an 'objectifiably knowable truth in itself', extrapolated from faith, which anyone could have discovered had they taken the trouble and been sufficiently open! So according to this argument, non-Christians lack good will, a view which has all kinds of baneful consequences.

But even dogmas which have become irrelevant with the passing of time remain theological, i.e. important for our understanding of faith; they even point the way. Even now, though without the consequences and implications of the council of Florence, we have to be able to explain why Jesus, confessed as the Christ, is the only way of life *for us*, though God leaves other ways open for others. We also have to explain why we are and remain sincere Christians without regarding non-Christians as heretics or discriminating against them. Finally, we have to explain, in sober humility and witnessing to theological truth, what we mean by mission.

The conclusion is that there is Christian identity *in* cultural breaks and shifts, and not an identity on the basis of what in a purely intellectualistic way used to be called 'homogeneous identity' (which cannot of course be proved historically).

Cultural shifts are therefore always times of testing, crisis and uncertainty for the Christian churches. This is part of the nature of Christian faith in its historical manifestation: the acclimatization of Christian faith to a 'new culture' or a new cultural phase in a particular cultural tradition, for example the Western tradition, is indeed full of risks, but it is the only way of presenting the gospel here and now in a living way. And that is what 'the church of God' is concerned with, not with the preservation or collection of 'cultural' relics by the churches as a memorial of the Christian past.

The result of these considerations may be clear: the Christian *perception* of the meaning of the offer of revelation comes about in a creative *giving* of meaning: in a new production of meaning or a re-reading of the Bible and the tradition of faith within constantly new situations of every kind. Interpretation and praxis *make* new traditions, in creative trust (as we can already see in the multiplicity of the Old and New Testament writings). That is the living transmission of the tradition of gospel faith to coming generations. Christian identity – 'what Christians hold in common' – as mediated through a variety of cultural and social worlds like those of Jesus, of Paul, Augustine and Athanasius, Pope Gregory the Great, Thomas and Bonaventure, Luther and Calvin, Teresa of Avila, Martin Luther King and Bishop Oscar Romero – lies in one and the same fundamental view of God and human beings and their mutual relationship, though this same perspective of faith was and is always present in historically divergent, different and even irreconcilable anthropological and theological views. Nevertheless, it is present in such a way that within the distorting cultural limits that are actually laid down, these limits are nevertheless 'delimited' and transcended by Christians in a way which is difficult to conceptualize. So we can recognize the authentic Christianity of, for example, the Christians named above and at the same time, in our situation, nevertheless reverently exercise criticism on particular forms of the practice of faith and views of faith in former times which do not hold for us.

This last, of course, also applies to the present, given the time-warp that can now, too, be found among believers. Above all non-Christians often tell Catholics that if they have criticisms of the church, the Pope and other church leaders, they ought to leave their church; others press our Catholic identity on us. They often use the analogy of a football league: if you don't observe the rules you ought to leave and for example go and play baseball. Such an argument makes a downright category mistake. In that case Augustine with his many new ideas and also Paul, indeed all the evangelists in their time, should have left the church. The basic mistake in this argument is that people fail to recognize that a church, as the organized form of a religious experiential tradition and as the community of 'a way of life', is also of course an 'interpretative community'. It certainly also knows rules and criteria, but they cannot be compared with those of other, non-interpretative, clubs or societies; they allow pluralism of belief within one and the same society of faith within particular limits which are difficult to define. I do not want to spend more time on the empty arguments I have just mentioned.

## CHAPTER 2

# Men and Women in Search of God, God in Search of Men and Women

## 1. Why God has become a problem for Western men and women

It has now ceased to be the case, at least in the Western world and the sectors of other parts of the world which are influenced by it, that men and women believe in God as a matter of course. It is possible to indicate not only external factors for this but also internal factors, associated with belief and its institutionalization in the church.

### I External factors

#### A. No need for a 'dualistic' posing of the problem

Sociologists of religion usually talk of the collapse of the social 'credibility structures' of belief in God in a secularized Western world. That means that in such a society the personal convictions of believers are no longer given any social support; human inwardness is no longer confirmed or encouraged by society as it is: rather, it is disturbed and made uncertain by society. But this modern liberal distinction between interiority (the private sphere) and externality (the public sphere) needs first to be subjected to criticism, including theological criticism, for at the same time it distorts the problems surrounding belief in God. Since Max Weber and Talcott Parsons this distinction has regularly been the starting point of many forms of sociology of religion, including the school of Peter Berger, though he already qualifies it in some respects.

Since modern times, every citizen of the Western world has spoken of human inwardness and, alongside it, of the more superficial side of being human, namely one's conditioning by social and economic situations.

This Cartesian dualism characterizes the whole of modern Western culture and provided the picture of modern men and women with their inward and their outward sides. Once this emphasis began to be laid on human subjectivity, the human individual was understood as a kind of *homo clausus* (Leibniz's 'monad'), an individual 'I' which is separated from the outside world by a mysterious wall, by nature, society, culture, though no one was in a position to say what this wall really is. Our human body? Our skin? Individual and society were seen as two independent entities, though it was accepted that one influenced the other.

The individual 'I' also appears in dominant Western philosophies of subjectivity and consequently in most forms of modern sociology as something that stands outside society, living in its own internal little house, while on the other hand society, sometimes hostile, is located outside the individual: there are two independent entities which have some contact with each other. Consequently all the emphasis is placed either on personal human inwardness or on society. In both cases one of the two poles is secondary. So in one instance the personal individual is what really 'exists', what is real, while society is a kind of abstraction, a system without a subject. In the other, by contrast, this social system is the true reality, while what is termed the 'individual' is disqualified as being the 'abstract individual'. These terms, on the one hand the enclosed personality and on the other society without a subject, still dominate many forms of both liberal and Marxist sociology of religion.

In this view, while personal action and the social system influence each other, the starting point is the presupposition of separate forms of existence, which subsequently begin to permeate each other. Here the ideal picture of the ego, which is never achieved, is often that of a free individual independent of all other existence. I myself in no way want to reduce the individual to a sum of social relationships, far less reduce society to the total of individual actions. The critical question is whether this sharp dividing line between an inside and an outside in human beings is justified, and whether it does not saddle us with the wrong picture of what it is to be human. All this will prove to be of the utmost importance when we talk about personal belief in God in a structurally atheistic world.

The picture of the 'enclosed individual', glorifying itself, autonomous and personal, is still expressed most clearly in Kant: he thinks that human beings are not in a position from their a prioristic little inner house to penetrate to the 'Ding an sich', the thing in itself, to a reality independent of them. That is modern close-knit subjectivity! In fact it has an influence on many sociological theories in which a distinction is drawn between the social action of individuals and their so-called non-social action, which is then evidently imagined in purely individual terms. Moreover, this modern picture of humankind presents itself as the expression of permanent human nature, and for Christians it then often becomes a kind of dogma of faith. In fact we need to note that this is a very recent picture, produced by Westerners. It is a culturally determined view of humankind in a historical context, and one against which there is increasing resistance as time goes on. We should not give up the modern 'liberal' achievements of the human subject in favour of a subjectless world, but we should nevertheless try to work ourselves free from the one-sidednesses of the Western philosophy of subjectivity.


The human ego is itself a social and cultural process, and the so-called inner life is itself a living part of a cultural process. In an individual we read the history of a particular culture. There is no dualism, but the dialectic of two poles: neither pole can be defined in itself without the other, though nevertheless we usually contrast person and society in our spontaneous but pre-critical experience. However, everything about a person, including his or her inwardness, is social. On the other hand, that does not mean that a person is made up only of his or her social development: these are two different forms of expression. Even the deepest structure of our personality is social. From our childhood, even before there is personal consciousness, we human beings are socialized. Becoming a person is acculturation. That modern Western men and women are clammed up in an emotional inwardness and have come to be subjected to greater social self-control is entirely connected with this modern 'subjectivity'.

The modern contrast between object and subject also called for control over one's affections and emotions and thus heightened the impression of human inwardness over against the outside world of objects. The I then lives in a kind of cage. This also gave rise to changes of structure in the individual, as a result of which the accent was placed even more strongly on the I. Hence the solitarinesss of many Western people. The greater individualization and inwardness since the Renaissance, as a result of which the wall between the inner world and the outside world has become thicker, shows that this wall for the most part consists of a cultural self-control over human feelings which functions automatically; these feelings then develop more strongly within individuals. What is controlled socially is then spontaneously and intensively experienced as a person's own inwardness. But in fact the social control is the wall between what we call inwardness and what we call outwardness. The specific social life of modern men and women is made up only of this enclosed inwardness, since the structure of human personality never displays an inside and an outside: it is a dialectical phenomenon.

The conception of an absolutely independent individual, a 'monad', is an artificial product of a particular historical phase of Western man in *his* interpretation of his experience of himself (*her* experience was never expressed in this Western philosophy of subjectivity). On the one hand this artificial product is a day-dream of Western man: he wants to be completely independent; on the other hand the product is based on a reification of mechanisms of individual self-control, the wall between inside and outside. Norbert Elias has been able to verify all this in a large-scale analysis by the precise decoding of the eating and living habits of modern men and women.[1]

This new view is concerned to form a picture of humankind through many mutually interdependent people who form 'figurations' with one another (family, neighbourood, district, nation, state, etc.). Here society is not an abstraction of the properties of individuals living separate lives, far less a system without subjects or an independent totality outside or alongside individuals. It is made up of individuals, but not intended or planned by anyone: a web of mutual dependencies. According to Elias, social dance above all can show us what social configurations are. Social dance does not exist outside individuals and is not an abstraction; the dance figuration is nevertheless relatively independent of the specific individuals dancing here and now, though not independent of individual subjects as such. Such a dance shows us how a feudal, a capitalist and a communist society are also configurations.

Societies have come into being, and have done so in a way which none of those involved have foreseen, intended or planned, or even achieved. Many social processes have a relative autonomy from the wishes and intentions of those who set them going and give them shape; they have the character of 'developments', of a structured process, and therefore lend themselves to scientific investigation. These very structures also form the structure of the personality of individuals in a particular society. The consequences of this non-dualistic anthropology in connection with belief in God in our time will emerge directly.

## B. Difficulties over belief in God in the modern Western world

A characteristic of modern times is the transition from living under a relative pre-programming to living by choices.[2] In pre-modern times people could generally say: 'Things are like that: that is how one lives, that is how one marries, that is how one dies, that is one's religious life', and so on. What was experienced as socially unavoidable was interpreted as necessity: that was how things had to be. Any deviation from that was dangerous for society. By contrast, modern life 'pluralizes', and this pluriformity is also expressed in a plurality of institutions. Moreover, in line with overcoming the dichotomy between inwardness and outwardness we can discover a direct connection, which can even be analysed in sociological terms, between institutional and social changes and cognitive changes in personality.

Men and women require their convictions to be endorsed by society. Because modernity has given rise to a multiplicity of world-views and institutions, and it is no longer the case that one, specifically Christian, view of the world is given social endorsement, the world has become a kind of market place in which different and divergent views of the world and humankind are on sale, from which one can choose. That is the way in which many sociologists speak. But even their expressions like 'credibility structures' and 'all kinds of views were on offer' still betray the ongoing influence of the old dualism. The terms presuppose one's own convictions about life as a kind of autonomous, inner independence which subsequently is either supported or weakened by external factors. If we strip what is correct in this sociological view of the remnants of a dualistic anthropology, we have to say that in a pluralistic society even the personality structure of belief has changed in modern men and women.

Modern men and women live in a world with many possibilities for choice, as a result of which they are more than ever thrown back on their own inwardness. However, the impression of a distance between the so-called enclosed 'I' and the external multiplicity of the views of life on offer has been intensified in modern experience. People feel more solitary in their choice. They feel more heavy laden, or, in other cases, unfettered and carefree, at home in the supposedly free world with the offer of newspapers, radio, television, magazines and discos. What is forgotten here, however, is that this multiplicity of possibilities has also become an internal qualification of a person's convictions about life. This multiplicity does not lie 'outside' a person as in an open market place but is internalized throughout human consciousness. The heavier burden or the superficial matter-of- factness does not simply come from outside, but also from within, from the modern structure of personality itself. A person's inner conviction is perhaps just as strong as ever as confirmation, but of course more modest, more reserved and in this sense to some degree 'relativized': modern believers know that there is also truth in other convictions about life.

The possibilities of choice do not lie outside believers: the modern structure of religious personality has even become different from before. Men and women experience themselves as beings with divergent possibilities. 'Atheism' then becomes a personal possibility and not just an external offer of packages between which the individual can choose. Such a situation was completely alien to pre-modern men and women. The answer to the question 'What can I know? What can I believe and hope?' is no longer just given 'objectivistically', as it were dished up in advance by a society which formerly recognized only the Christian view (or what went for that). Nor is the answer any longer present subjectively, because the structure of the modern personality has a greater openness, has even itself become pluralistic: the other also seems possible for me. That is not to deny that in particular protected milieus the structure of personality has not changed; here too there are often time-warps. The question here is: how long can one live in such a protected milieu within a pluralistic society without finding oneself in a ghetto?

For anyone who takes part in a modern society (however critically) and lives authentically in it, the other possibility of living is part of the structure of his or her own personality: the unshaken certainty that one continues to possess the truth oneself while others are mistaken is no longer a possibility. So the pluralism is not just institutional; pluralism is to be found within us as cognitive reality. That modern men and women, including believers, as it were spontaneously reject the theory that 'salvation is to be found only within the church' points to a spontaneous, pre-theoretical position as part of the structure of their own personality structure. They themselves think in pluralistic terms and know that no one has rights over the truth – although in that case there is then a threat of what is called indifferentism: to each his or her truth. At all events, modern men and women live in a world of uncertainty, which is only interrupted in fits and starts by a new philosophical construction or a neo-religious movement which passes by at greater or lesser speed.[3]

So we have more than simply the collapse of what sociologists call social 'plausibility structures'. The social inwardness of individuals, including believers, has changed. A different structure of individual personality has come into being. With this basic qualification we can then largely agree with the sociologist Peter Berger that there is a relationship between the secularity now socially dominant and the fading of the religious consciousness, which can be analysed by sociologists.[4] The dominant culture of, for example, a great city exerts a strong cognitive pressure on the religious awareness of country-dwellers, who formerly lived in a very uniform religious milieu and have now moved to a great city. But this is not so much a merely external pressure; the inner structure of people's personalities is also gradually changed by it. That also emerges from the divergent course of such a process of de-Christianization: some people abandon their belief in God quietly, becoming secularized before they themselves are aware of it; others do not submit so easily to the social pressure from within and from the outside; yet others begin to 'haggle' with their belief: they give up particular practices and save others.

In this connection there is initially a break or gap between the cognitive presuppositions of the religious consciousness (the personality structure of the believer) and the cognitive presuppositions of the dominant social milieu around them, which is in fact secular. In large cities, belief in God is almost 'deviant behaviour', sometimes even treated with some compassion and contempt; it is praised by others to the degree that religions function as a factor which 'provides social stability'. In place of the former social 'religious *a priori*' the dominant feature of modern societies is more a social 'empirical *a priori*' as a result of the prestige of science and technology, which not only dominate our society but have also changed the individual structures of our personality. There is not only a modern society but a modern conscious-ness, and these two form one whole. For many people, this changed structure of personality is the starting point of their life; they were born into a secularized society and become acculturized into it. Many people no longer believe; not out of unwilllingness, but because culturally they are incapable of doing so.

We must not, however, strain ourselves over what many people call the now-valid *a priori*, 'the modern consciousness'. For this *a priori* is purely a historical given, and thus in no sense a privileged awareness, as some people think. It is one element in an ongoing cultural history. Moreover, to argue on the basis of our dominant so-called secularized world that all belief in God is finally over seems to me to be an uncritical identification (on neo-liberal or Marxist lines) of the present, or one's own time, with the eschatological climax of the whole of history. Even Hegel knew at least a dialectical follow-up.

'Modernity' is in fact a relativizing factor and therefore a challenge to belief in God; but as modernity it is itself also a historical and conse-quently a relative phenomenon, and thus open to change. It may then be statistically true that those who believe in God have become a cognitive minority in a modern society, but this statistical fact does not have any prognostic value as such. All this does not tell us anything about the truth and power of attraction that will continue to emanate from belief in God, though it does say something about the circumstances and the way in which truths prove more or less convincing; pastorally and indeed catechetically this is very important.

Nevertheless the problem of truth retains all its force. The modern consciousness has also made us experientially poor. Many cultural analyses show how, as a result of modernity, technological and bureaucratic Western society has suppressed all kinds of emotional, real aspects and depths in human beings to which people now seek to give due place in group dynamics, sensitivity training and so on, artificially and thus alongside real living together in society (which is left as it is), because these things have been suppressed in ordinary everyday life.[5] As it were laboratory projects are carried out as to what a human society should be and how it should be achieved.

On the other hand it does not makes any sense to see 'modernity' on the whole as a phenomenon between generations, the only correct answer to which is the conservatism of a pre-modern society. Instead of wrestling with problems which really exist, that is arrogantly to assume the attitude of 'these problems must not be'; this is an attitude of sheer but also disastrous 'counter-modernity',[6] which in some people conjures up unhealthy and irrational apocalyptic visions. Despite the terrors of the time, the French Revolution was essentially a process of liberation: it was the major influence in making the freedoms and human rights which we now treasure part of our modern personality structure. But this 'bourgeois liberation' in turn subsequently became oppressive and repressive. The present-day 'post-modern' question is not so much concerned with *my* freedom, often at the expense of the freedom of *others*, as with solidarity with all people, and above all with those men and women who are unfree and oppressed.

The conclusion may be that this approach in terms of external culture, which also says something about the individual structure of human personality, already does a good deal to clear the area under investigation. The causes of the crisis in belief in God, above all in the Western world, are also connected with the pluralistic structure of our society and with modern personality-structure. All this merely says something about the social and cultural context in which 'truth' can be recognized as truth.

## C. The present 'world context' of belief in God

In the first chapter I spoke about the deconcentration of the church in favour of the salvation that God seeks to bring about for human beings in our history: salvation from God in and through the action of human liberation, in many spheres.

Gustavo Gutiérrez and Jon Sobrino have repeated in a number of publications that talk of God in developing countries is basically different from talk of God in prosperous countries.[7] The conversation partner of the Western theologian is the secularized person, the agnostic or the atheist. By contrast the conversation partner of the theologian in the Third World is the non-person, the one who is poor and oppressed.

Although this observation is acutely correct from a particular perspective, it is nevertheless a half-truth, but precisely in being so it is a challenge to Western thought about God. Poverty in its most oppressive form is in fact the social condition of by far the majority of the world's population. Moreover, we know that this is not a matter of fate or natural law, but the consequence of all kinds of interactive human factors of a cultural, socio-economic and political kind – of a system which can, however, be changed.

There is good reason for the statements in the EATWOT conferences of Third World theologians that 'the believing but exploited people' in the Third World contrast with 'the secularized and exploitative West'.[8] The two problems are interconnected and cannot be separated. The existence of the 'non-person', the poor and oppressed, in a subcontinent like Latin America or a country like South Africa, lands which have been dominated by Christians for centuries, is a scandal for any belief in God. For many people it makes belief in God incredible. Therefore in the West we can no longer talk of God without relating our thought about God to the massive suffering of men and women elsewhere and anonymously among us (in the so-called Fourth World).

To speak theologically is also to speak anthropologically, at least in the Christian experiential tradition. Therefore I too think that the focus of Western talk of God, of theology, lies in our concrete universal history as a history of suffering and oppression and also a history of opposition to this oppression, a history of liberating action. What can it mean that I, as a Westerner who believes in God, claim to find salvation in my belief in God when two-thirds of humankind is unfree, enslaved and starving to death? Westerners who believe in God have often concealed this gnawing problem by referring to 'another', 'better', eschatological world, and have also covered it up under the so-called cloak of love which may not take sides, but because of a false concept of reconciliation, in so doing they are in fact taking sides with the oppressive system, which is disqualified at best through words, not through actions. Such a position is no answer to the question of the meaning of our historical existence *in* this world. Human existence, above all in modern conditions, is increasingly an 'interdependent' existence: social oppression elsewhere is, by virtue of my and their humanity, a challenge for all of us, including me in the West, as human beings and as Christians. This is not romanticism, but the sober consequence of 'being human' as solidarity with anyone who bears a human name. This applies above all to those who confess the universal will of God for salvation.

Therefore, for example in Latin America and Asia, liberation theology, despite or more precisely in its geographical contextuality, is a question of universal significance. Can there be authentic meaning in my history if the history of more than half the human race is meaningless and absurd? Is that not a threadbare regional, cynical egotism? That is where the problem of the 'crisis of meaning' lies today. It is not just a problem for the poor but also for the rich: a universal problem. The Christian option for the poor, taking their side, is therefore a contextual expression of universal love for men and women.

All this means that the present-day context in which we speak meaningfully and productively, in a liberating way, about God, is the existential context of oppression and liberation. It is not the only possible context, but in my view without this context all other possible contexts become detached from life and become incredible to many people.

## II   Internal factors

Quite apart from all these external factors there are also particular problems arising out ot the special 'object' with which we are concerned here: the reality 'God'. Granted these problems arise everywhere and at all times, but in a so-called modern and anti-modern or modern-critical time they bring out old facets of the 'question of God' in a new and heightened way. I want to point out a series of problems here. I would not claim that they are exhaustive. Bringing out these difficulties already helps us to guard against an ideological misuse of the name of God.

Here I am in no way starting from problems like those stressed by the critical rationalist Hans Albert in connection with Hans Küng's book *Does God Exist?*,[9] nor even from academic philosophical problems (although we cannot by-pass them either). My starting point is the problems specifically felt by present-day men and women, which make it difficult for them to believe in God, even if they themselves cannot express these difficulties of belief as such precisely.

### A. *'You are a hidden God' (Isaiah 45.15)*

The main problem is not so much the non-existence of God. Historically, affirmation or denial of this existence is inextricably bound up with the question of the nature, the character or 'the being' of God. For often the existence of God is denied because people hang on to completely wrong, humanly foolish ideas about precisely who God is. So I am not in any way referring to the etymology of the word 'God' in ancient or modern languages, but rather asking: what do believers mean to say, meaningfully and in a generally understandable way, when they take the word God on their lips and thus talk about God? In Christian and indeed other religious communities people can talk of God as a matter of course. But from the moment that one reads, for example in scripture, that 'God dwells in light inaccessible' (I Tim.6.16) and people never perceive God anywhere, this supposed matter-of-factness becomes more precarious.

For there is no place anywhere in the universe and in what we loosely call our 'inwardness' to indicate where God can be pointed to, as I can point to John or Anne standing near me. However, if nothing within our sphere of human experience can be identified as that to which or the one to whom we are pointing when we use the word God, the question becomes urgent as to what meaning the use of that word in fact has, what reality it refers to, and does so in such a way that even non-believers can at least say it with us in a meaningful way. What the word God means must be capable of being communicated meaningfully, even to those who reject what believers mean by it.

So we have to investigate the precise semantic context and also the grammar of the use of the word God, uncovering the context in which our human experience thinks it meaningful to use the word God, YHWH, Allah, and so on, and at all events what believers mean by it when they speak about 'him', 'it' or 'her'. We can also raise the question of the truth and the verifiability of an assertion prematurely, no matter how important these questions may be. First it will have to be demonstrated how relevant belief in God is to life. The question of the humanly meaningful, semantic significance of the word God is the necessary presupposition of the question of truth about God. The issue is then the context of human life in which the word God is used meaningfully and in an understandable way. We have to know what we mean when we are talking together about something. Otherwise talk of God, above all, becomes a chaotic adventure.

This does not rule out the possibility that such a semantic clarification can in fact coincide completely with what we call a theological reflection on belief in God. It will emerge from this that scientific reflection on belief in God and the existence of God is in no way identical with belief in God. This reflection is both at the service of and in contrast to actual belief in God. By participating internally in belief in God, any theological reflection distances itself critically from actual belief in God. Because church preaching has all too often begun from the evidence of what the word God means and paid virtually no attention to the semantics of the word God, many believers in modern society have been left out in the cold. That, too, is a factor in the so-called modern crisis of faith.

The word 'transcendence' used in connection with God is similarly full of difficulties. In using the term transcendence people are of course working with models: something surpasses something else. In itself transcendence is a 'this-worldly model', in other words, a model that says something about relationships in the world. Can this term be extended to say anything about something or someone who goes beyond all that is real or imaginable? Thus extended and applied to what or whom we call God, this concept still has many different meanings:

(*a*) Something can be transcendent in respect of our human thought (epistemological transcendence). In that case the transcendent is not just something that has never been conceived of by men and women, but also what is inconceivable and unimaginable to them. One can never invent *God* by oneself, but only idols. If that is the case, does it then become illogical to believe in God? Is not the notion of God contradictory? People may not usually put things in this way, but this problem is unmistakably part of their experiences.

(*b*) Something can be transcendent in relation to our human experiences. God is then that which cannot be experienced. But in that case how can we confirm the existence of God? Or can we state that God is experienced as the ground of all experience which is experienced alongside it; as the one whose existence casts its quickening shadow on everything that we experience?

(*c*) Something can also be called transcendent in relation to space and time, the whole of the universe. In that case God is the timeless one who can never be located in the curved space of the universe. Is God then the 'wholly Other'? But how can something that is wholly other than what we already know, experience and imagine, be believed in and celebrated? Talking about God as the wholly Other without further corrections like saying that he is wholly Near is logically inconsistent. Talking about divine transcendence without venturing to talk of radical immanence is logically already untenable and absurd.

So transcendence seems to be a model with all kinds of intrinsic problems. Therefore some forms of atheism are a justified criticism of traditional concepts of God, even Christian ones. The criticisms made by Feuerbach and others have taught us that a concept of God as the wholly Other is not only logically incoherent but in social and personal terms has no liberating, critical and productive significance. The wholly Other can legitimate oppression and dictatorship as well as human liberation.

Moreover we have to analyse the relationship between cognitive and emotional elements in belief in God. In modern times the tendency has been to contrast the two elements and in so doing wrongly to identify the emotional with the non-cognitive. However, analyses of emotion have shown that emotion has a cognitive value and thus discloses reality; it is not just a kind of meaningless concomitant of the scientific, which is said to have exclusive cognitive claims. The cognitive intentionality of belief in God cannot be identified with conceptual knowledge either.

On the other hand concrete faith in God without images and concepts is not meaningful or historically effective, although we have no divine concepts. All our concepts, including those which we use in connection with God, are suitable only for expressing non-godly, worldly things. There are no revealed concepts. Yet belief in God cannot be had without particular concepts of God. Can we, must we, say anything more than that what we call God is a mysterious unknown X? But what use is a mysterious Mr X to me? Or does the inconceivability of God mean that we do better to keep silent about God, in order to give him his due? But that means saying that all religions are irrelevant - which is far from obvious.

If all our images and concepts of God, without any exception (*pace* Paul Tillich), are in any case human discoveries and products, and we do not have a single positive and authentic concept of God, without the reality of God itself being our discovery and our product, the study of the so-called sociogenesis or the social process of the formation of our 'concepts of God' is also relevant to theology. An investigation of the structure of the social and historical configuration in which particular concepts of God have developed then becomes necessary. A theological analysis of authentic belief in God is certainly possible, but soon threatens to become ideological without an analysis of the society in which these conceptions of God function. You cannot isolate the social function of belief in God from its theological significance. It is never just a matter of religious good intentions, but of the visible consequences of belief in God at the level of our history. Even very abstract confessions of faith can have a very specific social significance and political function. And here the question is always *Cui bono?* Who profits from these particular concepts of God? And who are their victims?

Therefore we need not only a study of the sociogenesis of our concepts of God but also an investigation of the way in which concepts of God which came into being in a former social and cultural situation and functioned there well, or even optimally, relate to changed social and cultural contexts. Originally liberating images of God, like YHWH, could become oppressive in changed circumstances, as Jesus' reaction demonstrated in his time. Jesus did not attack the Yahwistic belief in God but the way in which this belief functioned socially in his time, to the detriment of the *anawim* or the poor. The way in which the interrelationship between God, human beings and the world actually functions in society is also part of the nucleus of authentic or inauthentic belief. The social misuse by power of the name of God is also one of the most important factors which makes things extremely difficult for believers now (when they recall what has happened in the name of God and the church).

Later, I shall analyse the fact that, however much belief in God must also have a critical and liberating function in society, one cannot and may not identify the distinctive cognitive dimension of belief in God with its social function.

## B. Belief in God and its institutionalization in the church

A new development in our day is the situation in which people continue to believe in God while being alienated from the institutional church or religion. In former times, despite many rifts, which have not yet been sufficiently investigated, religion, church and belief in God nevertheless formed one undisputed whole.

Belief in God has a basic tendency to form communities. But even marginal church membership remains a form of experience of a particular religion which always has critical and marginal tributaries outside the officially approved streams. These are part of the total phenomenon of any specific religion. The history of human religion teaches us that belief in God has little future outside a great tradition of religious experience.

The tension between belief in God and church membership is connected with something fundamental, namely the institutionalization of belief in God. On the one hand this is a sociological and also a religious necessity, and on the other hand at the same time it results in a degree of alienation from the original religious experience. The paradox here is that it is almost impossible to hand down living belief in God without some alienation from the institution. A religion is not only the expression of a fundamental religious experience but also a 'domestication', a taming of the overwhelming power of this experience. A religious tradition is a collective recollection of a particular experience of God. The original religious force of an experience which forms the basis of a community is certainly handed down in an institutional religion, but by that very fact it is also to some degree regulated, even incapsulated. The inexpressible is made capable of expression, even expression in institutional terms, through sacred writings, symbolic rites, codes of behaviour and so on.

We must not lose sight of the fact that belief in God, too, is possible only in the forms of the human condition. Precisely for that reason an institutional religion also always comes under the criticism of the power and freedom of the original religious experience. However, no one can live all day with the high tension of a religious experience. So religion makes the power of the religious experience as it were 'bearable', all through life. For the same reasons, the liturgy also periodizes the moments of high tension. The institutionalization of belief in God is essentially for the good of this faith.

However, things become different when the official religious institution, in its behaviour and attitude, above all as a result of explicit or at least *de facto* alliances with 'the powerful of this world', in practice leaves the little ones in the lurch and in one way or another contradicts the message which it preaches. In that case the institution becomes incredible and a stumbling block to belief in God. What is thus done in the service of belief in God is then a hindrance to many people. The challenging character of religion or the church then disappears. So in fact the churches as institutions themselves make belief in God difficult today. Perhaps this is one of the most striking reasons why many of those who believe in God turn their backs on the church, though in so doing at the same time they run the risk of letting their belief in God become dishevelled and vague.

One can say that Christian faith as proclaimed by the churches today is no longer endorsed by and from human experiences. Those outside the church are contining to look for a 'religious more', an existential surplus, but the churches cannot in fact give it any form for them. With the disappearance of any endorsement from human experience, specific church practices no longer perform this function; they become irrelevant. On the other hand the need for the gratuitous, the 'religious surplus', does not disappear as a result; men and women still feel that they are more than purely social beings and more than the social roles which are imposed on them. This question of the religious 'more' is connected with the human experience that we are not exhausted in (and therefore may not be swallowed up by) social relationships. The complete identification of men and women with their social relationships also alienates them from themselves and from others.

Without being filled out by the church or being made specific by historical religions, however, this question of the 'more' remains vague and unsatisfied; it then hangs in a vacuum and people begin to fill in the empty space in their own way – which is sometimes bizarre. Without a 'transcendent more', human beings seem to be the captives either of themselves or of society. Despite often inadequate and sometimes empirically criminal manifestations of religion, this 'more' takes specific historical form in various religions or 'church societies'. Despite possible misuse and the wrong effects, the ecclesial institutionalization of this belief remains essential for belief in God.

## C. Belief in God at odds with official church morality

In connection with a variety of human realities (above all in the sphere of sexuality, marriage and the family) many committed Christians have arrived at new ethical views as a result of which they are alienated from the official morality of the church, though they remain firm and practising believers. For around twenty years there has been a considerable gap between the ethical practice of many believers and the official 'moral doctrine' of the church hierarchy. The new factor here is that people no longer feel guilty in engaging in this new practice, but feel perfectly in harmony even with the church's belief in God. Many believers have in fact abandoned the sexual morality called for by the church hierarchy yet nevertheless – for example as divorced and remarried people – continue to receive the sacraments without being troubled.

Here, however, it is often forgotten that a change in ethical view also brings about changes in one's image of God. Those who cling on to old pictures of God then find themselves involved in all kinds of clashes with new ethical values, so that in the long run the abandonment of the 'old morality' also affects belief in God, on which people also turn their backs. For the presupposition is then that belief in God is essentially bound up with the old morality. Legitimate changes in ethical appreciation must therefore go hand in hand with new conceptions of God if in the long run people are not to experience some dichotomy or schizophrenia.

A new responsible ethic also has consequences for the life of faith itself, though these consequences often take some time to develop. What happens then is that some believers ultimately turn their backs on belief in God, thinking that this does not go with their new ethical views which have cost them much struggle and doubt. (So this also has to do with the institutional church.) For many people, the official morality of the church hierarchy is thus the first stimulus towards a rejection of the church and in some cases, via this first step, towards abandoning all belief in God.

Although this really calls for a separate discussion, I also want to talk here about the belief in God which has expressed itself in the symbols of a patriarchal culture. Above all for women believers, belief in God has been made more difficult over the last twenty or thirty years because of the patriarchal setting in which – specifically in historical terms – the Jewish and Christian revelation of God and thus talk to and about God have come to us. Jewish-Christian religion has as its focus God the Father and the man Jesus of Nazareth. It is not so much the religious symbolism itself which is a stumbling block for many feminists, as that it also has a symbolically and socially oppressive effect, and that it arose in a society which was oppressive to women. So theological symbolism has in fact further intensified social and cultural discrimination against women.

I simply mention this fact within this list of the difficulties which modern men and women have in believing in God. Many believers, above all women, have the impression that they are being asked to believe in a God who injures and belittles people, above all women, through religion. This last is really alien to the deepest intention of the message of the gospel, but it is difficult to deny that discrimination against women can be found in the official preaching of the churches and in many forms of theology. I have already pointed out above that the way in which people are belittled by it is one of the most sensitive points over which modern men and women turn their backs on belief in God. This is true above all in connection with the feminist criticism of masculine talk about God.

## 2. Religions as the concrete context of talk about God

In the first introductory chapter I said that our secular history is the original place where God brings about salvation in and through human beings in a history of disaster, but that in the various religions this salvation is expressed specifically and explicitly as salvation-from-God. In this sense the religions are themselves the context in which the use of the word God essentially belongs, though never apart from the salvation and liberation brought about by men and women in the world. A listing of the different contexts in which men and women use the word God is therefore itself of great theological relevance.

### I   Talking about and to God within the context of a tradition of religious experience or a religion

First of all the word God is used by communities of faith and within a specifically religious activity, which we can sum up as an articulate confession of belief in God, the witness and the ritual, cultic or liturgical activity of the celebrating community, and finally ethical admonition (on a smaller or larger scale). This in fact means that the human use of the word God belongs primarily in a context in which people do not so much talk about God as to God, and therefore in a context of worship and reverence and further in a context of confessing and witnessing to God; and finally in the praxis of 'following God'.

So a philosophical context is not the most appropriate place for using the word God. We are concerned with a milieu in which God is addressed and in which the community of faith is addressed by witnesses, above all by the foundation documents of its religious tradition. This is at the same time a context in which the community of faith bears witness to its wrestling with God and with ethical questions. For 'to believe in God' is to wrestle with God, as Jacob/Israel once wrestled with God's angel. The context is not one of explanation and exposition, a context in which there is a philosophical quest for the conditions under which human thought and human action are possible.

The authentic context in which the word God is used is that of the individual and social prayer of living men and women to God. The word God is used there in an 'auto-implicative' religious context – a learned word to express the fact that this talk relates to the whole of a person. It says as much about human beings as it does about God. We cannot get pictures of human beings and pictures of God separately. Talk of God says as much about human commitment as about the commitment of God.

At the same time we note that in their religious context human beings speak to God in different ways, bear witness to him in different ways and celebrate him in different ways. There is a multiplicity of actual religions, a broad spread of possibilities in the primary context of talking to and about God. This fundamental pluralism in religious talk of God will also remain an important fact for us; is it a fact that can be overcome? Or, given the inexpressibility of God, is it as it were a matter of principle? And if that is the case, what does 'Christian uniqueness' mean?

## II  Talking about God within philosophical reflection on one's own religious attitude

Secondly, still within the communities of faith, there are many forms of theological reflection on this religious talk to and about God. That is already a more remote context, but one which follows on from the primary context; it is as it were the second context of talk about God. Here there is talk reflecting on 'talking to God'.

As on the first level, on this second, reflective theological level we can also see a multiplicity of divergent reflections. Not only right through all religious cultures, but even within one and the same religious tradition there are different, sometimes conflicting, theological schools and trends: both within the Christian experiential tradition and that of Islam, Buddhism and other traditions. Here we must not overlook the fact that theological reflection within a religious tradition does not coincide with this religious experiential tradition, just as one cannot identify the study of a particular religion with a study of religious ideas and theories.

## III   God: as a so-called 'extra-religious', autonomous philosophical question

There is an even wider context in which men and women use the word God, namely in philosophical reflection, as reflection on the totality of human experience: in rational reflection on the ultimate ground and source of all reality, Aristotle's 'unmoved mover', Plato's 'supreme idea' which synthesizes all ideas, Thomas's 'first cause' of all that exists, lives and moves, Spinoza's *Deus sive Natura*, Kant's 'condition of possibility' for human ethical action, Hegel's 'absolute Spirit', finally 'God' as the inspiration of social and political liberation movements, and so on. In this philosophical sphere, too, talk about God is very divergent and pluralistic. Most of these at least Western philosophical systems in which God is mentioned are historically inconceivable without the tradition of Christian religious experience in which believers pray to God. Although philosophy is a rational enterprise, in fact the religious use of the word God was always the wider context here. In other words, in these philosophical traditions we have either a rationalization or a theoretical thematization of an already existing belief in God, or the rationalization of an already pre-existing atheistic tradition. The philosophical denial or endorsement of the existence of God are not in fact conclusions from these philosophies as such. Belief in God or unbelief are already their starting points, and not really their conclusion.

So we have to say that even philosophical talk of God can be understood only against the background of a religious tradition, just as an atheistic or agnostic philosophy can be understood only within an agnostic experiential tradition. This can be demonstrated in historical terms and confirms the view that religions are the primary context of the use of the word God. In a rational philosophical analysis one is in fact simply uncovering the cognitive intentionality of a particular religious belief in God, or on the other hand of a *de facto* non-belief. That was also the basic significance of Thomas's so-called 'five proofs of God', just as Kant's *Critique of Pure Reason* was inspired by the same intention.

## IV  The 'theological passive' in talk about God in a secularized world

I must also mention the silent use of the name God, in what exegetes call the 'theological passive', in accordance with Jewish usage: for example, 'it was given to me', or, in a modern context, the closing sentence of a speech from the throne by the Queen of the Netherlands, 'we ask that the power may be given us'. Anyone, including the agnostic, can fill this out as he or she pleases. For believers this is a 'theological passive', through which the fetishism of the name of God is avoided, while its religious significance continues to be maintained.

## V  'Good heavens', 'My God', as echoes of a religious society in a secularized world

For the sake of completeness, I must finally also refer to the 'secular' use of the word God in, for example, curses (goddammed), or in the more friendly secular use of 'good heavens', 'my God' and so on. This use can also be understood on the basis of an originally religious context, but it has become an essential part of a culture in such a way that the word God often continues to be used in this secularized culture. One might also think of the German 'Grüss Gott', the French 'Adieu' or the English, 'For God's sake, you can't do that!' Neither belief nor unbelief is any longer involved here. But the fact that people begin to curse in situations in which their personal commitment is radically thwarted is linguistically a recollection of the fact that the original use of the name God was not a neutral, value-free assertion, but that in its primary, particularly religious context, it challenges the whole person: in that case one *praises* or *curses*.

It emerges from all this that the use of the word God in its primary context at the same time implies a very specific human pattern of action. 'To name God' is to say something about God, but at the same time also something about human existence. Belief in God implies both a theological and an anthropological expression. Here 'saying God' stands under the primacy of human action or commitment.

### Conclusion

It also follows from all this that the primary and most obvious description of what God is, is that which, he who, or she who is worshipped, confessed and celebrated by religious communities.[10] God is the one who is celebrated, and sometimes therefore also the one who is cursed.

But what is the meaning of worship or reverence for God? Worship or reverence appears in the first place as a conscious human action. Psalms, and in other religions all kinds of hymns, certainly say that even the sub-human world, because it too is dependent on God, celebrates God's glory in its own way, but one can hardly call this worship. Worship of God calls for an activity of the consciousness and thus of language and speech, and only human beings are capable of this, at least within our experience. Moreover worship of God is not a purely theoretical, detached activity; it is a performative awareness leading to realization; it is an activity involving the conscious integration of a person's life and all the thoughts, projects, evaluations and meanings that go with it.[11] This integration is brought about not only by knowledge but above all by the dedication of oneself to that which, or the one who, is worshipped as 'pure grace' (in whatever way), gratuitously, as the one who 'comes over' us and thus can be called the source and ultimate ground of human life. This activity of integration can be clearly recognized above all in the so-called high theistic religions: 'You shall love the Lord your God with all your heart, with all your soul and with all your strength.'

Through the activity of worshipping God a conscious relationship is established between human beings and a higher reality, which is worthy of utter human dedication and of being addressed as pure gratuitousness; this reality is therefore the ultimate source of all love and of human integrity, freedom and wholeness – while, thanks to this God, even apart from any sense of God, human meaning and happiness are to be found and in fact have been found through men and women. A 'priceless' divine discovery!

## 3. The mystical or theologal depth-dimension of human existence

I   Are faith in God, prayer and mysticism one?

It emerged in the previous analysis that religion and above all prayer are the real context of meaningful use of the word God. But it is striking that mysticism has its own peak periods in both place and time: for example Rhenish, Flemish and Dominican mysticism in the fourteenth century; Spanish Carmelite mysticism in the sixteenth century; the mysticism of the French School in the seventeenth cenutry; contemporary mysticism in the context of the second half of the twentieth century, with all kinds of mystical spectrums in between. Whatever the intrinsic nature of mysticism, at all events it seems to be a particular answer to a crisis or a question from a particular social and historical context.

One example may make the social and historical context of all mysticism clear. From the seventeenth century on, in the West the cosmos or nature became disenchanted as a result of the rise of the natural sciences; nature became one transparent, great clock, and was no longer a mysterious and numinous universe that could prompt mystic raptures. So in the seventeenth century, spirituality became a mysticism of inwardness; a mysticism of the subjective way of the soul to God.

For modern men and women the source of the rationality of the world no longer lies in the world itself, as it did for the Greeks and the people of the Middle Ages, but exclusively in the human spirit, which imposes its own concepts on reality. The modern development has limited reality to objectivity, i.e. has given it meaning through the human spirit. From now on the giving of meaning becomes far more a form of control than handing over to a pre-existing rationality. There is no longer any mystery in the nature of things. People then find in the world only themselves and what they have made. But this 'self' is already shrivelled up there.

Max Horkheimer once said: 'The more we look at nature as a pure object over against a human subject, the more this subject, which is thought to be autonomous, loses its content until ultimately all that is left is a name with nothing to name.'[12] A subject that has no other task than to *give* objective meaning to a reality which itself no longer has any sense ultimately also loses its own content. In the end, the pure subject becomes the empty subject. The autonomous subject is no longer in a position to be related to itself in any other way than as to an object. For structuralists and, for example, Michel Foucault the concept of the human is a modern invention, which must disappear as soon as possible. Nietzsche already said that modern human culture is a decadent phenomenon.

This modern focus on subjectivity results on the one hand in the disappearance of an authentic transcendence. One cannot pray to the God of modern transcendental philosophy, i.e. to God as the postulate of practical reason, God as the condition for the possibility of human thought and human freedom. At the beginning of the modern age it became clear that human beings no longer need God to explain the world, nature; later in our modern age, however, it was also concluded that we no longer need God to explain human beings: men and women seem capable of leading very good human lives without believing in God, lives at least as human as those of religious and Christian people. 'God' is not necessary, for nature, for human beings or for society, though God nevertheless has to do with human beings, nature and society.

On the other hand, precisely this modern rational and technological culture which caused the transcendent to disappear made a new longing for mysticism at least possible. A new category came into being as a result of dissatisfaction with a purely technological culture: that of the sheer gratuitousness of God. There is no need of God. God does not come into the category of what we need, but that of desire and love: the purely gratuitous, as when someone gives us a bunch of flowers and we honestly reply, 'You needn't have done that'. But that is the authentic wealth of life: the wealth of the unnecessary gift of a bunch of flowers!

I think that the present revival of mystical tendencies in knowledge and art, the new shift towards religion and myth, is connected with a reaction against the dualistic-Cartesian, modern rationalism of the West. This revival is also connected with the experience of impotence in the social and political sphere after the late 1960s, when above all the young had thought that they could change the whole of society. When I was a visiting lecturer in the University of Berkeley near San Francisco in 1968, the university city was full of left-wing political groups which had meeting-places all over town, various houses where the strategy of political democratization was discussed and mapped out. When I gave some more lectures there in 1980, twelve years later, I noticed that all these former strategic centres had now turned into meditation centres. Both facts on the one hand point to the effect of fashion, but on the other hand they must not be reduced to just a fashionable trend: social and cultural factors also underlie them, and these are more fundamental than mere fashion.

The Brazilian bishops rightly point out that the mystical movement makes an active appearance precisely where the churches become socially and politically aware. Often there is a link between mystical sects and propagandists of the ideology of the National Security state. Often these mystical communities are supported by fundamentalist and right-wing groups. So mysticism seems on the one hand to go with a more emotional religious group-life among the population, but at the same time to tone down opposition to social impoverishment. That is one more reason for asking what mysticism is.

First of all some definitions of terms, which must make it clear what we are really talking about. Since the seventeenth and eighteenth centuries 'mysticism' has become a kind of term of abuse to describe alien and mysterious, occult and irrational phenomena. In the second half of the nineteenth century and in the twentieth mysticism was again approached positively. However, in the tradition of Catholic spirituality, as far as the positive definition of mysticism was concerned, two trends came to the fore.

1. The Thomistic-Carmelite and also Dominican interpetation of what mysticism is. This sees the essence of mystical life in an intensive

form of the theologal life of faith, hope and love. In other words, mysticism is in line with the three divine virtues.

2. According to a primarily Jesuit (I deliberately say 'a', and not 'the'), more voluntaristic, conception of spirituality, mysticism is not on the same wavelength as theologal life but covers a separate sphere of all kinds of unusual and sometimes suspicious phenomena: visions, ecstasy, levitation and the like. In that case mysticism is a quite separate, distinctive sphere, which cannot be reduced to the ordinary Christian life of faith.

I myself define mysticism along the lines of the first trend, in which case mysticism falls within the ordinary life of faith; thus mysticism is an intense form of the experience of God in faith. However, if there is a particular psychosomatic disposition in that direction on the part of the believer, this can be coupled with extraordinary phenomena – physical repercussions like a loss of the senses in rapture, levitation, ecstasies, even stigmatization – but these are then non-essential concomitants of the authentic mystical life of faith. The so-called extraordinary presupposes a special psychosomatic substratum which it has also been possible to clarify clinically. So only the context can demonstrate whether such concomitant phenomena derive from an authentic religious source. These extraordinary phenomena are religiously neutral: they can be produced by drugs (e.g. LSD and mescalin).

From a Christian perspective, mysticism is essentially the life of faith, and therefore not a separate sector in Christian life to which only a few, or individuals, are called. As the life of faith, mysticism cannot be reduced to ethics either. Although mysticism is also found in ethics (both socio-political ethics and so-called personal ethics), it is essentially meta-ethical, in fact theologal. In other words, on the basis of its mystical depth, Christian faith transcends the political and personal ethical commitment of Christians; but it is a transcendence by implication and not by exclusion. In this sense one may not translate the Christian gospel exclusively into our Christian responsibility for a better world; in that case one would again be reducing belief in God to its utilitarian function for this world and failing to recognize its gratuitousness.

As well as ethical, communal, ecological and socio-political dimensions, the Christian life of faith also has a mystical dimension, i.e. an aspect of cognitive union with God. I term the aspect of faith which touches on God the mystical side of faith. This cognitive dimension of believing has two aspects: that of the confessing conceptual or image-producing conceptions of faith, for example faith in God confessed as Creator, Redeemer or Liberator, and the aspect of cognitive contact with the reality of God (a particular mystical tradition in fact speaks of *thigganein*, the Greek word for 'touch', contact). Mysticism in the more special sense is then an intense form of experiencing this cognitive element which binds us to God in faith, in which the conceptual elements move right into the background and even disappear completely.

Given the distinctive character of God, which transcends all concepts and experiences, mysticism always has something of a 'dark night'. Here we are confronted with the paradox of both the life of faith and mysticism. Belief in God without conceptions of God is meaningless and even impossible, moreover it is historically ineffective; while on the other hand God's absolute presence shatters all our images and conceptions of God. The Bible, both the first or Old and the second or New Testaments, is full of pictures of God and at the same time full of the breaking of these pictures. Therefore I must first go rather more deeply into this paradox of faith, which is also the paradox of all mysticism.

Basically, we have here belief in God's grace, i.e. in the saving real presence of God with us; this is not a separate sector, for example of human inwardness, but embraces the whole of the reality in which we live and of which we ourselves are also part. From God's side this absolute nearness is direct, but for us the immediacy is mediated, while remaining immediacy. (I know that this is nonsense in the context of inter-personal relationships, but that is not the case when it comes to the reciprocal relationship between a finite and an infinite being. An appeal to 'immediate experiences' can be very misleading! See Chapter 1.) Therefore in my view the whole problem of mysticism can be summed up in the term 'mediated immediacy' (though if mystics express their experiences of 'immediacy', analysis reveals that the immediacy is mediated, above all with John of the Cross and even with Eckhart). Mysticism is on the same wavelength as prayer; it is prayer in which an attempt is made to transcend the elements of belief which are also mediated through politics, ethics and concepts, in order to place just oneself in the immediate presence of God. Now by the very nature of God and the necessarily manifold mediation of any belief in God's absolute saving presence, that cannot be done. So the highest peaks of mysticism manifest themselves as 'dark nights' (John of the Cross) or, even more daringly, as 'dark light' (Ruysbroeck).

Without mediation, mysticism in fact threatens to be pursuing a void, a *nada*, as John of the Cross puts it. But in authentic mysticism this is a *nada* or 'nothingness' of overdefined 'fullness' which cannot be embraced in concepts or images – a fullness which, however, can show itself to the human spirit as such only as a 'dark night' or 'dark light'. At this level of mystical prayer there are no longer positive supports or positive mediations: there is only the mediation of negativity, revealing itself as a black hole or, as Thérèse of Lisieux says, 'like a wall'. Mysticism is a dialogue in which both conversation partners are intensively at work, but in which one partner, God, seems to be silent, for all his active influence.

Mysticism is essentially not just a cognitive process but a particular way of life, a way of salvation. So before we discuss mysticism as a 'key problem' it is necessary first to describe what mystical experiences are. On the basis of descriptions given by male and female mystics of their mystical life, I can see three constants here (with all kinds of qualifications).

1. Mystical experience is a source experience. There is a sense among mystics that something fundamental has happened: a sort of sense of 'illumination'. In it, the old familiar picture of the world and self (the 'ego') of the person concerned is radically shattered: his or her old world collapses and he or she has experienced something completely new, overwhelmingly new, which changes the whole of his or her life. Even the old words are no longer enough; the new experience calls for new words if it is to be described or articulated. To sum up, it is a kind of breakthrough, a collapse of the old world; an experience of something completely new: light or fire, a glow of love, or *nada*, or a 'You'. We also find paradoxes like 'all' and 'nothing' among the mystics, side by side; most characteristic is Ruysbroeck's expression 'dark light'. This is something transcendent and at the same time all-embracing: the source both of all objectivity and all subjectivity. It is an unconditional experience of salvation, an experience also of totality, of reconciliation with all things, despite connotations of suffering and lack of reconciliation.

2. Then usually follows a second phase: the first great love seems to disappear; there is a gnawing doubt. Was it all authentic? There comes what many mystics call the phase of 'purgation'('catharsis'), through a heightened concentration; also processes of love in what is experienced as human wounding, though this does not hurt those involved but rather raises them up. This second phase usually ends up in a night and a wilderness; authentic mysticism is often not a good thing, but a torment.

3. And yet! For ultimately there is a discovery of the features of the divine love, albeit only in the trace that the beloved has left behind in the being of the mystic. There remains a mediated 'immediacy'; there is the pure presence of the divine, but also the natural presence of the mystic with God. 'Mystical union', mutuality. And yet, this is always with a painful feeling of absence: not-seeing.

This mystical way of life can be experienced in a variety of contexts and situations. Some have these experiences of and in nature; others, like Buber, in the family or, like Rosenzweig, through visiting the synagogue

again after many years (where Rosenzweig rediscovered his old warm
nest); others, like Francis, in society and the world; others in reading
the Torah or scripture, or in confrontation with Jesus confessed as the
Christ; others in the experience of the 'you' of their fellow men and
women; others again through sinking into their own being (the so-called
mysticism of being). In our time, for many people mysticism is the
experience of the 'situation of the oppressed poor'. Yet it is always an
experience of totality, a kind of feeling of the presence of the whole of
reality, indeed the source of the whole. At all events, the Inexpressible
that is experienced is more real than the chair on which the mystic is
sitting, more real than all that the mystic regards as reality. Mysticism
in no way means 'God and only God'. Francis's Hymn to the Sun makes
this clear, when Francis says, 'Be praised, my Lord, with all your
creatures!' The mystic will, however, first let everything go, give up
everything, even himself or herself, but in the gratuitousness of God
find everything, including himself or herself, restored a hundredfold.
Authentic mysticism is never flight from the world but, on the basis of
a first disintegrating source-experience, an integrating and reconciling
mercy with all things. It is approach, not flight.

## II   Mystical silence and mystical talk about God

In a never-ending game of 'yes it is, no it isn't', people can assert that
God does not exist or equally simply argue that he does exist. However,
they cannot deny that in fact all human cultures have a name for the
divine and that even so-called secularized cultures hang on to a God,
an 'ultimate concern' (Paul Tillich). Religions belong to the historical
image of what humanity has shown us of the varied facets of living men
and women in human history and still continues to give us in secular
societies.

But only through the horizontal dimension of our changing human
history – through human beings, freedom and chance, convergence and
determinism – does God come into view for thoughtful men and women.
That already means that we can and must make a distinction between
what can be called the 'real referent' (in this case the reality of God
himself) and the 'ideal referent' or even the 'available referent' (our
conceptions and images of God). This distinction is not peculiar to
religious knowledge. It can be found in all forms and at all levels of
human knowledge, spontaneous and scientific, though it need not
necessarily have been reflected upon. I must demonstrate that in more
detail.

In human experiences we can say: the names Anne and Peter denote those two there. The real referent is demonstrable. This already becomes more difficult with figures from past history. For example, take William of Orange. Who is the real referent of this name? At any rate we can no longer point to him, except through all kinds of historical documents and reports. Through them we get only a reconstructed picture of the real William. It is not the real William but the historical picture of William, the 'ideal' referent, who evokes particular patriotic feelings among the Dutch and the Flemish. I believe that here we come upon a fundamental model which is also important for our talk of God: the distinction between the 'real referent' (for example, William of Orange, who was living at a particular time) and the 'available referent' (our historical image of William the Silent). Moreover, it then emerges that as William of Orange has a certain relevance for the life, for example, of Dutch citizens, it is not directly the real referent but the available 'ideal' referent who motivates patriotic actions. There is never an uninterpreted William the Silent. No Freudian or follower of Jung, like Erikson, who wrote a book on Luther, would ever make a distinction between the 'Luther of history' (the real referent) and the 'Luther of Jungian interpretation': for them the Luther of history is the Luther of this Jungian interpretation. For these reasons I use the same term, the referent, for the two elements, even though they can be distinguished, sometimes in the sense of the real referent and sometimes in the sense of the available referent.

However, it can also happen that history hands on names to us, in other words that we are given an available referent, for example, St Christopher, patron saint of travellers in difficulties, who according to the findings of contemporary critical scholarship never existed. So the possession of available referents cannot in itself allow us to argue to the existence of a real referent. The fact that humanity has so many religions with all kinds of images of God does not in itself tell us whether or not God exists. In Chapter 1 I already said that for believers, the reality of God is independent of our human consciousness, independent of our expression of God; on the other hand, our talk of God is also dependent on the historical context in which we talk of God. However, the question is whether this talk of God by men and women is itself independent of the real existence of God, or whether it is impossible or even inconceivable without the existence of this reality. At all events, here, too, we can immediately draw a distinction between God as the real referent (which at all events God is for those who believe in God) and all our images of God (the 'ideal' referent).

God is the reality to which at all events believers point by means of the images of God which are put at their disposal by the history of human religious experience. By analogy with a historical figure the reality of God is 'absent', i.e. out of our control, unavailable for observation or for scientific experimentation. So from this perspective God is an unknown X, a limit-concept without content for us. Moreover, as reality God transcends all our thought and reflection; nowhere do we hear his voice or see his face. As a reality God cannot be verified; he is even a matter of controversy to human beings.

However, the most decisive content of the available referent in connection with God, in other words, the most sensitive point of all our images of God, is precisely the way in which the reality of God is not at our disposal. This already says a good deal about God's reality. The rebound effect that God, the real referent (if God exists), has on our images of God is to demonstrate the inadequacy of all our experiences and all the images that we make of God: they fall short. The gap between real and available referent in this case is infinitely greater than that between a historical figure and our historically reconstructed image of him or her. That means on the one hand that the real referent, by virtue of what he is, in fact has an influence on our images of God: these are provoked by divine power, though 'in' the action of men or women who give meaning in faith. Presupposing the reality of God, the first and basic influence of the real referent on the 'ideal' referent consists in stripping these images of God of all power to express God's reality adequately and in an appropriate way through the real presence of God. The explicit sense of the radical deficiency of our images of God is therefore the most striking feature of these referents which are at our disposal here. The real referent as it were rejects all available referents out of hand. We can rightly say that there is an experience of God as that which cannot be experienced, without there being any contradiction here (though there is perhaps a paradox). The totality which gives meaning, and its ground, are also experienced indirectly in what can be experienced directly in the world.

*By being God in absolute freedom,* God thus reveals to us that all our images of God (not God's reality itself) are in fact human products and projections, which as such are incapable of describing the divine reality. This most sensitive point of all our images of God, namely the sense that we have no control over the reality of God, is not a human construction or projection, but rather (as believers may interpret and do in fact interpret it) a projection *from God on to us* through worldly, historical intermediaries. On the basis of God's reality itself, all our projective images of God are rejected and depotentiated. In this repercussion on all our images of God, in the way in which the picture of God which we produce is constantly broken, there is revealed that which stands over against us in and with respect to all our projections.

Anyway, this is the structure of our images of God as they have been and are experienced in most religious traditions, and this can also be tested in an appropriate way in deeply human experiences. If we pray to the real or living God, we have in mind only 'images of God' which in the act of praying are shattered by the real referent to whom we pray. When we speak to God, we nevertheless do so in terms of images of God. This does not mean that we pray to an 'image of God'; that would be idolatry. On the other hand it is precisely these images of God which, as the available referent, have a direct and significant influence on the action, thought and life of believers. It even makes a difference to our action and belief whether we experience God as liberator or as a pantocrator who continues the existing order. In prayer, the real place where the name of God is used, we are made aware of the difference between the 'real' and the 'available' referent. But this means that our knowledge in faith of the real referent is also mediated through our projective images of God, which are at the same time radically relativized by the inexpressible presence of God. Therefore it is never possible to offer a compelling proof against agnosticism and atheism. What God may mean for all believers is another matter: at all events, it follows first and foremost that God can never be demonstrated in our world; he never has been and he never will be. Moreover, the real referent of the name God is not to be confused with the objects of our experience, far less with our constructions and projections, though these play a role in any belief in God.

Because of this twofold structure of the real and the available referent in connection with the name of God, a conversation about images of God between believers and those who call themselves unbelievers is often asynchronous: the agnostic identifies all conceptions of God with projections of the human mind; by contrast, the believer refers to the real God who is envisaged in our projections. He is not himself a projection, but rather projects himself on to our conscious history, from which we produce images of God. However, this implies that our pictures of God in faith, in so far as they are legitimate, not ideological (this is the critical issue!), are in no way arbitrary: in spite of everything, as projections, authentic images of God must be aimed at something, i.e. they must say something about the reality of God himself, if we are not to form God in our image and likeness.

There must therefore be non-projective elements of reality in our belief in God which determine the direction of our images of God. Therefore the Jewish-Christian tradition defines God as pure positivity; in other words, it rejects all names and images of God which injure and enslave human beings instead of liberating them. Precisely in this concept of pure positivity we maintain the transcendence of God, for we do not know what God ultimately is and what the *humanum*, humanity, can ultimately be, and reserve this for God; or rather, that is God's own divine proviso on all our thought, action and reflection.[13]

But if we have constantly to shatter all the images of God with which we talk about and within which we talk to God, would we not do better to be silent about God? Does not talking about God or being silent about God ultimately amount to the same thing? My answer would be 'No'. Not speaking about God produces an empty stillness or a still emptiness. In that case there is no speaking *to* God, no prayer (though this is the essence of all religion). Mystical silence about God, i.e. speaking to and about God in conceptions of God which are constantly broken, is a filled space: one can hear the language of silence. There is presence here. This is quite a different experience from the experience of an empty silence, and not just another name for one and the same experience. In order to give some expression to the ineffable nature of this most deeply religious experience, the mystical tradition rightly speaks of a *triplex via*, a threefold way of life:

1. The *via affirmativa*: believers use names and images of God (conceptions of faith). For example, they say that God is good, God is the future, God is the liberator. But if we look more closely, it becomes clear to us that these positive predicates of God say more about ourselves and our expectations than about God. God is good, certainly, but God is not good in the way in which human beings are good. God is a liberator, but not in the way in which human beings are liberators. In that case we must also deny God these names which we rightly assign to him. That is,

2. The *via negativa*. We are right to do this, but not in order to make God anonymous or even to fall into a meaningless silence. For by virtue of the dynamic of the reality of God beyond our control, a dynamic which reveals itself in our experience, this denial is itself denied in a third instance, namely,

3. The *via eminentiae*: God is beyond all names and images, but in an eminently divine way which we cannot describe he is at least all that is good, true and delightful in the world of human beings and their history. That means that on the basis of God's being God we are as inexpressible in our creaturely depth which God wills to bring to salvation as God is himself – with (and on the basis of) the inexpressibility of God himself.

In the depth of everything that is, the mystery of creation and the mystery of God coincide in an indivisible way. The boundaries – which there certainly are – are only on our side (see below) and not on God's side. *We* are limited, not God. For Eckhart, God and the soul were therefore literally 'undividedly one mystery'. This cannot, of course, be grasped in concepts. We continue to talk in a stammering way about God, but in doing so in fact talk about the reality of God and not just about conceptions of God.

Properly understood, this *via eminentiae* brings us not to a Greek, purely contemplative, view of mysticism, but to a Christian view of the kind formulated by Eckhart. Here it is not the inwardly contemplative Mary, but Martha, whose concern for God makes her solicitous for human beings, who is seen as the model of all true mysticism. (Fourteenth-century mysticism was then, of course, the only possible form of emancipation and liberation for women and those who were not clergy, hence the mistrust of mysticism on the part of the church hierarchy.) The *via eminentiae* is not a philosophical or purely conceptual, dialectical thought-process, but is revealed to us in the Jewish-Christian, biblical tradition, in which the nature or the character of God is made known to us as love for men and women with a disinterested partisan preferential love for the poor, the oppressed, the excluded and the voiceless. On the basis of the historical story of men and women who on the basis of their converse with God see new and alternative possibilities, earlier images of God will constantly be shattered and new possibilities will come to life. Thus we do not learn to know the *via eminentiae* beyond affirmation and negation in and through a conceptual interplay of thought, but in and from the history of solidarity, justice and love made by men and women in a world of egotism, injustice and lovelessness.

In our experience of God – by worldly and historical mediation – as the one who is beyond all experiences, what I would call an 'absolute limit' ultimately plays a mediating role.

## III   The absolute limit

At least in our modern times, believers and non-believers have the basic experience of an absolute limit, of radical finitude and contingency. I am not talking here about particular 'limit situations' in human life to which philosophers and theologians sometimes refer in order to 'give religion' to men and women at moments in which they feel most vulnerable and hopeless: in sickness and death, plagues, Aids and so on. There are also evidently people who do not recognize any kind of absolute limit: they are champions of an unlimited belief in progress in a world of inexhaustible possibilities. But the economic crisis and the destruction of our natural environment stand in radical contradiction to this naive optimism.

Of course, the simple and abstract notion of a limit does not take us any further. Confronted with limit-experiences primitive people believed in a fantastic kingdom beyond the absolute limit within which we live, and filled this 'other world' with mysterious powers and forces which intervened from above in human life and kept this world under their control. But if we are confronted with an absolute limit to all our experiences and knowledge, with what right can we then speak of the existence of something that lies beyond this absolute limit? In that case is not agnosticism not only a modest but also a more reverent attitude?

Recognition of radical finitude as such is no longer a religious concept, as it used to be, but is usually a generally recognized reality of human experience. No one has analysed this radical finitude of being human in this contingent world better than an agnostic who was originally in fact a militant atheist, Jean-Paul Sartre. There is both an atheistic and a religious experience of our radical finitude. The experience of contingency is the unexpressed heart of human life, but it is not a 'direct experience', as is that of someone who comes up against a wall at full speed, experiences a relative limit in a painful way and collapses with concussion. The radical experience of a limit is mediated through all kinds of experiences of relative limits in our life. Here I am rejecting Schleiermacher's direct datum of a 'feeling of absolute dependence'; this theological concept is too much a reflection of nineteenth-century liberal and social circumstances.

Far less is the experience of an absolute limit a kind of generalization or extrapolation of immediate experiences of very specific limits. Rather, in my view it is an experience of an absolute limit *in* the constant experience of all our relative limits, in all kinds of sectors and at all human levels. In each particular experience of a limit, in the long run we experience that we are neither lords nor masters of ourselves, far less of nature and history. There is a radical contingency or finitude at any moment of life within what are nevertheless many kinds of positive possibilities. Since the experience of transition from relative limits to an absolute limit is above all a philosophical problem, here I shall leave any technical analysis on one side. For I am not concerned to provide a so-called 'proof of God', but to make sense to some degree of what believers call God.

The question then is: are we imprisoned this side of an absolute limit, like a prisoner within his relative limits, the walls of his cell? Or is this imprisonment purely fictitious? In other words, is an absolute limit something that really bounds us and thus keeps us as it were captive within this limit? Do we have to say metaphorically, but really, that the absolute wall around our limited existence in the world is a reality, for believers and agnostics? Can we say anything more about this absolute limit than that we ourselves are radically finite? We ourselves are this limit. The absolute limit is our limit, not a human product, not a human projection, but a real fact. In whatever way, we ourselves are posited as finite beings, as Heidegger puts it.

Our finite existence in the world is not itself a human product or project. In other words, if God exists, the boundary between God and the finite is not on God's side, but on the side of the finite. Agnostics like Horst Richter, a Marxist-Freudian psychotherapist, see unreadiness to accept our absolute limit or 'finitude' as the cause of the sickness of modern Western men and women and also as the foundation of all reasons of state and dictatorships:[14] finitude and all human limitations, including the possibility of suffering, are argued away and smothered. But the reality of the absolute limit remains, despite all human boasts of greatness, and this then introduces neurosis into a culture.

The real fact of this limit also compels us to interpret it. What is the structure of such an interpretation, whether in a religious or an agnostic sense? Because of the absoluteness of this limit, our interpretation of it, however it is made, is at the same time a particular view of humankind and the world, a particular understanding of reality. In other words, here, in and with the utmost silence, in the vacuum of the absolute limit, not only all religious but also all other non-religious, agnostic views of humankind, the world and history arise, which on the whole are enclosed within this absolute limit or, more correctly, are themselves this absolute limit. For the modern concept of 'absolute openness to the future' is also subject to optical illusions. In that case, the surface or the perimeter of the absolute limit is stretched, perhaps to infinity. But that does not remove this absolute limit. Present, past and future fall within the absolute limit of all that is finite.

This absolute limit is thus a basic condition of our whole human existence; the divine and eschatological proviso is here simply its religious expression. As experience, however, this proviso is secular, human and universal. The structure of any human interpretation of this boundary that we experience seems to me to be the same for the two directions that human beings can take. The situation is often, wrongly, put like this: there is a fundamental and universal datum of experience (experience of contingency, experience of an absolute limit); the unbeliever accepts this and leaves it at that, while those who believe in God also envisage a completely new 'other-worldly kingdom', a kind of superstructure above experience. Imagined in these terms, this is a false estimation of the interpretations of both believers and unbelievers.

Is the experience of contingency by the person who believes in God and the atheist already a fundamental experience for both, a concrete experience which both share in common? Some say, 'There is no neutral basis of experience which can be interpreted in both a theistic and an atheistic way',[15] since the interpretation is an integral part of experience itself and can never be detached from it. That is true, but it is only a half-truth, for it is clear that the believer's experience of contingency is fundamentally different from that of the agnostic. For the believer, this is concrete, albeit mediated through this experience of contingency or absolute limit, an experience of God's absolute saving presence throughout his or her life, while the agnostic is shut up alone with fellow men and women within this absolute limit. These are at the same time two fundamentally different experiences. But it in no way follows from this that one cannot speak meaningfully of the same sort of experience with two possible interpretations. It certainly does not mean that there is a neutral common experience which is simply interpreted in two different ways. It means that there is no uninterpreted experience of contingency, but in the whole of this interpretative experience there is a pre-linguistic element of experience which is universally human, although the specific totality of this experience is experienced and interpreted in a religious way by Christians and in an agnostic way by humanists. Both interpretations are specifically part of the experience itself. But although both interpretations are an intrinsic part of the experience of contingency and thus colour this experience as a whole, the experiential aspect of contingency *qua* contingency is not itself identical with the interpretative element and is thus human and universal.

Contingency, accessible to both a believing and an agnostic interpretation, is thus itself at the same time an experience which is held in common. Here we have an experience which in its pre-linguistic experiential element (at which we can never arrive separately) is accessible to everyone. Therefore this religious interpretation can be tested by our dimension of experience which is shared by all men and women. We do not develop the divine out of ourselves, but the divine freely manifests itself in profoundly human experiences.

The mystical 'direct experience of God' also ultimately has to do with the experience of God through the mediation of our 'absolute limit'. Hence Ruysbroeck's brilliant religious talk of the experience of God as dark light, mediated immediacy!

## IV   The rationality of belief in God

### A. *Christian, Jew, Buddhist, Muslim by birth – or 'nothing'*

The Christian tradition says that belief in God is a gift of grace. On the other hand, we know from the previous chapter that religion is always a secondary discourse, i.e. speaking about something which in whatever way has already been expressed to some degree in our human experience. Belief in God includes worldly experiences in which something calls to be put into words, though it can only be expressed in the language of faith. The positiveness of revelation is in fact silent about precisely this mediation.

On the other hand, faith is not based on rational arguments which are meant to show the superiority of religion to other solutions of the questions of life. Such apologetic procedures overlook the fact that the fundamental orientation of the life of a person is based on a whole cultural history and not on a rational argument; they fall too short in their consideration of the self-awareness of belief in God as that has taken shape in a particular religion, for example in Christianity, which in fact acquired its knowledge of God from a specific history of salvation, from the life of a particular people and particular men and women among this people. Procedures to account for faith must rather be developed in close contact with the self-understanding of each religion and the social and cultural roots of particular believers. People never arrive at the deep decisions of life on their own. Hopefully critical, they stand and live within a particular cultural, religious or non-religious tradition, whether this is in a large-scale or a small-scale milieu (in the latter case, perhaps the family).

Men and women are 'cultural beings': they inherit and leave legacies; no one begins from zero as an absolutely certain starting-point. We live in the present, from a past to a future. The structure of thought or memory in human life is striking here: we also allow our actions and experiences to be defined by the dialectic of present and past, or past and future: memory and hope, tradition and prophecy. History is a process of learning, the handing down of culture, and at the same time it is planning: it is both tradition and experiment. Human beings are vehicles of culture and hand on the true, good and attractive humanity that has been offered them. But human beings also create tradition. Here the dialectic of theory and praxis plays a role. Men and women are never determined solely by their past; they also shape history to their desires and longings and create new traditions.

That for example a person is and remains a Christian because he or she was one originally and wants to remain one out of a 'desire for the nest' is a social and historical fact that need not in any way be judged unfavourably. However, the fact that others turn away from their own desire for the nest, flee it and look elsewhere indicates that the real determining factor is not merely what is 'familiar from the beginning' (without further qualification). The determining factor is whether people 'feel happy' in this home, or whether it compels them to throw it off as an enslaving yoke. The determining factor is not 'the original', but the meaning, the dynamic and the enriching power which has emanated from this 'domestic tradition' to the invididual (here one might also take painful recollections into account; in that case these are not determinative).

'Feeling at home (despite everything)' in a religious or non-religious tradition which one has inherited from the beginning is also a decisive factor in whether or not a person believes in God. (This standing in a religious tradition in which one has constructed one's own identity is then in fact the concrete form of what believers call a 'grace of God'. Grace does not stand as a dilemma in opposition to freedom and tradition!) The believer and the non-believer need not be judged here in different ways: the personal convictions of both are connected with the tradition in which they respectively stand. For the non-believer, too, this tradition (hopefully with the same critical attitude) has become his or her own flesh and blood. This tradition is also part of his or her personal identity. This applies to Christians, Buddhists and Muslims, and also to agnostics. The fact that a person is also culturally determined by a fundamental view of life does not in itself tell either for or against the truth of this conviction.

In a pluralistic society with conflicting and even diverse religious traditions of meaning, the necessity of a response of faith in fact becomes more urgent. We need to be aware that no one can demonstrate by rational arguments that his or her conviction of faith is more 'rational' and better than atheism or other religions, unless the other's conviction contains confessional elements which injure and dishonour men and women (for example, a religion which called for human sacrifices) or plays down human values. Men and women cannot come fully into their own in just any religion or view of life. (Religious indifferentism on the basis that all religions are equal is therefore anthropologically already open to attack before it becomes a 'heresy'.)

However, apologetic under the sometimes sympathetic mask of 'open questions' is often a way of showing that, despite everything, one's own faith is unassailable. In that case, it is not an attempt, under the pressures of one's own time, to purge one's own belief in God of all kinds of historical accretions and distortions, which perhaps even have serious consequences for faith itself. The most responsible form of apologetic is to uncover the 'intelligibility' or the comprehensibility of faith. For 'mystery' does not mean an appeal to a truth which cannot be understood and is claimed ideologically to be immune from criticism – though it is often used in this sense by clergymen as an excuse. A responsible faith is not a matter of looking for rational proofs for faith, but of making understandable to fellow-believers and non-believers what is meant by talk about God.

## B. The meta-ethical or religious basis of the human praxis of justice and love

### 1. In search of a criterion

We saw above that the original and authentic use of the word God is to be found in the context of worship (in the sense of revering, adoring, praying to God). On the other hand it emerged that religion is 'second-order' talk which (for example in Christianity) explicitly confesses that we live in a history in which God is at work for human salvation, in a history in which God has made a covenant with humankind and in which human beings present themselves as the main mediators of salvation history. God is 'transcendent' precisely in the determinisms of this world, in coincidences and in free human interventions (i.e. God is in some way involved in these and yet stands above them); that is, he is creatively present here, albeit only for good, and every day he seems to be greater than he was yesterday. He is also always ahead of our actions through his initiative.

The action of God in world history is thus (within the single, all-embracing yet one act of creation) always the divine activation of worldly, historical and human powers and possibilities. There must therefore be places 'in the world' where religious talk of God is meaningful and can also be understandable to others, as it were 'assignable', if not provable: the others must also look in the direction which you indicate, as one who believes in God. At one time almost any feature of our daily experience could disclose some religious significance, because almost everyone looked at the world through a religious framework of reference. Things are no longer taken for granted in this way (in the Western world).

I have already said that for many people 'finitude' is no longer a religious concept but a secular one. Because no compelling arguments can be given for God as a source of universal salvation, some people claim that the postponement of the theoretical question (perhaps for ever) clashes with praxis. The question is whether the need to decide for or against is not an urgent human matter which brooks no delay. The argument goes like this: given that the concept of God is bound up with human praxis, the need not to postpone this decision becomes humanly urgent. For if God exists as salvation for men and women, and if we keep in mind the importance of religious belief in salvation from God, we may not postpone a decision about this. By contrast, an indefinite suspension of purely theoretical judgments is possible and usually responsible.

However, as people argue, if a person opts to postpone for an indefinite period the theoretical decision about the question of God, there will still come a particular moment when he or she in practice begins to live as if there were no God, even while there are no convincing arguments for *not* believing in the God of human salvation. The point of this argument is that the theoretical decision is anticipated in practice. The decision to suspend the theoretical judgment is then in practice a decision to live as if there were no salvation from God.

The flaw in this argument is that it is a vicious circle. Anyone who believes in God and thus in the relevance of the concept of God for praxis naturally accepts this argument, but not anyone who does not believe in God as salvation for men and women. Only if you believe in such a God are you confronted with the importance of God for your own human action. The agnostic does not accept this importance; not to believe in God is to deny the importance of God for any human action.

In contrast to this false argument, an honest justification for faith is possible only on three associated conditions. It must be possible to assign a human experience, or experiences, which 1. all men and women unavoidably share with one another and 2. at the same time is an experience (*a*) which does not necessarily calls for a religious interpretation while (*b*) it is nevertheless experienced by all men and women as a fundamental experience, namely one which affects human existence most deeply, and 3. which is helped in the understanding of this fundamental character, which so deeply affects human existence, by the word of God.[16] I say, 'is helped'; not, 'gives a better understanding of' this experience than the agnostic explanation (and in so doing I am correcting the views of both Shepherd and Kuitert and my own earlier view), since to say that this interpretation is 'better' is the claim of a believer who precisely because he or she is a believer cannot convince someone who believes otherwise, though that person may then know what the believer means. So I am talking about universally shared experiences which are fundamental to any human existence, which by the introduction of belief in God's saving presence manifest a distinctive comprehensibility which can be understood by others (even if they do not accept them), which is not present in other interpretations in which belief in God is not expressed. In this way we can see a distinctive, meaningful possibility of understanding, even if it does not amount to a rational and universally conclusive proof.

I have already referred to the experience of contingency (the experience of an absolute limit) which is in fact generally shared by human beings and yet can be and in fact is interpreted in both a secular and a religious way, while as interpreted in religious terms it uncovers a specific and distinctive comprehensibility or intelligibility.

On the other hand, this experience of contingency may not be formalized so that it becomes an abstract which lies outside any context. So contextually we can set this experience within the present-day experience of men and women who are fighting for greater humanity, for salvation and liberation, in search of ever-greater justice and humanity. In that case, what does contingency mean? Stage by stage, I want to demonstrate (schematically) that believers can first make this quite clear to themselves (i.e. justify it in terms of their own rationality) and then also make clear to non-believers what they mean when they use the word 'God' for the interpretation of particular experiences and ultimately even for all experiences.

## 2. *Experiences of the aporia of God's omnipotence and helplessness*

We have only human words for talking about God and the 'omnipotence' which is constantly associated with the term God, words which are exclusively adapted for talking about human and worldly things: we do not have a divine language at our disposal. Therefore if we are to be able to speak about God, we must metaphorically rebaptize and extend all our words. Above all the word 'power' has been seriously infected by human beings. Human power can certainly also be liberating and productive, but it is often destructive and enslaving, imprisoning and manipulative. Precisely because we usually experience relationships of power in this sense, modern men and women are wary about using the term 'omnipotent' for God; it conjures up too much the dictatorial power which enslaves men and women. And the wariness about using the term 'omnipotence' of God applies all the more, the more it becomes clear that in the course of history the Christian churches have flocked to the side of the 'powerful of this world' and in a religious context, too, have treated as nobodies and enslaved those who were already poor and oppressed in society, often with a reference to God's omnipotence. So if we speak of God's omnipotence, it must be of a liberating omnipotence, a good omnipotence. Otherwise it is better not to use such words in connection with God.

The word 'defencelessness' or 'impotence' does not indicate precisely what the 'defenceless superior power' of God really means, either.[17] But human experiences of defencelessness and vulnerability allow believers to expect God to be present among vulnerable and defenceless men and women and also to make himself vulnerable along and with them. That is certainly one aspect of the problem that we are discussing, even a comforting one. However, we shall soon see that this is not enough to bear the full weight of the problem.

In asking whether God is omnipotent or powerless we shall have to avoid four possible approaches.

(*a*) We cannot talk about God's omnipotence in the abstract, as in speculative mediaeval trains of thought. If we do, we arrive at the craziest questions like: can God make a square circle? Can he make the past never have happened? Can he create a world in which there is no evil and suffering? Moreover, such questions and possible answers have never been much use to anyone. When God is involved, so too are the salvation and happiness of men and women. So anyone who asks about God's omnipotence or helplessness without at the same time asking about human salvation is already on the wrong lines and occupied with pseudo-problems.

Peter de Rosa, a Briton who has produced many scripts for religious programmes on the BBC, wrote a short but sensitive book, a kind of reverse parable of the creation story, *The Best of All Possible Worlds*.[18] God wants to create the best of worlds, in which there is no suffering and no evil, nothing that can cause irritation. You see him drawing up his blueprints: always perfect creaturely beings. According to the plan, nothing can go wrong. And indeed in reality everything goes without a snag. But imperceptibly, in the long run there is a stir among these perfect creaturely robots: they rebel against God, they want some adventure, something that cannot be forecast, a risk; they want to venture something with the chance of suffering and things going wrong, with the chance even of eventual success or total fiasco. In any case, all the creatures ask for an 'adventurous life' in which life and death have a place and not a pre-programmed computer world which has no meaning. Selma Lagerlöf, a Scandinavian novelist who was accused of writing only about human evil and suffering and not about the good, replied: 'Don't you know, only evil makes history?' The good is so obvious that one has almost nothing to say about it. It even *is* gratuitous. But evil has a very turbulent history.

(*b*) Still less can we think along the lines of the popular book by the American rabbi Harold S.Kushner, *When Bad Things Happen to Good People*.[19] This book has rightly comforted many people; for many people it has rightly done away with the idea that God is tormenting and nagging them with suffering for their own good. But one of the basic presuppositions of this book is that God has absolutely nothing to do with human evil and suffering: he stands above and outside them. It is true that God does not want evil or human suffering, and that must be emphasized and repeated, but this does not mean that God has nothing to do with them. Kushner's answer is too easy and too superficial.

(c) A while ago, above all in North America, some theologians wanted to seek the solution in a theology which took the 'death of God' as a starting point: the process of history liberates people from the oppressive figure of the omnipotent God. God has to die so that man may live (T.Altizer). The mistake of this theology lies in the way in which it makes the absence of God in the Western secularized world a normative theological concept without analysing the social and historical reasons for this absence, namely the context of the exploitation and annexation of property for the benefit of a few. By means of Western power, Christianity has made God play the role of an oppressor: it has transposed its own cultural, economic and political imperialism to God and forgotten the subversive figure of Jesus of Nazareth. However, the God of Jesus is a God who is involved in the history of the struggle against all oppressive power.

(d) After people had been talking for centuries about the omnipotence of God, in the last forty years, beginning with Bonhoeffer, stress began to be laid on God's defencelessness and powerlessness. Facts like Auschwitz have become a symbol for the defencelessness of God. People began to put the emphasis on a God who shares in suffering, a God who endures suffering along with the poor and oppressed. That may be true, and I too shall lay stress on it, but it is not enough: it does not make clear *to what extent, how* and above all *whether* God is still a redeeming and liberating God. A God who only shares our suffering leaves the last and definitive word to evil and suffering. In that case, not God but evil is the definitive omnipotence. And in that case what does God mean for men and women?

So we shall have to look in a different direction from these four approaches.

To talk meaningfully about God is possible only on the basis of human experience. For Christians, the basis of talk about God – alongside the general basis for their experience and interpretation of this, our created world, in which they live – is above all (and specifically) Israel's experience of God and Jesus of Nazareth, an experience affirmed in faith, which from God's side is called 'revelation'. And this experience was handed down in an interplay of interpretation and new experiences. Not fifty years ago, but now, we in fact raise the question whether God is omnipotent, whereas people formerly took that as a matter of course

or proclaimed it in a purely authoritarian way. For our human experience
in the second half of the twentieth century this omnipotence is no longer
so obvious. Does not the whole history of humanity tell against this
omnipotence? Does not Auschwitz – as the symbol of so much satanic
evil in our history – tell against this omnipotence? Or all the innocent
suffering and injustice in this world, or the distress of the Third World?
Or, if we look on a smaller scale: does not the dashing to pieces of just
one innocent baby tell against God's omnipotence? If we are inclined to
answer such questions and cries solely by saying that God's omnipotence
will only appear in the end-time, above history – one day all the evil of
this world will be overcome in a post-earthly existence – then we must
take into account the fact that the more time goes on, above all Western
Europeans with a *fin de siècle* mentality are getting increasingly weary of
the question of the messianic future and its excessive expectations; they
seem to be dissociating themselves from the idea of the 1960s that there
must be a positive connection between the kingdom of God and the
beginning of the overcoming of evil, here and now, already in our world
(I find this among fellow theologians). And yet for a Christian it must
be clear that there is a positive link between the 'kingdom of God' and
the 'kingdom of human freedom'. If here and now we nowhere experience
where and how God's power is at work against evil, belief in God's
omnipotence is sheer ideology, a loose statement the meaning of which
cannot be verified in any way. First I offer a short historical survey of
how this problem arose in the tradition of Christian religious experience.

Although the so-called Apostles' Creed begins with the confession of
God's omnipotence, 'I believe in God, the Father Almighty, maker of
heaven and earth', it would be a great mistake to think that the
omnipotence of God is central to the Old and New Testaments. Quite
the contrary: the history of God with Israel is to a large degree the
history of one who constantly sees his plans failing and has constantly
to react afresh, tactically and strategically, to the disobedient initiative
of his partner, without evidently having the power or being willing to
compel this partner to do his will. Evil seems so to have the upper hand
that in Genesis 6.6 God himself says that he 'regrets' having created this
humankind, given the abundance of evil and suffering that it has caused
in the good creation. And things are no better in the New Testament.
There we are confronted with the worst nadir of all: the Messiah who
was to bring salvation to the world hangs defenceless on the cross.
There, free but rebellious human beings triumph, while Jesus, the
bringer of salvation, cannot or will not free himself, and his God
maintains complete silence.

Only in the Greek translation of the Old Testament does the use of the term *pantocrator*, ruler of all, for God come to the fore. From the patristic period onwards, God's omnipotence becomes something that is taken for granted and is never discussed. This tradition is summed up well in the question *de divina potentia* in the *Summa* of St Thomas. But Thomas already recognizes a certain limitation of God's omnipotence: he draws a distinction between God's absolute omnipotence (*potentia absoluta*) by which he can do anything that is meaningful (anything that comes under the *ratio entis*) and on the other hand his power conditioned by the creation (*potentio ordinata*) (q.25 a.5 ad 1), in which he takes account of the divergent and distinctive nature of all created things, the peculiar nature of things and persons.

Some centuries later Humanism and the Renaissance laid greater weight on human freedom and autonomy than in the Middle Ages. The consequence of this was that from the end of the sixteenth century to the seventeenth century enormous tensions arose in theology over the relationship between God's omnipotence and human freedom. The central question was whether or not human freedom can limit God's omnipotence. Jesuits and Dominicans got into one another's hair over Molinism, with their views of how these two were to be reconciled, until in 1607 the Pope intervened and for a time banned all polemic on this question.

In the meantime the Reformation encountered the same problem: in particular Remonstrants and counter-Remonstrants fought over the question whether human beings with their free will could or could not withstand God's grace. The Remonstrants seized on Acts 7.51, 'Stubborn and uncircumcised of heart and ear, you always rebel against the Holy Spirit as your fathers did before you', and thus claimed that this was possible. But they were condemned in the Canonical Rules of Dort (III/IV, esp.10-12). The question was thus whether human beings can develop an initiative of their own to resist God's election to blessedness (the term then used).

With the Enlightenment in the eighteenth century the accent was put even more strongly on humankind come of age, even in respect of God, than at the beginning of modern times. And in that connection people then began to talk about the 'self-limitation of God'; these theologians were called 'kenoticists' on the basis of Philippians 2.7, which mentions a self-emptying or kenosis of God at the incarnation. But among the kenoticists this 'self-emptying' was often understood as a kind of 'self-obliteration' of God, something like an anticipation of the 'death of God' theology.

Finally, in a work which has become famous, written in a Nazi prison, Dietrich Bonhoeffer was one of the first to write 'Only the suffering God can help.'[20] God himself is thus seen as a victim of human autonomy and a world come of age. In Christ God dies to human autonomy. Inspired by this, the Dutch New Catechism of 1966 associated the confession of God's omnipotence with the confession of God who suffers and fights in a world of coming-to-be and sin.[21] That is a general outline, which is largely known, of a historical survey of the problem with which we are concerned.

Given all this prehistory, I would prefer to speak, not of the impotence or powerlessness of God but of his defencelessness, because power and powerlessness contradict each other, whereas 'defencelessness' need not *per se* contradict God's power. We know from experience that those who make themselves vulnerable can sometimes disarm evil!

For Christians, perhaps faith in creation is not the focus of their belief but the background and horizon of all Christian belief. Christians confess that we are created in God's image. To be created is, on the one hand, to be taken up as a creature into God's absolute gratuitousness and saving nearness, but on the other hand, seen from God's side, it is a sort of 'divine yielding', making room for the other. This non-godly, protected space of one's own is necessary if God is to make this other his covenant partner. True partnership presupposes a contribution, freedom and initiative from both sides; otherwise there is no partnership. By giving creative space to human beings, God makes himself vulnerable. It is an adventure full of risks. Daring to call human beings to life creatively is from God's perspective a vote of confidence in humankind and in its history, without any condition being placed on human beings or any guarantee being asked of them. The creation of human beings is a blank cheque which God alone guarantees. By creating human beings with their own finite and free will, God voluntarily renounces power. That makes God to a high degree 'dependent' on human beings and thus vulnerable.

This does not do away with the saving presence of God, his immanence in creation. But this creative power of God never breaks in from outside. God's power is inwardly present; Augustine even says *interior intimo meo*: God is more intimate in me than I am identical with myself. Therefore the divine omnipotence does not know the destructive facets of the human exercising of power, but in this world becomes 'defenceless' and vulnerable. It shows itself as a power of love which challenges, gives life and frees human beings, at least those who hold themselves open to this offer. But at the same time that means that God does not retaliate against this human refusal.

The sin in the world of creation in fact renders the Creator defenceless in the extreme. Moreover the rule of evil seems universal and ineradicable in our history; the theory of original sin bears witness that Catholicism, too, and not just the Reformation, has laid stress on the degree of sinfulness in our world. If human beings prefer to use their freedom to remove themselves from the communion with God intended by him and from mutual human solidarity; in other words, if people use the freedom and room given by God for themselves, they make themselves adversaries of God and put limits on God's power. 'Behold I stand at the door and knock,' says the book of Revelation (3.20): God stands on the threshold and knocks at the door, but if we do not freely open it, he does not come in. Out of respect for our freedom God refuses to force the door of our heart and our free will. But God continues to be present in redemption and forgiveness: God does not go away, and continues to knock. In other words, this limit is not God's limit but our limit: the limit of our finitude and above all of our free sinfulness. But God is also present to save beyond this limit, if necessary as the final judge. Meanwhile he is indeed defenceless.

Christians must give up a perverse, unhealthy and inhuman doctrine of predestination without in so doing making God the great scapegoat of our history. We must give up a world history laid down 'from eternity' and 'manipulated' by God, without allowing God himself to be checkmated by our history. Nothing is determined in advance: in nature there is chance and determinism; in the world of human activity there is the possibility of free choices. Therefore the historical future is not known even to God; otherwise we and our history would be merely a puppet show in which God holds the strings. For God, too, history is an adventure, an open history for and of men and women. If I claim to believe in God who has taken the risk of creating the world, then my trust means that ultimately the world will be the expression of God's will in a way which is still not true and is now even contradicted by empirical experiences. So at this point we can never identify God's will in detail. One of the basic mistakes made by some of those who believe in God is to pretend that they know in detail what is 'the will of God' here and now. Some people saw the storms which swept the Netherlands in 1953 as a divine punishment for sin or at least as a divine admonition, just as nowadays some of those who believe in God explain Aids in the same way as a divine punishment. If I am a believer, I am no longer a believer in a bizarre 'first innocence' like these people, but in the phase of a 'second naivety', which has been subject to criticism.

## 3. *Ethics as a* religious *challenge*

First of all, a couple of definitions to avoid misunderstanding. By 'the religious', 'the mystical', 'the theologal' I understand everything in Christian life that has God himself as an explicit object. By 'the ethical', on the other hand, I understand here directly everything which has as an explicit object the humanization or the furtherance of human beings as human beings. In Chapter 1 I said that the ethical has an autonomous consistency, but that on the other hand the ethical as taken up into the mystical dimension of the life of faith is 'transfinalized'; it becomes one expression of the coming kingdom of God. I now want to clarify this further.

My starting point is given by the Christian experiential tradition that the love of God and the love of humankind are not calculable: they both form one and the same divine virtue, although in a degree of tension. That also applies to the negative side of ethics, i.e. to that which is unworthy of human beings, what in religious terms we also call sin. The moral failings through which we mar and wound human beings and the environment are an indication that we are in the process of banishing God from our lives. There is no encounter with God (whether faith or sin) which is not mediated through an encounter with the world as it is. It is therefore always dangerous to talk about sin in terms of a human rejection of God or as sin against God, if we do not at the same time indicate where this rejection also damages our humanity.

Just as the religious or theologal also finds expression in the ethical, which then becomes a sign of the authenticity of our love of God, so in turn ethical rationality becomes a criterion that can unmask ideologizing aspects of the mystical or religious life. For, given its particular structure, Christianity is constantly threatened by a twofold danger, either the swallowing up of the human in the divine (along the lines of ancient monophysitism) or through a reduction of the divine (here the theologal) to the human (here the ethical, above all in its more large-scale ethical or political dimension). But the christological model shows us that 'the divine' does not manifest and express itself alongside and above 'the human' but actually in it, and the converse is true: sin against God also alienates men and women from themselves; to transgress human rights is at the same time to trample God's rights under foot.

The 'problem of God' continues to pursue us, and compels us to ask increasingly more fundamental questions.

In modern times, the universal human experience of the ethical demand, not as an abstract principle but as the reality of the other person in need which challenges me, summons me and lays a claim on my freedom, emerges as 'a privileged place' in which there can be a meaningful experience of God. E.Levinas in particular has analysed this phenomenon. The manifestation or epiphany of 'the other' breaks off the pretence of my totality and ego-relatedness: the other is really other, transcendent.[22] 'In my going to meet the other openly the attachment of my freedom comes to be loosened.'[23] So the ethical demand has a priority over the religious appeal. A religion which enslaves or crushes men and women is by definition a false belief in God, or at least a religion which is interpreting itself perversely and has lost contact with its own authentic roots.

First of all comes the face of the other person as an ethical challenge to my free subjectivity. Above all in our modern human experience, the priority of the *humanum* or human worth is the specific context in which the problem can be put in a valid and also a meaningful way. Is there a God of salvation, who then has enormous consequences for the praxis of human life? In our experiences there is a dimension which breaks through all the totalitarian demands of the empirical sciences, namely the ethical experience of the underivable demand that the other person makes on me. To encounter the other in an ethical way is in no way to encounter him or her as an *alter ego* in accordance with the Kantian demand 'Do not do to others what you would not want others to do to you' (the logic of fair play from the bourgeois Enlightenment); nor is it encountering him or her as an element of a 'totality' (the member of a state, of a society, or of the human race). It is encountering him or her as an original, unique, transcendent other, to whom I am related in an asymmetrical relationship. That means that I can encounter the other person as someone whose existence can make demands on me, demands which are not to be derived from the moral demands I can make on the other.

No doubt I can subsequently generalize this absolute demand from the person of the other in his or her transcendent otherness into a general ethical principle and draw the conclusion from it that there is also a demand on him or her not to harm me, as Kant did. But the principle that the innocent other may not be harmed is based on the underivable concrete phenomenon of personal otherness, and I cannot use this principle to serve my own interests simply because I too can be the unique other for others. E. Levinas arrives at the perceptive insight that what the other person can demand of me is not a consequence of what I can demand of him or her.[24] Another person's ethical personhood is in a kind of non-reciprocal relationship to me; it is not the same as the relationship of my personhood to the other. Fundamentally, this is more a phenomenon of transcendent personal otherness than a matter of sharing in purely communal interests.

There is something special in the relationship of another person's freedom to my freedom. This relationship is ethically asymmetrical.[25] The other person is not transcendent because he or she should be as free as I am. His or her freedom enjoys a superiority which comes from their transcendence.[26] Levinas is here reacting against the I-relatedness of Sartre's *pour soi* (the I).

'The other allows himself to stand as a demand which dominates my freedom and therefore is more original than anything that takes place in me.' 'The other person whose exceptional presence is expressed in the ethical impossibility of my killing him or her indicates the end of the powers. If I can no longer have power over him or her, it is because they absolutely go beyond any idea that I can have of them.'[27] This is the opposite of modern bourgeois freedom since the Cartesian *cogito*, which posits itself independently of 'the other'.

The priority of the ethical then implies that there can be no knowledge of God without social relationships. For Levinas, the other is not an intermediary, not an incarnation of God, but through the features of his or her face is the manifestation of the level at which God reveals himself.[28] And he concludes from this that what cannot be reduced to an interpersonal relationship is ultimately a primitive form of religion: 'the face-to-face remains an ultimate situation'.[29]

However, Levinas' view leads to a cul-de-sac or aporia. The other is not only the origin of an ethical claim on me; he or she is often also potential violence and injustice, as I am to him or her. In order to rescue the meaning of the ethical demand I must thus accept that it is worth the difficulty, indeed is ethically obligatory, to obey the ethical demand for justice and the recognition of the other, even if the other is in fact the source of injustice and violence. Here, rightly, Y. Labbé,[30] among others, takes up one of Kant's inspired thoughts: if only the human being, only the other, is the source of value and meaning (as Levinas says), then there is no guarantee whatsoever that evil will not have the last word on our existence as ethically responsible beings. If human beings are the only and ultimate source of ethics we therefore find ourselves at an aporia. And this is above all the case when the ethical relationship between the other and my freedom is seen as asymmetrical; the other is always the constantly threatening, possible source of injustice.

A dramatic illustration can show what I am getting at. Imagine that in a dictatorship a soldier in a firing squad is ordered to shoot dead an innocent hostage, purely and simply because, for example, he is a Jew, a Communist or a Christian. He refuses to carry out the order for reasons of conscience. He is certain that he himself will then be shot along with this hostage (who will be shot by someone else). But in this refusal the soldier recognizes that the humiliated bewilderment of the hostage is an unspoken and perhaps inexpressible moral summons which he experiences as a demand. The other lays claim on his freedom: he experiences the ethical impossibility of his killing this man and therefore refuses to carry out the order.

In this disarming act of conscience which on the one hand (as Levinas puts it) demonstrates the 'end of the powers' through the disarming death of the soldier, there is on the other hand a paradoxical element, one which even borders on the absurd. For the moral gesture of the soldier is not only to be regarded as ineffective so far as the life of the hostage is concerned (someone else shoots him) but also means the immediate end of his own life with all its unrealized possibilities (he too is shot). So the soldier seems to be under an ethical demand which is at the same time unquestionably absurd. That is defencelessness to the nth degree, and yet in it lies 'the end of the powers'.

That the other person is an ethical demand on me thus leads to an aporia: on the one hand there is no guarantee that evil – violence and injustice, torture and death – will not have the last word about our finite experiences of the world, and on the other there is a certain absurdity: an evidently useless gesture which is no use to anyone. Two ethically honest 'solutions' to this aporia are possible. On the one hand one can talk of a 'heroic act', as Sartre and Camus would do in this case: a gratuitous heroic action for the sake of the *humanum*. On the other hand the reply could take a religious direction, though equally on the basis of human values.

Both solutions conjure up a view of reality in which by holding fast to the *humanum* – the specific person in his or her invulnerability – human beings become victims of empirical factuality, but at the same time put it to shame. On the basis of a person's positive answer to someone else's ethical appeal, against all the appearances, the gratuitous action gains the victory over the empirical triumph of the facts. In both cases we have to do with hope for the ultimate victory of the good: faith in human beings despite everything.

But then the question arises: what is this hope founded on? What are the theoretical truth-conditions of this hope? In the religious answer God himself is the ground of hope and there is well-founded hope. But what are the grounds for the non-religious, humanistic hope in the final victory of good over the apparent triumph of actual evil? Just a 'postulatory' hope, a hope that is positivistically postulated against all hope by our own free will? That is all very well, but is it just a daydream?

Belief in humanity despite everything cannot be a mere positivistic act of will, for in that case people would be trying to drag themselves out of the mire by their own hair. The possibility of a total, emancipatory self-liberation is contradicted by the fact that men and women are not only grace to their fellow human beings but also threat, violence and annihilation, time and again, sometimes with refined technical means. To say that martyrdom is not in vain and that coming generations will reap the fruits of this earlier suffering may be true for some, or even many, people. But the case of the soldier can repeat itself time and again in the future. So while one can indeed interpret the soldier's refusal in a secular sense, as a prophetic action in hope of the eventual triumph of humanity, if one does, one must be aware that there are no grounds for this hope in history or anthropology.

Is it a postulatory hope? Of course such hope can have beneficial social and historical effects. The brave action of the soldier is capable of articulating and mobilizing the aspirations of an important group of people in society.

But one may not draw too absolute a contrast between the humanistic-agnostic and the religious interpretation of such a martyrdom. The humanistic hope is not just a postulate; it has a foundation in an autonomous ethical conviction. At any rate one can argue that there is hope for the triumph of the human because the sacrifice of the soldier has the consciousness of justice on its side, which is not on the side of those in power. The human conviction that justice is superior to injustice in fact gives ground for such a hope. However, this human conviction is just as true for believers, and is the way through which their faith in God is mediated.

Religions and agnostic humanism continue to trust that justice is greater than injustice and evil. According to the testimony of Simone de Beauvoir, the agnostic Jean-Paul Sartre, once even a militant atheist, said on his death bed, 'And yet I continue to trust in the humanity of humankind.' The humanistic hope is thus not purely postulatory: the conviction that one is on the side of justice provides grounds for this expectation; the hope is founded on the rights of justice, despite the fact that the experienceable world is constantly an empirical contradiction of this.

However, the humanist does not know in the end whether reality itself will prove our ethical conviction of standing on the side of justice to be right! The great difference from the religious view is thus that hope with a purely ethical foundation offers a perspective on perhaps a higher degree of humanity for some or even many people in the future, but forgets the many sacrifices which have been made and the countless victims who will still fall. The fallen themselves then experience no liberation or redemption; they have lived so that in the future other people may perhaps not have to undergo the same fate.

In the experience in faith of this extreme ethical situation the person who believes in God sees and experiences reality with its absolute limit in the last resort not as a blind fate nor as wild chance, but as being in fact personal, namely supported by God's absolute saving presence.

In situations which are not willed by God nor even tolerated by him, but which are in fact absurd, God is nevertheless near, to bring salvation. The absurd is not argued away, far less understood rationally or approved of in religious terms, but for the believer it does not have the last word: believers entrust the absurdity to God, the source of pure positivity and the transcendent foundation of all ethics; the mystical source of any ethical commitment, which still gives hope to the actual victim, who outside the religious perspective is written off for good. It is not that the martyr offers his brave death in order to get 'an eternal reward'. Certainly his or her historical action is itself stronger than death; this act itself is praxis of the kingdom of God and bears within itself the germ of resurrection. The one who believes in God sees faith in the superiority of justice and goodness to all injustice **as an** experience of the meta-human (for people clearly cannot produce it in their history), an experience of the absolute presence of God's pure positivity in the historical mixture of meaning and meaninglesness which is called the 'human' phenomenon and its history. This is no belittling of the human by making an appeal to a completely alien factor, God. For this appeal to God on the one hand takes the form of the human conviction that justice is superior to all injustice and on the other hand is an appeal precisely not to that which is completely alien, but to the ultimate, innermost source of all justice: the intimate presence of the exclusively positive reality, 'God', a God who does not want death but life for his people and for all.


Here we also have a pregnant expression of the fact that for those who believe in God, above all Christians, faith in God in one and the same movement frees men and women for love of God and love of their fellow human beings, and above all for love of the maltreated and the outcast (Matt.25.40).

This commitment to one's fellow human beings, even to the point of ethical martyrdom, is to be seen as a context with which human beings can empathize, within which (in a massively secular world) a humanly relevant, philosophically meaningful notion of God's defenceless victory can find a place, and which has its own possibility of being understood, a possibility that can be recognized by others.

The answer to the ethical appeal sketched out here, which is given by both the secular humanist and the person who believes in God, thus lies in a gratuitous or 'vain sacrifice', whether in a heroic sense or as a 'vain offering of love', in a deeply human sense of trusting in God in a holy, non-heroic way, despite everything. These are two possibilities for human life, both of which have their own rationality and comprehensibility. For the believer, the religious interpretation is the more understandable and the more rational. The non-believer sees more rationality in the agnostic interpretation. But within this context, what believers mean by God is also understandable to non-believers. The believer finds

sufficient signs of this faith in his or her human experience, and does so
without these experiences losing human reality.

Although in no sense the only way (there are many ways from and to
God), for those who are seized with bewilderment and sometimes anger
when they see what is done to their fellow human beings, this is the most
obvious, modern way to God: to give a warm welcome to our fellow
human beings in this our wicked world, both on an interpersonal level
and by changing the structures which enslave human beings, men and
women. In other words, we need to encounter fellow men and women
in a liberating way, inter-personally and through political structures.
Moreover, this is not a purely theoretical or speculative approach to
God (ontological foundations, or proclamations of free subjectivity
calling for a decision), but a meta-ethical, i.e. religious or theologal
interpretation, and above all the praxis of an ethical human possibility
on a small scale and on a large scale. This is no metaphysic of being or
of free subjectivity. One can oneself, in openness and perhaps readiness
for sacrifice, accept passively all the misery of the world, but one cannot
remain passive when others are affected by that suffering and violence.
I know that bewilderment and anger in a secular world are not *per se*
religious or holy anger, and do not themselves cry out to a God except
where the religious, and above all Christianity, is already present.
Theology cannot provide any proofs of God; it is reflection in faith on
the praxis of justice and love and its implications. But I shall come back
to this thorny problem later, when we discuss the uniqueness of Jesus
of Nazareth as the Christ.

What is at stake here is not simply the ethical consequences of the
religious or theologal life; rather, ethical praxis becomes an essential
component of a life directed to God, of the 'true knowledge of God': 'He
judged the cause of the poor and needy; then it was well. Is not this to
know me? says the Lord' (Jer.22.16). God is accessible above all in the
praxis of justice and love. 'No one has seen God; if we love one another,
God abides in us and his love is perfected in us' (I John 4.12).


## Conclusion

Mediated through the human conviction that one cannot treat good and
evil, justice and injustice on the same footing, and thus that right is on
the side of the good, belief in God provides the theoretical mediation
between the human hope for the victory of the *humanum* and the concrete
reality of our history. The practical mediation between this hope founded
on God and the world which can be experienced in history comes about
through the praxis of those who believe in God, changing and improving
the world; at the same time there is an awareness that where this fails

through human injustice the last word has not been said, because the practical mediation is taken up in trust in God, whose future for us is greater than our historical future. Thus belief in God is the basis of a prophetic praxis which renews the world. The praxis of faith bears the promise of hope. Finally, for Christians, the historical mediation is brought about through the eschatological recollection of the death and resurrection of Jesus, which is itself a promise for humankind that has not yet been fulfilled but is nevertheless well founded. So the hope of belief in God is dialectically reconciled with the experienceable world – 'reconciled', not in an undialectical model of harmony, but through the critical and productive praxis of living men and women which brings salvation and through belief that there is always a surplus of hope with respect to the world that can be experienced and that resists us. For believers, this surplus of hope over and above what is constantly realized in history is grounded in what they call God's creation-for-his-saving-purposes: God's absolute saving presence in what he has called to life. Precisely this gracious presence, mediated in our experience in and through our essential finitude and through both experiences of meaning and negative experiences of contrast, remains an inexhaustible source of never-failing potential for expectation in humankind which cannot be secularized. Life without belief in God is not quite the same thing as life in a world from which the effectiveness of God's active work of salvation has disappeared (although only believers could make such a distinction)! Belief in God is thus both affirmation and criticism, and therefore not purely negative criticism or 'divine proviso'. Precisely because this faith is consolidating and confessing, and also productive and liberating, it has a critical force which can subject all forms of lack of freedom and disaster to criticism. Any positive filling out of what definitive salvation is which claims to know better runs the risk of either becoming human megalomania or belittling God's possibilities.

## 4. Letting God be God

Above all in our day the terminology 'mediated immediacy', which is challenged by some but which I have used for a long time, is taking on a new accent.

Since, and above all after, the Enlightenment, it has become clear that God is not necessary for the world, for human beings and their society. The life of men and women seems to make sense without belief in God. Jacques Pohier has analysed this in a convincing way.[31] The consequence of this is that we can no longer think of God in terms of need and function, of importance and utility for men and women. In this sense God transcends the category of the necessary, the useful and the contingent. I myself have already said, 'There was no need for God'! Even people who do not believe in God find their life in the world meaningful. Human life is meaningful even without belief in God (which is not the same thing as 'without the existence of God'): that is the great gain of modern 'unbelief' (for believers as well). In other words, God is not to be reduced to a function of human beings, the world or society; in this sense the religious and metaphysical theism in which God stood as an ideological guarantor of a particular view of human beings, society and the world is at an end. We shall now have to speak of God in terms which go beyond both theism and atheism. The short-lived American 'death of God' theology at least had the advantage of making this clear: the hypothesis of God is useless in all kinds of areas.

So in the end believers will have to speak of God by avoiding the ideological function of the old, classical political theologies,[32] but on the other hand they cannot get caught up in the pretended or so-called neutrality of the classical confessional theologies. Only then is liberating talk of God, and thus liberation theology, possible, meaningful in religious and human terms, and necessary. In the religions finality and ultimacy is at stake.


That God is experienced as dark light implies that the infinite God is not exhausted in his interpersonal relationship to men and women, even if he calls this relationship to life in an absolutely free way, with a freedom which is identical to his own absolute being! In this sense he is at the same time impersonal and more than personal. However, the fact that we have to deny a limited individuality to God's personhood has consequences both for his divine identity and for his personal relationship to men and women. The interpersonal relationship between God and human beings is not to be envisaged on the model of two persons who in their limiting and limited individuality stand over against each other and encounter each other as finite beings. God does not know this limitation: in the I-thou relationship between God and humankind God himself includes the human I.

Therefore, prayer is addressing oneself to God, but in the sense that God was and is already most deeply present with and in our being in the world before we turn to him (*interior intimo meo*, says Augustine). Thus there is a mystical substratum in and before any prayer, and any prayer in turn finally also calls for mystical submersion in this primal ground and horizon of life. Mysticism, including Christian mysticism, is therefore concerned with the divine 'supra-personal', but precisely as the trinitarian foundation and source of what above all the Jewish,

Christian and Muslim tradition calls the interpersonal relationship between God and human beings.

However, the paradox is that from a Christian perspective this 'divine supra-personal' must again be interpreted as absolute freedom, the sheer gratuitousness of the triune God. One cannot draw a distinction in God between a zone of freedom and a zone of necessity. All that God is and does is absolutely free, with the absolute freedom of the divine eternal being himself. There is no natural pressure or natural need in God. Both the being of God and God's existence in three divine persons is God's absolutely free choice ('aseity' in terms of absolute freedom), because we may not and cannot identify 'freedom' and 'contingency' in God. God's tri-'personal' being and action in creation and covenant transcend the categories of need and contingency and of creaturely freedom of choice; his being and his action are absolute freedom, and therefore for us are 'every moment new', unpredictable.

Therefore the 'inner-divine Trinity' in a certain sense transcends the so-called 'economic' Trinity, i.e. the triunity as it shows itself in the history of human salvation (= *oikonomia*). But here too we have a transcendence through implication and not a still deeper 'hidden being' (a kind of 'essential Trinity' as opposed to the 'economic Trinity') which would threateningly correct or contradict its revelation in history (in a perverse understanding of the 'eschatological proviso'). If the Christian revelation makes any sense, then in this Christian view God, as he is in himself, is precisely as he has shown himself in our history in the man Jesus of Nazareth. That is the reason why Christians call this man Christ, God's anointed and beloved. So we gain sight of his true and only, real divine countenance (though this is not fully visible and exhaustive, since it goes through the prism of Jesus' human limitation and thus is to some degree refracted). The human face of Jesus not only reveals the face of God in very clear contours, but at the same time veils the face (because it is a revelation of the inexpressible God through Jesus' real-human, historical, and thus contingent and limited expression). Only thus does Jesus himself already point out the way to the invisible, the inexpressible and the unnameable Father (the divine Arche or divine absolute freedom: by expressing in words or picturing for us fatherly and motherly features which we can barely express). Precisely for that reason the christological revelation lets God in his freedom also show other aspects of his riches elsewhere. However, this already brings us to a third chapter: God the Creator and Father of Jesus Christ.

# CHAPTER 3

# Christians find God above all in Jesus Christ

## Introduction

It has emerged from what has been said so far that all men and women, including Christians, have a good deal to say about God and thus about the salvation and well-being of men and women in connection with God, apart from Jesus Christ. This already makes Christianity fundamentally open both to the secular world and to the other world religions. In other words, the kingdom of God, the central term in Jesus' religious message, is broader and richer than Christianity and the churches of Christ.

In this third chapter we will often be confronted with difficult problems. There is the problem of the by no means minor distinction between the profile of Jesus of Nazareth (which is theocentric) and the picture of the New Testament Christ, who is thus the 'Christ of the church' (which is christocentric). Secondly, there is the problem of the necessary (but sometimes alienating) mediation of faith in Jesus Christ by the church. And in a pluralistic encounter of divergent cultures and religions there is above all the problem of the reconciliation of belief in the uniqueness and universality of Jesus Christ with a positive evaluation of other world religions, without Christianity being able to regard itself in a superior, let alone 'imperialistic', way as the one true religion which excludes all other religions (and then in fact also often annihilates them), or includes them by annexing them (Buddhists, Hindus, Muslims and others are then called implicit or anonymous Christians without being asked and without their desiring this title).

The expression of the uniqueness of Jesus Christ on the one hand without discrimination against other religions but on the other hand without falling into 'religious indifferentism', suggesting that all religions are equal, is also part of the task of this chapter.

# 1. Unity and tension between 'Jesus of Nazareth' and the 'Christ of the church's faith'

## Preface

In what they want to say in specifically Christian terms about God, Christians speak of him on the basis of Jesus, whom they confess as the Christ, the Lord, the Son. On the other hand, according to the Christian experiential tradition, no one can confess Jesus as 'the Lord' except in the power of the Spirit of the risen Christ (I Cor.12.3). Finally, human talk of Jesus as the Christ today – and thus christology – is possible only in and through the mediation of the church. In and through the church, through the mediation of fellow men and women, we continue to hear the story of Jesus.

The story of Christ in the church is the story of a Jew who appeared in our human history and who after his death was confessed by fervent followers as 'the Christ, God's only Son, our Lord'. In that story, set down in writing for the first time in what Christians call the second or New Testament, we read how particular people reacted to the historical phenomenon of Jesus and how as a result they began to lead a new and different life. In it we also read how other people, in an equally radical reaction, fiercely rejected the same Jesus and even did away with him by executing him.

Through the New Testament, as in a reflection, we can discover historically the essential features of who Jesus was, how he lived and what inspired him. For these church communities tried to follow him. We have no writings, no direct documents, from Jesus himself. Only in the reflection of the way of life of his followers do we get a profile, a portrait of Jesus. So there seems to be a dialectical interaction between our understanding of the historical Jesus and the faith and praxis of 'the church of Christ'.

The later followers tried to understand for themselves what Jesus had meant for his first disciples and what he also means and could mean here and now for their own lives. This first process of interpretation, at least in part, issued in what we call the New Testament. From New Testament narratives it emerges that what emanated from Jesus' earthly life was such that it compelled people either to follow him in a radical way or to reject him fiercely.

We continue to see that the whole history of the churches in its ups and downs consists in a constantly new process of following Jesus, walking in his footsteps, and in a process of interpretation, constantly going further, in which Christians, confronted time and again with other situations and problems in the church and the world, with confidence in the tradition handed down to them, in faith and yet critically accept what previous generations handed down.

The identity of the 'historical man Jesus' with the 'Christ of faith' or the 'Christ of the church' is a basic affirmation of the New Testament. There are no exclusive alternatives. Certainly we have begun to see more clearly that at the same time they form a relationship in tension without which Christianity is not Christianity and the gospel is not the gospel. For Christians there is no Jesus outside the confession of Christ in the church, just as there is no church confession without the liberating appearance of the historical Jesus of Nazareth for humankind.

## 1. Jesus of Nazareth and Jesus Christ

In Part 1 of this trilogy, *Jesus*, I analysed this relationship at length. No really new insights have emerged from the considerable amount of literature which has appeared on this theme since then (often also along the lines of what I had written in 1974). But people have become more sensitive to some of the tensions and implications.

Originally the term 'Jesus Christ' was not a proper name but a double name which at the same time expresses a confession, namely that of the earliest community in Jerusalem: the crucified Jesus is the promised Messiah, the eschatological anointed of the Lord: 'God made him Lord and Messiah' (Acts 2.36; see Rom.1.3-4). That 'Jesus Christ' is a confessional name indicates the basic structure of all christology: this confession is the foundation and the origin of the New Testament.[1] Without this confession we would never have heard of Jesus of Nazareth. That Jesus has thus become known in our history is also essentially a result of the Christian confession.

But in turn the confession points to a being from our human history: Jesus of Nazareth. This confession is as it is because Jesus of Nazareth was such that he could evoke it. All the statements about Jesus in the New Testament, even when they are recollections of historical facts from the life of Jesus, have a confessional character. People talk about Jesus because they believe in him, and not out of purely historical interest. What is important here, however, is the fact that this confession is about a historical man, with a very particular situation in our history: Jesus of Nazareth, no other, and not some kind of mythical being.

Christology without a historical foundation is empty and impossible. This appeal to history is in modern times at the same time an expression of Christian opposition to the ideological misuse of the name of Jesus Christ, since the church's use of the name 'Christ' is subject to the criticism of the name Jesus: under the criticism of his message and the distinctive nature of his way of life, in the service of righteousness and love, to the death.

## 2. What the historical-critical method teaches the believer

I have already pointed out that the modern interest in the historical Jesus is not the result of the modern 'historical consciousness' but a question which is essential for Christianity because a historical person, Jesus of Nazareth, and not a mythical figure, is confessed to be the Christ.[2] The clear break which many have noted between the 'historical Jesus' and the 'Christ of the church' is thus not so much the consequence of modern historical-critical methods as of the loss of the church's grip or influence on society and culture. Thanks to this emancipation, the historical-critical method had its chance; before that the church-confessional interpretation of scripture had a monopoly.

A scientific study of scripture is possible which is not subject to the authority of the church: that is a manifest achievement of critical exegesis, which studies the Bible as literature, accessible to anyone who wishes to read it. Initially there was a fierce reaction on the part of the churches to scientific exegesis, because it demonstrated a 'break' between Jesus as he was reconstructed by the historical-critical method and Jesus as the churches confess him. Historically, on the basis of the rationalistic element in the origin of 'historicist positivism', this did in fact have a critical impact on the church's tradition and in favour of the negation of the Christ of faith. The fact of the modern, free scientific exegesis of New Testament texts has revealed a latent underivable structure of christology: the tension between Jesus' actual way of life as attested by the four Gospels and the honorific titles confessed in these same Gospels. I myself have stressed that the meaning of Jesus must be discovered not from these honorific titles but from Jesus' particular career, by which all the existing honorific titles are 'broken'.[3] The tension between Jesus and Christ is not the result of the modern historical-critical approach, but structurally a peculiarity of the New Testament and all christology, in this sense: the distinctive character of 'otherness', being indissolubly connected with all historical and thus contingent reality, makes different interpretations of the figure of 'Jesus Christ' possible and necessary. On the basis of this tension between the 'Jesus of history' and the 'Christ of faith', no one can claim Jesus for themselves.

The historical-critical method only became subversive of church belief by freeing it from all authoritarian pressure. This also led the Christian churches themselves to favour the historical-critical method, but in an apologetic sense. It was thought that historical studies could show the continuity between the Jesus of history and the Christ of faith.

But precisely at that point there is a danger. Here is something which history just cannot do: a purely historical approach never brings us from Jesus to the Christ.

The church began to use the weapons of its rationalist foe in order to prove itself right. Modernism was itself opposition to such ecclesiastical domestication of historical methods, the concern of which was to use scholarship to legitimate an authority which people were getting rid of in the social and political spheres. I agree with C.Duquoc that all the polemic over the Jesus of history and the kerygmatic Christ, or the Jesus of church belief, was historically less a christological question than a fight against the exclusivist patent of scriptural interpretation, by whomever it was made.[4]

So despite all the one-sidedness of Bultmann's position, we must not too quickly forget the grain of truth in his basic intuition, namely his denial of a smooth continuity between the Jesus of history and the Christ of the church's faith. In the present situation of the churches, which use historical studies of Jesus of Nazareth apologetically to show the continuity between 'Jesus' and 'Christ', Bultmann continues in a renewed way to fulfil a critical role in respect of the church's faith.

The historical method is free and independent of any external intervention that is alien to it. For the churches, that in fact means that they have no other authority for their witness than their 'own kerygma' and thus are not measured by the autonomous, historical methods of scholarship. In Bultmann's position 'Jesus' belongs to the inner core of a church family. Is this not of inestimable worth? Bultmann was at the same time on the track of a correct insight![5] The retort, however, is: does that not demonstrate that the proclamation of faith is 'immune'? Does an intimate Christian in-group not also have enormous disadvantages?

The break (or better, the striking difference) between the Jesus of history and the Christ of faith is not only a modern question, but has its basis in the text of the New Testament itself. The historical dispute between scholarly interpretation of the Bible and the church's interpretation of the Bible has disclosed a fundamentally theological and 'christological' problem: the historical figure of Jesus of Nazareth is in no way homogeneous with his identity as this is expressed in and through the proclamation and dogmatics of the church.

It emerges from history that any period makes its own picture of Jesus. Jesus thus seems to be manipulated by divergent human needs and interests. By mocking this fact, one runs the risk of at least overlooking, or even ridiculing, the fourfold difference in the Gospel story of Jesus' life. Or there is a concern to monopolize Jesus or use him as a standard by reducing him to what Duquoc wittily calls 'an official vulgate';[6] in other words, this one legitimate interpretation of Jesus is then allowed, and no other interpretations (which is contrary to the New Testament).

Precisely what historical study of the literature which is called the New Testament has discovered has fundamental significance for any christology. Speculative theories about christology from above or christology from below overlook the real problems which arise here: they are often shadow-boxing with a series of all kinds of mutual mis-understandings. Historical studies have made clear to us that there is no smooth continuity between the Jesus of history and the Christ of faith. On the other hand, the affirmation of the identity between Jesus and the kerygmatic Christ is a basic position of all the New Testament.[7]

Identity and diversity show that the biblical story has possibilities and perspectives which only emerge through the mediation of present-day challenges: the multiplicity of pictures of Christ is essential for the figure of Jesus as the biblical narrative describes him. Jesus is in fact a historical and therefore a contingent being: his historical career must explain the biblical expectations and so-called honorific titles and not vice versa, and precisely this is what happens in the New Testament. Jesus is not just the illustration or concrete embodiment of religious ideas and conceptions that were already present; in that case there would in fact be nothing original about him and Jesus too would be caught fast in one interpretation.

The personal career of Jesus of Nazareth interprets what Messiah, Son of God, Lord, means, and these are not interpretations which Jesus himself gave during his earthly life. We do not know in advance what Son of God means in connection with Jesus; nor can the fact that the king of Israel was himself called Son of God in Israel itself tell us in what sense Jesus can and must be called Son of God. Jesus' own career must explain what this term or honorific title implies. The same goes for the expression 'Jesus is our liberator'. Neither old nor new contents of liberation can be any use here except under the criterion of Jesus' career from the biblical narrative, albeit in relationship to the need for liberation in our present situation.

*3. The process of the growth of scripture as a witness to the church's mediation in the transition from 'Jesus' to 'Christ'*

In the first chapter I spoke of 'old biblical and new present-day Christian experiences'. In that chapter, in connection with the concepts of experiential tradition on the one hand and situation on the other, I indicated the need for historical mediations, but at the same time (in order not to anticipate this third chapter) I deliberately left one aspect of this mediation implicit. I now want to bring out this aspect which was left implicit then, namely the mediation of all christology through the church, or ecclesiologically.

In that first chapter I said that understanding of scripture, the understanding of faith, involves a critical and hermeneutical enterprise. I mentioned a reciprocal-critical relationship between the Christian experiential tradition (scripture and its exegesis down the ages, and also Christian praxis) and the present situation. Scripture as the story of the life, death and resurrection of Jesus tells us of a unique 'one-off' event which cannot be repeated in the further history of the church. On the other hand, a relationship with the present is an essential part of the understanding of scripture, while this relationship, i.e that between the story of scripture and our present situation, is 'extra-scriptural', at least in the sense that scripture does not know the situations in which we now live and therefore cannot make any direct statements to us about them. Moreover, by the fact that it is put into writing, in other words becomes text, what is said is liberated from the precisely situated constriction of a localized inter-personal relationship between speaker and hearer. So we and our situation ourselves form part of the text's sphere of reference. It follows from this that an intrinsic element of the distinctive meaning of a text is that it is open to an indeterminate number of readers and for that reason open to divergent interpretations.

The multiplicity of possiblities of interpretation is connected with the semantic autonomy of the text, as a result of which it transcends any limitation to a public which was perhaps originally circumscribed (e.g. the Christians of Corinth in Paul's letters) by its potentiality to address an unlimited number of readers and thus interpreters with their own horizons. We ourselves as readers are part of the horizon of scripture as text.

Therefore present-day believing (present-day believers and the realization of the gospel in praxis) is also the result of the making of all kinds of comparisons between present and past, depending on both the expression of faith and praxis then and now and the situation then and now. There is thus inevitably a creative (and in this sense discontinuous) element in any interpretation of faith. The church community (believers and their leaders), therefore plays a direct part in the actualization of faith; i.e., in concrete believing here and now. We see that already happening in the formation of scripture itself.

For Christians, the New Testament confession of Jesus Christ is the norm of interpretative Christian faith in Jesus of Nazareth. But since his death Jesus has been absent from our history. We can reach him as such only through a text which itself expresses the faith of the earliest Christian church communities in Jesus. Moreover, this text is far removed from us in time and culture. This raises all the more sharply for us the question of the 'christological norm': does this lie in scripture? Or does it lie in the pneumatic working of the Spirit of the absent but Risen Christ in the church? Here there is a threat of biblicism on the one hand and of irresponsible, almost objectifying and automatic, magisterial or charismatic appeals to the Holy Spirit on the other.

We can read the answer to this question from the structure of the New Testament. There it becomes clear that the authors of the New Testament put all kinds of words on to the lips of Jesus which he never spoke historically. In a creative way they adapt what Jesus said in another situation to new situations, which Jesus did not or could not know in the Palestine of his time. The New Testament authors act in this way, and do so correctly, because they were convinced that in the present, Jesus, who according to the Christian conviction of faith was taken up to the Father after his death, from where he sends his Spirit, himself speaks to believers, who live in a quite different situation from the first disciples in Jesus' time.[8] Believers began from the fact that what Jesus had said in very definite, particular situations was also significant in other particular situations and thus also retains its significance even now. The 'universal significance' of Jesus' message which was also established in this way therefore of course calls for adjustment to the present in different situations, for actualization.

In its varied subjects the church community is the vehicle of this actualization: it knows that Jesus lives in his church through the gift of the Spirit. This actualization and even adjustment in faith in no way does away with the historical memory of what Jesus had said and done. The church community living now bears witness to the living actuality here and now of Jesus' gospel which was recorded definitively in scripture. Scripture thus remains the necessary reference text, but the churches make the text into a living word here and now on the basis of maintaining a dialectic between the New Testament story of the career and death of the historical Jesus on the one hand and the life of God's Spirit, recognized as the Spirit of the risen Jesus, in the church of today on the other.

Therefore we cannot speak meaningfully about God 'as Christians' without christology and we cannot speak about christology without pneumatology. And it is impossible to speak about either christology or pneumatology without a living church community, and thus without at least an implicit ecclesiology. But although for Christians God and Christ, spirit and church (and thus theology and christology, pneumatology and ecclesiology) are already closely connected, it will emerge that we cannot regard all these entities as identical without further ado.

From these brief considerations it thus emerges that scripture itself provides the proof that the Christian revelation cannot come to us without the mediation of the church. The actual presence of the church in what happens here and now in the world - the situation (and there are other things and events than in Jesus' time, indeed incomparably different situations) – is therefore the necessary mediation of the actuality and productiveness of the gospel of Christ here and now.

But to note the need for church mediation in the actualizing of Christian faith is in no way to make a plea for ecclesiocentrism or to give the teaching office (in its fallible and infallible aspects) a central place in the church. The whole of the living church community in its confession, prayer and praxis is the subject of this mediation. Moreover there is even quite a considerable difference between the unique, 'one-off' situation of the earliest Christian communities and the situation of the church after scripture (in terms both of leaders and of the community as a whole). The church is certainly both now as it was then the 'sequel' to Jesus, a community of believers who follow Jesus; as such they seek, walking in the footsteps of Jesus, to be a visible and tangible, socio-historical sign of liberation. But the church no longer produces new gospels. Moreover there is often unfaithfulness to the gospel.

The evangelical, apostolic testimony in scripture has a simple uniqueness which the creative witness of present church communities in present situations can in no way claim. Church mediation now is therefore very different from church mediation then. This should never be forgotten, above all by a Catholic ecclesiology which is often grounded almost exclusively in papal and episcopal authority. The relationship of the earliest church to scripture is at the same time different from the relationship of present-day churches to this same scripture, which remains the constitutive area within which all churches live, within the earthly sphere of the world of our human history, in which these churches also live.

The appeal to the Spirit is at the same time an appeal to the mediation of the whole of the believing church community; it is in no way an exclusive appeal to authority or, on the other hand, to an internalized individual charisma of the Spirit. And that appeal to the Spirit, at work in the church community, is at the same time an appeal to scripture. An unavoidable dialectic is involved here.

## 2. The career of Jesus, confessed as the Christ

I   The theocentric focus of Jesus' message and career: the kingdom of God as the real 'cause of Jesus'

*A. The message of the kingdom of God and renewal of life (*metanoia*)*

Kingdom of God, a key word in Jesus' message, is the biblical expression for God's being: unconditional and liberating sovereign love, in so far as this comes into being and reveals itself in the life of men and women who do God's will. One could also just say 'God', but in Jesus' time people avoided naming God directly.

Kingdom of God, literally even realm of God or rule of God, is a term which does not come naturally to us modern men and women. Nor are we bound to the terminology, though we are to what is meant by it. One can take the term 'kingdom' in our modern sense and then give it biblical content. In that case kingdom means a geographical sphere which is inhabited by citizens, members of the kingdom, who have a common legislation and rule. In that case kingdom of God is the whole of the worldly sphere, the ecumene or the inhabited human world, in which the 'rule of God', creator of this universe, means that peace, justice and love prevail there among men and women, who are also at peace with the whole natural ecological environment – provided that they assent in freedom to the kingdom of God.

According to the New Testament confession, the 'approach of the kingdom of God' is closely connected with *metanoia*, or the renewal of human life: 'The time has elapsed (= is fulfilled) and the kingdom of God is at hand; repent and believe in the good news' (Mark 1.15; see Luke 11.20; Matt.3.2; 4.17; 10.7). The followers of Jesus experienced in and through their *metanoia* that with Jesus the kingdom of God had come near to us; through their belief in Jesus their life became completely different.

What particularly did Jesus mean by this conception which is strange to us? That emerges from the whole of his life, from his words, parables and actions. For the whole of his life was marked by his message and praxis of the kingdom of God: 'Seek first the kingdom of God and his righteousness, and then all things will be added to you' (Matt.6.33). Before we analyse this 'praxis of the kingdom of God' proclaimed and practised by Jesus, we can sum it up as follows. The kingdom of God is the saving presence of God, active and encouraging, as it is affirmed or welcomed among men and women. It is a saving presence offered by God and freely accepted by men and women which takes concrete form above all in justice and peaceful relationships among individuals and peoples, in the disappearance of sickness, injustice and oppression, in the restoration to life of all that was dead and dying. The kingdom of God is a changed new relationship (*metanoia*) of men and women to God, the tangible and visible side of which is a new type of liberating relationship among men and women within a reconciling society in a peaceful natural environment. The kingdom of God is God's revealing and saving presence in the world, a presence of which I have spoken in the two previous chapters. The kingdom of God is 'a kingdom of men and women', a human kingdom, in contrast to the kingdoms of the world which are symbolized in Daniel 7 by animals, kingdoms in which the strongest holds sway. The kingdom of God is the abolition of the blatant contrast between rulers and ruled (also where God is seen as such a tyrannical ruler).

The concrete content of the kingdom of God transcends our human power of imagination. We get a vague idea of it on the one hand through human experiences of goodness and justice, of meaning and love, and on the other hand as reflected in our opposition to situations in which we feel the human in us, personal and social, to be threatened, enslaved and dishonoured. However, from the Christian perspective these experiences come to stand out only against the horizon illuminated by Jesus' life: his message, conveyed above all in parables of the kingdom of God, his personal pioneering of the praxis of the kingdom of God which he maintained to the death. Here the vision of what the kingdom of God can be for men and women takes eloquent shape. The kingdom of God is essentially connected with the person of Jesus of Nazareth himself. The New Testament states this in one of its earliest recollections, when it says that with Jesus the kingdom of God, God himself, comes very close to us.

So the kingdom of God has to be defined further in terms of the life of Jesus: in terms of the fact that where sick people came to Jesus they were healed; in terms of the encounter of 'demonic spirits of sickness' which become whole in their encounter with Jesus; in terms of his table-fellowship and dealings with 'tax collectors and sinners' who in his time were those who were marginalized, discriminated against and even excommunicated; in terms of his beatitudes on the poor; and finally in terms of all the oppressed. Jesus finally sums all this up in a simple gesture, protecting children whom his disciples think are a burden to him: his reaction was that the kingdom of God belongs to those who are like such children (Mark 10.13-16; Matt.19.13-15; Luke 18.15-17). When John the Baptist sent his disciples to ask Jesus whether he was the Messiah, Jesus replied: 'The blind see and the lame walk, lepers are cleansed and the deaf hear, the dead are raised and the good news is preached to the poor' (Matt.11.4-5; Luke 7.22-23), and Luke makes the so-called public life of Jesus begin with a sermon which he preaches in the synagogue on Isa.61.1-12 and 58.6: 'He has sent me to preach the good news to the poor' (Luke 4.18). Also: 'Blessed are you poor, for yours is the kingdom of God' (Luke 6.20). The main significance of the poor both in the books of Isaiah (3.4; 10.1-2; 11.4; 14.32; 26.5-6; 29.19; 32.7; 41.17; 51.21-22; 54.11; 58.7; 61.1; 66.1-2) and in the New Testament (Mark 14.5-7 par.; Mark 10.21 par.; Luke 14.13-21; 16.19-22; 19.8; 21.1-4; John 12.5-8; 13.29) is that they are those who are really socially and economically poor, exploited and oppressed.

Now the fact that Jesus' proclamation and praxis of the kingdom of God represent good news for these poor and oppressed people does not mean that 'the kingdom of God and his righteousness' (Matt.6.33) brings these poor people direct liberation from poverty, exploitation and oppression. It means that Jesus rescues the poor from their sense of shame at being outcast; he restores their worth as human beings, children of God. Those members of a society from which they are as much outcasts as lepers, who meet someone like Jesus, who gives them a warm welcome and offers table fellowship, are rescued from their sense of shame at their expulsion from society. A humiliated, despised or outcast person who is welcomed and invited in to drink a glass of wine with someone once again feels a member of the human race, feels finally accepted and able to laugh again. So the poor and the despised are redeemed and liberated by Jesus. As a result of this the poor can ultimately distance themselves from the scale of values in the society which had so humiliated them. And this new situation of authentic liberation is at the same time the possible beginning of social self-liberation, for adherence to a social system of values which is based on humiliation is the greatest barrier to the self-liberation of the poor and the oppressed. The fact that, as I have repeatedly heard from Latin American liberation theologians, there is more laughing, dancing and celebration among the poor and oppressed is a clear indication, in keeping with Jesus' beatitude, that the kingdom of God now already belongs to the poor. This blessing of the poor is not a consolation of the gospel that keeps them from becoming socially subversive. It is rather the divine promise that Jesus gives them so that they may stand up proudly against a violent society as particularly beloved children of God. They, the poor, are not to blame for being poor (though being poor is a discredit and in no way an honorific title, not even from God); the blame does not lie with them, the poor, but elsewhere, and it is precisely the poor who are the victims of what others are to blame for. By feeding the crowds with just a little bread and a few fishes Jesus seeks to demonstrate that in the kingdom of God the praxis of brotherly and sisterly sharing applies, not the will or law of a particular social system as a result of which the poor become steadily poorer and the rich steadily richer. Precisely by taking sides with the poor and those who are discriminated against, the kingdom of God is at the same time a challenge to the rich to abandon their self-interest and adopt the course of brotherly sharing. The parables and life of Jesus will make this clearer.

The conclusion may well be that it is only against the background of an acute sense of the sinful situation of the world, a state of injustice and an absence of peace, a state of structural poverty, unnecessary suffering and sorrow, that we can understand Jesus' proclamation of the coming kingdom of God and of the need for renewal of life or *metanoia* on the basis of his experience of 'a God concerned for humankind' (to repeat a key phrase from my *Jesus* book).

*B. Parables of the kingdom of God*

Jesus clarified what he meant by 'kingdom of God' and thus by 'God' above all in the language of parables.[9] The originality with which Jesus talks about God does not diverge substantially from the Old Testament image or concept of God. But particular accents above all from the prophetic proclamation of what and who God is take on such a distinctive profile in Jesus' preaching, to the point of almost being over-emphasized, that other aspects of the traditional picture of God are constantly forced into the shade. Generally speaking, we can say that according to Jesus, his God – the God of Abraham, Isaac and Jacob, the God of Moses, the God whom Jesus called his 'Father' – is a God who does not let himself be claimed by a caste of pious and virtuous people who know that 'they are not like the tax-collectors and sinners' and are sure of a commensurate reward for their faithful observance of the law. No, all parables rule out this view of God; Jesus shows that God comes to stand on the side of those who are pushed aside by the 'community which thinks well of itself': the poor, the oppressed, the outcast and even the sinful. But this 'God of the poor and sinners' is not an indulgent God: he lays claim completely on men and women and asks them to follow him with a undivided heart.

This already emerges from the parable of the lost sheep (Matt.18.12-14; Luke 15.4-7): the behaviour of the shepherd illustrates God's action as Jesus lives it out for us. Here is a God who is more concerned about a benighted sheep than about the ninety-nine who are safe. The parable of the 'lost son' further stresses this (Luke 15.11-32). The utterly surprising attitude of the father towards the prodigal son promptly provokes the indignation of the oldest son (Jesus' first listeners). But

Jesus teaches them that the sinner remains their brother or sister and that they all must share in God's joy over the conversion of the sinner. In the parable of the Pharisee and the publican (Luke 18.10-14), the pious Pharisee who in fact keeps the law scrupulously and thanks God because he is not like this sinner is turned away by God. The publican who feels unworthy to appear before God goes away 'justified'. Moreover in the parable of the workers employed from the eleventh hour (Matt.20.1-15) Jesus presents a very provocative picture of God: God remains free in handing out his gifts and favours. No one is so justified before God through good works as to stand in the way of God's goodness to those who have no good works to offer, or at least have few 'merits'. This attitude of God then becomes all the more challenging for pious and virtuous people since it is really about sinners. To offer forgiveness to one sinner causes God more joy than the salvation of ninety-nine righteous.

The parables finally speak about God, although he is almost never named. They teach us that God does not mean to be a guarantor of privileged positions in bourgeois or religious society. In contrast to the dominant and conformist images of God in his time, Jesus presents a God who shows special love towards those who are handicapped, crippled, oppressed and marginalized, even sinful. For it is not the perhaps hidden spiritual or ethical nobility of the poor and outcast which moves Jesus to this special love. He looks around in the first place for particular people because these handicapped, crippled, poor or burdened people are sick. It is precisely these people who accept his message, while the wise and intelligent elite rejects it. In the parables Jesus shows 'the other face of religion (or the church)': his way of being the 'God of men and women', of all men and women, makes him primarily the God of the outcast and the excluded. Anyone who cannot hear that from the New Testament, above all in the parables, has understood nothing of Jesus' message of the kingdom of God. It is perhaps our own bourgeois acclimatization over the centuries, our membership of the 'community which thinks well of itself', that has made us blind to the plain meaning of Jesus' message and the parables which clarify it. The God of Jesus is a God who does not allow himself to be pocketed by the lobbies of pious people. That is one of the basic elements of Jesus' gospel. As followers of Jesus, we must follow God, 'who makes his sun shine on the good and the evil' (Matt.5.45). The behaviour that Jesus requires of his disciples must distinguish them from the tax collectors and Gentiles (Matt.5.46-47), and from the sinners (Luke 6.32-24). Therefore it is required of Christians that they should 'Be merciful, as your Father is merciful' (Luke 6.36); not cast out even sinful brothers or sisters. Anyone who opposes any form of discrimination whatsoever has Jesus on his or her side. The commandment 'love your enemies' (Matt.5.44-45; Luke 6.35) is on the same wavelength as the radicalism of Jesus' love of the neighbour. Anyone who follows that commandment will be called son of God (Matt.5.9).

On the other hand this God of those who have been rejected by their fellow men and women is at the same time a God who lays complete claim to the human heart, radically, but without any compulsion or violence: 'Seek his kingdom' (Luke 12.31, cf. Matt.6.33) and all the rest (our basic need for food and clothing) will be added to us (by God). From a parable, that of the master and his perfect servant (Luke 17.7-10), it emerges that even the most complete trust and service of God does not bestow any right to stand before God. Jesus proclaims the spirituality of trust in God for rich and poor, not the pseudo-spirituality of an appeal to one's own good works, by which one screens oneself and stands aside in an elitist way from 'those sinners there'.

Precisely because of this trust in God, Jesus goes especially to the poor. 'Salvation is preached to the poor.' To a great extent Jesus' action consisted in establishing social communication and opening up communication above all where excommunication or expulsion was officially in force: in connection with public sinners like tax collectors and public outcasts, the possessed and the lepers – in short, all who were thought unclean. They are precisely the ones whom Jesus is seeking, all of them. For the official Judaism of the time the God of Jesus is a dissident God. That not only emerges from Jesus' message and parables, but is also corroborated by his way of life.

## C. Jesus' praxis of the kingdom of God

The kingdom of God is a new world in which suffering is abolished, a world of completely whole or healed men and women in a society where peace reigns and there are no master-servant relationships – quite a different situation from that in the society of the time. As things are there 'it may not be so among you' (Luke 22.24-27; Mark 10.42-43; Matt.20.25-26). However, the coming of this new world does not take place without human action, in which Jesus has preceded us.

For alongside Jesus' proclamation there is his action, and in particular the New Testament miracle stories. Historically there can be no doubt that in the time of Jesus and the early church phenomena were produced by religious preachers which their contemporaries adjudged to be miracles. The separate stories in the New Testament reflect the awareness of the narrators that Jesus did miracles, although they express this awareness in forms which do not correspond to our understanding of these events. It is certain that people experienced fullness of life in Jesus' company in a way that immeasurably transcended their everyday experiences. In this context the miracles are signs of the 'whole', healed and sound world of the kingdom of God which is made present in them. Moreover the proclamation of the nearness of the rule of God and the miracles of Jesus belong inseparably together.

By both the parables of the kingdom of God and Jesus' praxis of the kingdom of God it becomes clear how Jesus relativizes the human, sometimes hard-fought principle of justice. Jesus' praxis and parables often offend our sense of justice even now. The worker at the eleventh hour gets just as much as the worker at the first hour (Matt.20.1-17), and from the person who has nothing will be taken away even what he has (Matt.25.29). Jesus here wants to teach us that the rules for the praxis of the kingdom of God have nothing to do with the social rules in our societies; this is an alternative form of action. Jesus does not defend immoral or anarchical people, but he does go and stand alongside them. He unmasks the intentions of those who are zealous for God and righteousness; he takes from these zealots even what they have: a zeal for God and the law which excludes men and women. He points to the perverse effects of virtue like that of the oldest brother of the lost son (Luke 15.11-32) who is overbearing about the repentance of his youngest brother. Jesus reacts sharply against those who manipulate the social rules. Strict righteousness can involve the excommunication of men and women who are already public outcasts. The coming of the kingdom of God does not know the human logic of precise justice. Jesus wants to give hope to those who from a social and human point of view, according to our human rules, no longer have any hope.

There is something subtle and killing in a particular kind of virtue. The subtle vice of 'perfection' has not yet disappeared from church life. People defend so-called unassailable laws, and in so doing injure already vulnerable fellow men and women. Jesus showed that up. The effect of this zeal is often to deprive men and women of room to breathe. Jesus opposes worldly practice when the law has the effect of excluding the other person. If the law reduces people to despair, it forfeits all authority. For Jesus, the poor and the outcast are the criterion of whether the law is functioning creatively or destructively, as the will of God for the benefit of men and women.

Even the tradition of Jesus' Jewish people, of Israel, is not the final authority for him. For him, this tradition has a human legitimacy, but he does not submit to it unconditionally.

The novelty of Jesus' attitude to law, to tradition, to the existing pictures of God, does not derive directly from his transcendent authority, which puts itself in the place of Moses. If that happens, the new features that emerge in Jesus are derived without any intermediary directly from his divinity, and the critical power of his human choice, the reason why he was condemned, is completely trivialized. For Jesus, God is not the guarantor of society, of prosperity, and of the family.

Jesus' picture of God is determined by the thirsty, the stranger, the prisoner, the sick, the outcast; here he sees God (Matt.25). In all his behaviour, Jesus rejects righteousness as the 'absolute imperative' (Matt.20.15-16). In his view righteousness is not the last word. Jesus takes the part of those who have no advocate but many accusers, who with their references to the law, pointing their fingers, expel men and women and thus kick them out.

In all this Jesus is aware that he is acting as God would. In and through his life he relates God's action to men and women. In his parables he is concerned with the one lost sheep, a lost coin, a lost son. To fellow believers who are offended at his dealings with unclean people, Jesus seeks to make clear through his actions that God turns towards lost and vulnerable people; Jesus acts as God acts. So in him there is a claim that God himself is present in his actions and words. To act as Jesus does is praxis of the kingdom of God, and moreover a demonstration of what the kingdom of God is: salvation for men and women.

That Jesus' activity in healing and performing cures, along with all his conduct which frees men and women from need and misery, is part of his task is also shown by the fact that he send out his disciples not just to hand on his message of the forgiveness of sins and eternal life but also with the task of 'curing and healing people' (cf. Mark 3.14-16; 6.7ff.). The kingdom of God includes forgiveness of sins, but it is more than that. The people who can experience salvation from God in Jesus are also themselves called to do this after Jesus, to an even greater degree (John 14.12), in unconditional love towards their fellow men and women. The foundation of the life of the disciples of Jesus lies in the life which Jesus himself led in his day.

## D. *The kingdom of God and Jesus' career*

So what is striking in Jesus' career is the essential relationship between the person of Jesus and his message of the approach of the kingdom of God. Moreover there is an intrinsic connection between the message and the proclaimer, just as there is an intrinsic connection between this message and Jesus' consistent action in accordance with it. By his person, his message and his way of life, Jesus stands as guarantor for the liberating God who loves men and women. From Jesus' career it becomes clear to the believer that the God of Jesus, the God of Israel, fully accepts people and in this acceptance tries to renew them in relation to themselves and others, in a world which is worth living in for men and women.

All this presupposes that Jesus himself also lived in the conviction of being affirmed and recognized by God. The Christian tradition formulated this in sharper terms in the expression of its belief that Jesus is related to God as Son to Father: he is Son of God. But the basis of the possibility of using this church name lies in the historical reality of Jesus himself, above all in his 'Abba' experience, which, in contrast to what he experienced in 'this world', was the source of his message and practice of turning to those who were suffering.[10]

Jesus' message of and about God was so integrated into his active dealings with his fellow men and women, which liberated them and established communication, that his proclamation and his way of life interpret one another, while together changing and renewing people, liberating them for their fellow men and women in love and solidarity, just as after his liberating encounter with Jesus Zacchaeus the tax collector lets the poor share in his posessions. In turning to both the rich tax-collector and the outcast and to vulnerable children, the sick or the possessed, the crippled and the poor, Jesus immediately demonstrates what he is talking about; and in so doing he anticipates eschatological salvation, the kingdom of God, here and now.

## E. The career and death of Jesus

The proclamation of the travelling teacher whom people called rabbi explained the law – which he recognized even more strongly than the Pharisees as the will of God – as intended for the *benefit* of people; this did not leave Herod Antipas and the priestly authorities untouched. The tradition according to which Simon, a Pharisee, warned Jesus of the threat to his life from Herod (Luke 13.31), is historically particularly credible, above all because of the anti-Pharisaic tendency in many New Testament texts after the 70s. At all events, at a particular moment, as a result of many events Jesus came to understand that his career too, like that of John the Baptist, would inevitably end up in painful rejection and death.

In one way or another, perhaps in the dark night of faith, but conscious of his task, Jesus related his impending death to his proclamation of the kingdom of God. Despite this threat of death he remained faithful to his message and bade farewell to his followers at a festive meal: 'I shall not drink again of the fruit of the vine until the kingdom of God has come' (Luke 22.18). After this he was executed, by a Roman crucifixion, 'under Pontius Pilate'. There is good reason for this to appear in the Christian creed. It implies a political element, quite apart from any theological significance of the crucifixion.

We may not isolate the death of Jesus from the context of his career, his message and his life's work; otherwise we are turning its redemptive significance into a myth, sometimes even into a sadistic and bloody myth. As soon as we fail to take account of Jesus' message and the career which led to his death, we obscure the Christian tenor of the saving significance of this death. The death of Jesus is the historical expression of the unconditional nature of his proclamation and career, in the face of which the significance of the fatal consequences for his own life completely paled into insignificance. Jesus' death was a suffering through and for others as the unconditional validity of a praxis of doing good and opposing evil and suffering.

Both Jews and above all the Roman authorities were involved in the legal murder of Jesus. For particular Jews, above all the Sadducean priestly caste, who as masters of the temple had an understanding with the Romans, Jesus' criticism of what was done on the sabbath, to the detriment of the poor and the outcast, and also his attitude towards the temple and his criticism of it (think of the cleansing of the temple), was a great thorn in the flesh. This criticism was also to be heard from fellow-Jews from the Diaspora. Despite everything it emerges from the later New Testament passion narratives, for all the distortion in them, that the theme of the 'destruction of this temple' by Jesus was unmistakably a factor for certain Jews in their condemnation of Jesus (for the significance of the sabbath obligations, Ex.31.12-17, see John 2.19; Acts 6.14; Mark 11.15-17 par.; Mark 13.2 par. 15.29; Matt.26.61; 27.40 and Rev.21.22, which stresses that eschatologically there will no longer be a temple). However, it was not so much the Pharisees (who throughout the Gospel narratives are wrongly depicted as Jesus' opponents – because of their dominant position in Palestine, though that really came about only after the Jewish war), but above all the Sadducean, pro-Herodian and in fact pro-Roman clan, who played the dirty trick of handing Jesus over to the Romans as a dangerous political case. In the passion narratives the Pharisees do not appear once.

We have to see the life and death of Jesus as one whole; we cannot consider the significance of his death by itself. To give one's life for others is in fact the greatest sign of love and friendship, but only if any other solution is in practice excluded and is thus impossible. God, who, according to Leviticus, 'abominates human sacrifices' (Lev.18.21-30; 20.1-5), did not put Jesus on the cross. Human beings did that. Although God always comes in power, divine power knows no use of force, not even against people who are crucifying his Christ. But the kingdom of

God still comes, despite human misuse of power and human rejection of the kingdom of God.

## F. Jesus' message and career raise a new question

To believe in Jesus as the Christ means at its deepest to confess and at the same time to recognize that Jesus has an abiding and constitutive significance for the approach of the kingdom of God and thus for the comprehensive healing of human beings and making them whole. This significance is essentially bound up with the distinctive, unique relationship of Jesus to the coming kingdom of God as salvation for men and women, as all religions confess God. That with the coming of Jesus God comes near to us is a basic Christian conviction which must therefore be expressed in one way or another in the Christian creed.

What Jesus said and did, so that others began to experience decisive salvation, salvation from God in him, raises the question: who was he that he was in a position to do such things? If he mediates a new relationship to God and his kingdom to us, it is natural to ask: what is his relationship to God? And what is God's relationship to him?

It becomes clear from this that Jesus *in his humanity* gets his name from, i.e. is defined by, his relationship to God. In other words, Jesus' deepest being lies in his utterly personal bond to God. Our relationship as creatures to God is doubtless also an essential part of our common humanity. But this relationship does not define our being human in its humanity. Nothing, no creature, escapes this relationship: but that is not yet to say anything about the nature of this creature. With Jesus more is involved.

From the New Testament it emerges on the one hand that ultimately God can be 'defined' only from and in terms of the human career of Jesus, and on the other hand that Jesus as man in his full humanity can be defined most deeply in terms of his unique relationship to God and human beings. Thus God is at the same time part of the definition of what and who the man Jesus is.

However, God is greater than even his supreme, decisive and definitive self-revelation in the man Jesus – 'the Father is greater than I' (John 14.28). The humanity of Jesus thus points essentially to God and to the coming of the kingdom of God for which he himself gave his life, i.e counted it as nothing. For Jesus, God's cause – the kingdom of God as salvation of and for men and women – is more important than his own life. In this reference to God which disregards his own self, to the God whom Jesus called his Creator and Father, lies the definition, the real significance of Jesus. For Christians Jesus therefore (*a*) is the decisive and definitive revelation of God and (*b*) precisely in this capacity at the same time shows us what and how we human beings can, must and really may be. Therefore the man Jesus is indeed connected with the nature of God in the definition of what he is. In Jesus God reveals his own nature by being willing, through him, to be salvation of and for men and women. To take up the words of the church father Irenaeus: (*a*) the salvation of men and women lies in the living God, and (*b*) God's honour lies in the happiness, liberation and salvation or wholeness of men and women.

In the man Jesus the revelation of the divine and the disclosure of true, good and really happy humanity coincide completely in one and the same person. The nucleus of the whole of Jesus' activity is thus that the 'God of human beings' who is concerned for humanity wants to make us 'people of God' who, moreover, like God, are concerned for others and their humanity. What is striking about Jesus is the liberating humanization of religion which nevertheless remains the service of God.

In the Christian creed of the churches this view of Jesus is set against the background of faith in God as creator of heaven and earth. Christian belief in creation implies that God loves us without conditions or limits: for our part undeservedly and boundlessly. Creation is an act of God who on the one hand presents us unconditionally with our finite, non-godly human existence, destined to true humanity, and who on the other side, at the same time, in disinterested love presents himself here as our God: our salvation and happiness – the supreme content of true and good humanity. God freely creates men and women for human salvation and happiness, but in this same action he wills in sovereign freedom himself to be the deepest meaning, the greatest salvation and happiness of human life.

Therefore God, in whom we can trust, in all his absolute and divine freedom, is a constant surprise for men and women: 'He is the one who was and is to come' (Rev.1.8; 4.8). In creation God takes the side of all that is created, that is vulnerable. For those who in the Jewish-Christian tradition believe in the living God, the human cause is the cause of God himself, without in any way diminishing human responsibility for our own history. But at the same time, God's cause is also the cause of all men and women.

The article in the creed, 'I believe in God, creator of heaven and earth, and in Jesus the Christ', thus means that for the non-godly, for the vulnerable, God's being is liberating love in Jesus Christ. God, the Creator, the one in whom we can trust, is love that liberates men and women, in a way which fulfils and transcends all human, personal, social and political expectations. Christians have learned all this by experience from the career of Jesus: from his message and his life-style which matches it, from the specific circumstances of his death, and finally from the apostolic witness of his resurrection from the realm of the dead.

## II   From the theocentricity of Jesus to the christocentricity of the New Testament and the church

*A. From Jesus who speaks to us of God to the church which speaks to us of Christ*

After his death, Jesus the proclaimer becomes the one who is proclaimed, God's Christ. The message of the New Testament is unmistakably christocentric. But this does not mean that it is in any way unfaithful to Jesus. The proclamation of the kingdom of God was central for Jesus and he did not want in any way to give us a christology. To construct this is the task of his followers: 'Whom do *you* say that I am?' (Matt.6.15; Mark 8.29; Luke 9.20). But Jesus equally leaves no doubt that there is an essential relationship between the approaching kingdom of God and his own person and activity. In the church's proclamation of Jesus as the Christ the message of the kingdom of God is retained in full. In the New Testament Jesus in no way takes the place of God, not even in the highest christological statements (John 1.1; 20.28; Heb.1.8-9): 'You are Christ's and Christ is God's '(I Cor.3.23). For the New Testament, 'God will be all in all' (I Cor.15.28).

In Jesus' self-understanding, access to God is determined by the way in which people react to his message and appearance: 'I say to you that any one who confesses me before men, him shall the Son of Man confess before God's angels' (Luke 12.8-9 = Matt.10.32-33, see below). So if the kingdom of God has a world-wide significance, Jesus' relationship to that kingdom also has a world-historical significance: Jesus was aware of playing a special, unique role in the coming and the realization of the kingdom of God. The move from theocentrism to New Testament faith in Christ must thus be expressed on the basis of Jesus' own theocentric message.

Of course no historian can demonstrate or deny that Jesus' self-understanding corresponded to reality. It was believers who experienced that Jesus is the Christ in the change to their own lives. All the honorific titles in the New Testament take their direct origin from the experience of salvation from God in Jesus Christ, as a result of which believers saw their lives change. Jesus' followers experienced the connection between the coming of the kingdom of God and personal *metanoia* or change of life in their own life-renewing dealings with Jesus. It was Jesus who transformed their life and made them enter the kingdom of God.

However, there is a danger that Christians may forget the originally theocentric focus of Jesus' appearance and then either lapse into a Jesuology which says too little or introduce a reduction in which God is absorbed into Christ:[11] in that case his saving presence in nature and history, outside Jesus, in God's great word of creation, is in practice denied.

## B. *The saving significance of Jesus' life and death*

In the Christian tradition, the death of Jesus becomes a central theme, although in the New Testament there is a whole series of earlier levels at which no interpretation in faith of Jesus' death is given. However, we may say that the Christian proclamation of the saving significance of Jesus' death on the cross goes back to the basic tenor of Jesus' own proclamation. Jesus was opposed to the idea of a triumphal messiah. Only in a redefinition of the meaning of messiah, anointed, can this title be applied to Jesus.

Jesus' crucifixion alters the term Messiah: the crucified and rejected Jesus is the messiah. Like God, Jesus identifies himself *par excellence* with outcast and rejected men and women, the unholy, so that he too himself finally becomes the one who is rejected and outcast. This identification is radical. So there is a continuity between the career of Jesus and his death, and because of this continuity the saving significance of Jesus finds its climax in the crucifixion and does not lie in the crucifixion taken in isolation.

From the Christian perspective, God revealed himself in Jesus in and through the non-divine form of Jesus' humanity. However, this has been interpreted in quite different ways within Christianity. Above all within the 'two-natures' scheme of Pope Leo the Great, people often arrived at a kind of christology of paradox, between the extreme of the human and the extreme of the divine, passing over the actual narrative of the Gospels. In these theologies of redemption there is often an abstract dialectic between 'weak humanity' (*forma servi*, the form of a slave) and the all-powerful God (*forma Dei*), viewed in an unhistorical way. This forgets the sovereign free decision and choice of Jesus which resolutely rejects all ideology of power and therefore any attribution of a Jewish messianic title to himself. Jesus is not condemned because as a man he is said to have divine pretensions, nor for his weak humanity. It emerges from the Gospel narrative as a whole that he is condemned for his sovereign and free human way of life, which is subversive to any one who gambles and bets on power. His authoritative appearance was a challenge and led to his trial and condemnation: his behaviour compelled the powerful to unmask themselves. He criticizes the perverse effects of a particular zeal for 'God's cause' to the detriment of the 'human cause'.

In short, the clear choice of Jesus was his refusal of any messianic ideology which on the one hand liberates the oppressed but on the other hand mercilessly annihilates all the oppressors, which was a generally accepted apocalyptic model.

It emerges from the whole of the New Testament (despite some 'interpretaments' pointing in a different direction) that Jesus puts the emphasis on the gratuitousness of our redemption and liberation. Many existing theories of our redemption through Jesus Christ deprive Jesus, his message and career of their subversive power, and even worse, sacralize violence to be a reality within God. God is said to call for a bloody sacrifice which stills or calms his sense of justice. First sin must be avenged and only then is reconciliation possible. The rejection of Jesus by God is said then to reconcile us with God. That goes against the whole proclamation and career of Jesus. Jesus refuses to heal human violence in our history through 'divine force'. From his three choices in the wilderness it is clear that he resolutely rejects the title messiah, with all the Jewish expectations associated with it at the time.

To attempt to reconcile mercy and justice is to attempt to harmonize the irreconcilable. As a man, Jesus opts for mercy and gratuitousness, ruling out punitive sanctions on the oppressors and the evil. People seem unable to imagine that there is a generosity without any connotations or after-thoughts, and on the other hand that good and evil do not lie on the same level and that the consequences of evil therefore follow an internal logic of their own (I shall be analysing this internal logic later in this chapter).

Jesus did not want to be a messianic-political leader, but this does not mean that his message and his career did not have political significance. I would describe as 'subversive' actions and words which in fact undermine the authority of social and political institutions. The basic choice of Jesus was to refuse power, and so his words and actions take on an unparalleled authority. Accepting rejection and repudiation for himself, Jesus does not want to be the leader of the outcast. Here he seeks to stress that being outcast is not a privilege, but the perverse effect of an oppressive society. The silence of God when Jesus hung on the cross is logically on a par with Jesus' choice in rejecting any messianism of power. Jesus' death on the cross is the consequence of a life in radical service of justice and love, a consequence of his option for the poor and outcast, of a choice for his people suffering under exploitation and oppression. Within an evil world any commitment to justice and love is deadly dangerous.

The redefinition which Jesus gave of both God and humankind in and through his preaching and conduct takes on its supreme and ultimate significance precisely in his death on the cross: God is also present in human life where he is absent from human view. The vision of the kingdom of God, of a coming world in which the wolf and the lamb lie down side by side and a child plays on the hole of the serpent, could also have been understood wrongly. Before Jesus' death it sounded to the disciples like a triumph, almost too good to be true. But through and on the basis of Jesus' career they became wiser. Where the good triumphs and suffering and death yield, God is confessed in practice. Certainly, but there is more and also something else: Jesus points out that salvation can also be achieved in suffering and in an unjust execution.

Jesus told us so attractively to pray to his Father that his kingdom should come by us men and women hallowing his name here and now on earth, and doing his will as through the ages the angels had done in heaven. He also told us to pray that his and our Father should in fact perform the threefold function of a Jewish father by providing for the daily needs of his children, forgiving the evil they had done if they really regretted it, and protecting them against all evil. But on the cross, the Jesus who taught us to pray like this found that even his prayer was more like a lengthy monologue than a dialogue with a statement and a response. Even for Jesus it was true that those who authentically seek personal contact with God have the impression that in this prayer they are hearing only the empty echo of their own voices.

On the cross Jesus shared in the brokenness of our world. This means that God determines in absolute freedom, down the ages, who and how he wills to be in his deepest being, namely a God of men and women, an ally in our suffering and our absurdity, and also an ally in the good that we do. In his own being he is a God for us. I therefore can no longer attach any significance to the classic difference between 'God in himself' and 'God for us'.

In the New Testament there is a theological redefinition of various concepts of God, and also a redefinition of what it is to be human. God accepts men and women unconditionally, and precisely through this unconditional acceptance he transforms them and calls them to repentance and renewal. Therefore the cross is also a judgment on our own views: a judgment on our ways of living out the meaning of being human and being God. Here is revealed ultimately and definitively the humanity of God, the nucleus of Jesus' message of the kingdom of God: God who comes into his own *in* the world of human beings for their healing and happiness, even through suffering. God does not impose any conditions on us human beings, including the man Jesus, for his redemptive and liberating appearance: 'It was God who was in Jesus reconciling the world to itself' (II Cor.5.19). It was not God but men and women who put Jesus to death; at the same time, however, this execution is the material prepared for God's supreme self-revelation by human beings, as emerges from New Testament belief in the resurrection of Jesus.

## C. Belief in the resurrection of Jesus

To begin with, any meaningful statement about the resurrection of Jesus must be of such a kind that Jesus' shameful death is not trivialized in the light of the resurrection faith. Jesus' death is historically beyond question a defenceless event. To talk of Jesus' atoning death, or of the redemptive value of this death, can become sheer ideology without critical reflection. Paul says that the cross is not a sign of honour but a curse (Gal.3.13), an offence and a shame. The resurrection of Jesus does not do away with that. In Jesus' death, in and of itself, i.e. in terms of what human beings did to him, there is only negativity. In his case this is not an ordinary death, nor an instance of the universal human problem of death as a dialectic of death and life, as Bultmann and others assert, but of a shameful execution which is quite out of proportion to the actual career of Jesus – indeed is in flagrant contradiction to it. Thousands have been crucified, yet nevertheless their crucifixions have not been thought to have universal significance, nor have they been called atoning deaths. So the importance cannot lie in Jesus' death as such. Purely as the death of Jesus, this dying cannot have any redemptive or liberating force; on the contrary, death is the enemy of life.

My position is that if the career of Jesus does not show any anticipatory mark of the resurrection, his death is sheer failure and in that case resurrection faith is simply the fruit of human longing (as Jacques Pohier thinks). Without effective anticipations of the resurrection in the earthly life of Jesus, Easter is an ideology. The only subject of the statement of faith 'He is risen' is the historical Jesus of Nazareth who believed in the promise by giving it form in his message and above all in his way of life. Jesus' faith in the promise as the source of an original praxis is a historical anticipation of the significance of the resurrection and thus of God's overwhelming power over evil. In his career Jesus is an 'already', still of course within the horizon of death, but now that of a death which has already been overcome in hope. The power of God was already at work in the life of Jesus, and his death shares in that. Only on this presupposition is belief in the resurrection not an ideology! If only Jesus' death is a historical anticipation of his resurrection (this applies above all for Bultmann and to some degree also already for the apostle Paul), this resurrection is unavoidably the negation of a history.

Thus we cannot detach the defencelessness of Jesus on the cross from the free power and the positivity which revealed itself in his actual career of solidarity with oppressed men and women on the basis of an absolute trust in God. God is concerned with the happiness of men and women who live under the threat of nature, social oppression and self-alienation. Jesus is so opposed to this that his concern for his own survival fades away and even plays no part. Oppression may not be; the right of the strongest may not apply in the life of the human community. Oppression is injustice and a scandal. So Jesus refuses to regard evil as being on the same footing as good and acts accordingly. Jesus' career itself is therefore praxis of the kingdom of God, a historical anticipation of the resurrection, and his death is part of this career. So we can speak of his death as a defenceless superior power, disarming evil. Moreover, it was already the insight of the first Christians that even the earthly life of Jesus has to show positive anticipations of the resurrection if faith in the resurrection is not to be ideological; and that insight is acutely expressed in the story in which the Synoptic Gospels speak of a transfiguration of Jesus during his earthly life.

So we can understand why precisely at the place of the deepest disappointment, the cross, a liberating faith could break through among the disciples. Let us analyse its content more closely.

The psalm which Jesus prays on the cross and which begins with the words 'My God, my God, why have you forsaken me?' ends in a prayer of thanksgiving for God's abiding, albeit silent, saving presence. God was not powerless when Jesus hung on the cross, but he was defenceless and vulnerable as Jesus was vulnerable. The basic experience of the first disciples after Good Friday was that evil, the cross, cannot have the last word; Jesus' career is right and is the last word, which is sealed in his resurrection. Although the cross was on the one hand the sealing of the superior power of human beings over God, in the dying Jesus God is present, and indeed present as pure positivity, as he was with the living Jesus, In that case suffering and death remain absurd, and even in Jesus' case may not be mystified; but they do not have the last word because the liberating God was absolutely close to Jesus on the cross, just as he was throughout Jesus' career. But that was a presence without power or compulsion. Paul says that 'the foolishness of God is wiser than men, and the weakness of God is stronger than men' (I Cor.1.25); God's presence was near in power, but without the misuse of power.

So God can be present in reconciliation and we may speak of the redeeming and liberating career *and* death of Jesus. God conceals his superior power over evil and at the same time expresses it in his defencelessness in order to give us room to be ourselves in solidarity with oppressed men and women. In this defencelessness, however, at the same time God uses his superior power because his defencelessness is the consequence of his fight against evil in a wicked world. The messianic 'must suffer' of Jesus is not a 'divine' must. It is forced on God through Jesus by human beings, yet God and Jesus are not thwarted by it, not by virtue of the resurrection as such, which would then be regarded as a kind of compensation for the historical failure of Jesus' message and praxis, but because his 'going around Palestine doing good' was itself already the beginning of the kingdom of God, of a kingdom in which death and injustice no longer have a place. In Jesus' praxis of the kingdom of God his resurrection is already anticipated. The Easter faith expresses the fact that murder – and therefore any form of evil – has no future. Precisely for that reason death is overcome. The crucified Jesus is also the Risen One.

Only when we have seen the defencelessness of the cross can we and may we also look for the significance of Jesus' resurrection. Only a new action on the part of God – (although this newness is the eternally young, free being or the one act of God's being God, and not a 'second act' which as it were makes up for what has gone before) – could link Jesus' historical life, through his death, with the 'Christ of the church's faith', with the confession 'He is risen indeed'. In the resurrection from the dead, God's eschatological action with reference to Jesus the crucified one becomes God's own verdict on Jesus, and only in this way does God's evaluation of Jesus and his message, career and death also become clear to believers. The Easter faith presupposes a new action by God relating to the crucified Jesus. In the first instance this expresses how God is related to Jesus – in the reception and interpretation of Jesus' disciples. Paul understood this well when he explicitly said to those Corinthians who denied the resurrection: 'Some evidently have no sense of God' (I Cor.15.34).

Therefore the reality of the resurrection, through which alone the resurrection faith is brought to life, is the test of both the understanding of God preached through Christ and our soteriological christology. In the resurrection God authenticates the person, message and whole career of Jesus. He puts his seal on it and speaks out against what men and women did to Jesus.

Just as the death of Jesus cannot be detached from his life, so his resurrection cannot be detached from his career and death. To extrapolate the death and resurrection of Jesus so that they become the nucleus of the Christian message is ultimately to twist the prophetic content of the whole ministry of Jesus: that is a Pauline kerygma without the four Gospels, and Paul is canonical only within the New Testament as a whole. First of all we must say that Christian belief in the resurrection is in fact a first evaluation of Jesus' life and death, and especially a recognition of the intrinsic and irrevocable significance of Jesus' proclamation and praxis of the kingdom of God which nothing can undo, in the light of the gospel. We undermine the resurrection faith if we remove this first dimension.

But this belief comprises still more, and this 'more' is also connected with the life and death of Jesus. The resurrection of Jesus is in the second instance the breakthrough or manifestation of something that was already present in the life and death of Jesus, namely his living communion or communion of grace with the living God, a communion which could not be broken by death. This living communion is already on earth the beginning of what is called eternal life.

Thirdly, there is also in the resurrection an aspect of a divine judgment on what human beings did. Resurrection is not merely the extension of Jesus' living communion with God (beyond death); it is the germ of the establishment of the kingdom of God: the exaltation and glorification of Jesus to God. 'I believe in Jesus the Lord.' His message and career themselves have an eschatological significance and do not get this only from the resurrection.

But this threefold theological argument remains an abstraction which we cannot locate properly in theology if we leave aside the living, *pneumatic* presence of the glorified Jesus in his church. Through and in this Christian belief in the resurrection of Jesus, the crucified but risen Jesus remains effective in our history through his followers. Jesus' resurrection, his sending of the Spirit, the origin of the Christian community of God as the church of Christ which lives from the Spirit, the New Testament witness to all this and thus resurrection faith, define one another reciprocally, though they cannot be identified with one another.

We can say that the 'church of Christ' which came into being on the basis of the resurrection of Jesus is what is meant most deeply in the New Testament by the appearances of Jesus: in the assembled believing community of the church the crucified but risen Jesus appears, i.e. is effectively present. Moreover, where the church lives by Jesus Christ, lives by praying and liberating men and women in the footsteps of Jesus, belief in the resurrection does not undergo any crisis. On the other hand, I feel very strongly that it is better that there should be no belief in eternal life than that a God should be presented who diminishes people in the here and now, keeps them down and humiliates them politically with an eye to a better hereafter.

This spiritual presence of Jesus in believers has consequences for Christian life. Just as positive anticipations of the resurrection and thus of the superior power of the grace of God could be seen in Jesus' life (and must be seen, if resurrection faith is not to become an ideology), so the same holds true for Christians. Within the defencelessness of our own lives we must be able to *experience* the superior power of God: otherwise we accept it with a faith which is presented as purely authoritarian.

Anyone who begins to look for this element of present experience must, I think, first be well aware of the difference between our timebound existence and God's eternity. As human beings, we know that silence is an element of any dialogue, of any talking. Now how is that to be understood in a dialogue between human beings and God? What is a human life of at most between seventy and ninety years to the eternal God? A fraction in his divine life; a sigh, a moment in which we can say barely a few words to the listening God. Therefore God is silent in our earthly life. God listens to what we have to say to him. God can answer only when our fleeting life on earth is ended. Should the living God not be extremely interested in us all our lives, listen silently to our life story until we have expressed everything and each person has communicated his or her own life to God? Do we not all dislike being constantly interrupted before we have finished? Nor does God interrupt us, but for him the whole of our life, however important, is just a breath, and God also takes it seriously; that is why he is silent: he is listening to our life story. Precisely because he is greater than our human heart, he never speaks as a tangible human voice in our innermost being but only as a 'divine silence', a silence that only after our death takes on a distinctive voice and face that we can recognize. As long as the Eternal One is still listening to our life story of fifty or even a hundred years, the eternal God indeed seems to us to be powerless and defenceless. In this there is both a desperate trial for our historical existence and at the same time an experience full of hope and expectation.

In the light of this Christian view of Jesus' career, death and resurrection, both 'God' and 'Jesus' take on a critical and productive, liberating power for us. The criterion of humanization, proclaimed by Jesus and used by him in practice, beyond all human expectations of the *humanum* which they desire and which is constantly threatened, this desire for the humanity of humankind, for our soundness and wholeness, is something which is close to the heart of God, and not a reduction of the gospel. For the gospel is good news not just about Jesus but about the God of Jesus, creator of heaven and earth, the God of all men and women.

The message of Jesus embraces the kingdom of God in all its height and depth, breadth and length, not just the forgiveness of sins and eternal life, though it does comprise that, and indeed perhaps does so above all. Jesus proclaimed to the end the absolute, freely effective nearness of the God who creates and brings salvation to human beings in all their dimensions. We Christians learn, stammeringly, to express the content of what God is and the content of what men and women can be, in other words the content of human salvation, from the career of Jesus.

We are liberated to new, authentically human possibilities of life. From all that has gone before we can at least make the following list. Through Jesus' redemption Christians experience the freedom to accept that despite sin and guilt we are accepted by God; the freedom to be able to live in this earthly world without ultimate despair about our existence; the freedom to look death in the face as not having the last word; the freedom to commit ourselves disinterestedly for others in the confidence that such dedication is ultimately of decisive significance (Matt.25); the freedom to accept experiences of peace, joy and communication and to understand them as manifestations, however fragmentary, of the saving presence of the living God; the freedom to join in the struggle for economic, social and political justice; the freedom to be free from oneself in order to be free for others, free to do good to others. For Christians, all these experiences are a Christian experience of faith in the God who discloses himself in Jesus Christ as the sacred mystery of all-embracing love: experiences of salvation from God.

Christian redemption is indeed liberation from sin. But liberation from sin also has a cultural context. In our time the Christian understanding of sin also includes the recognition of systematic disruptions of communication like sexism, racism and fascism, antisemitism, hostility to and attacks on immigrant workers, and the Western cultural and religious sense of superiority. The Christian love which is the basis of community therefore also includes the necessity to recognize the need for deep involvement in present-day work of political, cultural and social emancipation.

### III  The kingdom of God: 'already and not yet'

#### A. Present-day experience of the kingdom of God as the foundation of a firm hope in a final consummation planned by God

Earlier in this chapter I said that where men and women encounter Jesus in faith, the sick are healed, demons are driven out, sinners are led to repentance and the poor discover their worth. In all these encounters with Jesus the kingdom of God is experienced here and now both by Jesus and the one who encountered him. The seed of the kingdom of God already germinates and ripens here and now on earth.

The kingdom of God is not an unearthly other world, but the completion of the restoration of this world, our world which is out of joint. Therefore the contemporary experience of men and women who as followers of Jesus place fragmentary signs of the kingdom of God in this world, our world that is out of joint, is also the foundation for a firm hope of a kingdom of God grounded in Jesus that will one day be completed. To what height and depth, to what length and breadth, will this ultimately completed kingdom of God, which began in this world 'as small as a mustard seed', finally grow?

The undefinable aspect of the *humanum*, i.e. the eschatological fullness and freedom of men and women, which is sought and constantly found in a fragmentary way, only to be constantly threatened again, can only be expressed in symbolic language, by speaking in parables and metaphors, though these reach further than the impoverished sharpness of our rational definitions (which we also need if we are not to lapse into chaos). Four great metaphors, presented in the Jewish and Christian Bible in many sounds and tongues, suggest to us the way towards what, according to God's dream for the happiness of men and women and all their fellow creatures, humankind will eventually be.

(*a*) The definitive salvation or the radical liberation of humankind for a brotherly and sisterly society and community in which there are no longer any master-servant relationships, in which pain and tears are wiped out and forgotten, and in which 'God will be all in all' (I Cor.15.28), is called 'the kingdom of God';

(*b*) In the Christian tradition of faith the achievement of the salvation and happiness of the individual (called *sarx*, body or flesh, in the Bible) within this perfected society is called 'resurrection of the body', i.e. of the human person including his or her human corporeality, this corporeality being the visible orchestration, the personal melody, of a person which others also enjoy (although this glorified corporeality has nothing to do with the body which is left behind, it has everything to do with the personal corporeality in which I lived on earth);

(*c*) The eschatological consummation of an intact ecological environment which human beings need for their life is suggested by the great biblical metaphor of 'the new heaven and the new earth'. This is not another world (that would mean contempt for and rejection of the original good creation), but our earthly world redeemed from being out of joint – though I do not know how to imagine this. Moreover, whether or not we can imagine this here and now is quite unimportant; there are many surprises to come.

(*d*) Finally, the normative role or significance of Jesus (in fact a man from somewhere in Nazareth), whom many Christians confess as the Christ, will become evident to all, being established on the one hand now already from fragments of the kingdom of God and, on the other hand, also in the final eschatological consummation of this kingdom; this is something that we can express now as the deepest concern and interest only in the biblical image of 'Maranatha' ('Come, Lord Jesus'). This eschatological picture (the parousia of Jesus Christ), which cannot really be expressed in human language, is nurtured by the experience of and recollection of what Christians now already (see the following exposition), albeit with some hesitation, and in fact quite daringly, call the uniqueness of Jesus Christ. What in Christianity is called Jesus' parousia or second coming is, in the final consummation of the kingdom of God, ultimately the becoming transparent to all of the real significance of Jesus of Nazareth, in the midst of so many world religions, in the eyes of God himself.

These four metaphorical visions of the eschatological future* envisaged by God for men and women now already influence the action of Christians in the world: not in an indeterminate or undirected way, but in a very definite direction, namely through the dynamic of the direction indicated by these four symbols: concern for a better society for all, above all for the outcasts and those who are stand by their side, for vulnerable men and women; and pastorally through communication as an incessant criticism of society and culture where there is clearly injustice; concern for the human body, for human psychological and social health; concern too for the natural human environment; concern for a sound attitude of Christian faith, hope and love; concern for meaningful liturgical prayer and a meaningful sacrament; concern finally for the individual pastorate, above all to the lonely and those 'who have no hope'(I Thess.4.13). The Christian spirituality with which Christians do all this draws both its power and its joy from this eschatological hope.

*B. Is there a counterpart to this fourfold 'heavenly' vision of the future for 'evil people'?*

In the Gospel of Matthew, in the story of the last judgment there is mention not only of the ultimate liberation of men and women but also of a condemnation: 'Depart from me you cursed ones, into the eternal fire that is prepared for the devil and his angels' (Matt.25.41). This in fact derives from the apocalyptic literary genre, in which alongside the

---

* Perhaps (though I am not sure, since biblical visions have something classical and immortal about them) in 1990 we must look for other more telling metaphors which suggest the same thing. For this we need poets who are tuned to the same wavelength as the sensitivity of the Bible.

exaltation of the oppressed all the oppressors are taken from their throne and annihilated.

However, Christianity did not take over this apocalyptic model in every respect. In fact the resurrection of Jesus did not have any of the effects that the apocalyptic Jewish visionaries expected. In order to 'gloss over' the absence of these effects, some Christians began to speak of a divine postponement of the parousia and the eschatological final judgment. Within an apocalyptic horizon one had to talk like this: within this thought-pattern the postponement of the annihilation of all oppressors goes with the final victory of the oppressed. But after Easter the history of oppression and violence went on in the same old way, and still continues to do so, as if there had never been a Jesus. People were disappointed in the apocalyptic expectation of retribution for evil ones and oppressors.

However, Christians look at the effect of the Easter event in the light of the Holy Spirit given by the risen Jesus, which bestows forgiveness. The sending of the Holy Spirit and the forgiveness which is given to us by the crucified and risen Jesus of Nazareth poses for us the problem of what happens to the oppressors in our history. Jesus himself does not speak of sanctions for oppressors, as apocalyptic did. He breaks with this apocalyptic model; the Christian experiential tradition speaks only of an eschatological judgment. But according to the liberation theologians, a liberation which does not already take a historical, albeit transitory form, in fact becomes an accomplice of violence, which continues in our world after the Easter event.

As Marx also said, the purely eschatological solution can in fact have an alienating effect in our history. The anxiety which prevailed throughout Europe between the fourteenth and the eighteenth centuries as a result of the vision of the last judgment is well known. Architecture, the graphic arts and literature are full of it. We also have visions of permanent suffering, damnation to eternity in the New Testament (e.g. Rev.20.10). Whereas in the same Bible we hear that God comes near to outcast men and women in Jesus, according to the apocalyptic vision a 'kingdom of the damned and suffering', a kingdom of those definitively cast out from the kingdom of God, a kingdom of permanently suffering men and women, will exist for ever alongside the kingdom of God. And this hellish suffering will continue for ever without any meaningful perspective, because by definition in hell no therapeutic significance can be attached to it. In that case it is solely the perpetuation of revenge: vengeance and retribution. In this view there will be eternal suffering, though it is that of the oppressor, while Dutch Christians now already have difficulty over the senseless rejection of the prisoners held since the

Second World War (and only released in 1989), the old and sick 'Nazi prisoners of Breda'.

Some Christians (like Peter Berger in the United States) have in fact said: 'There is so much evil crying to heaven that there must be something like a hell.' One could think in that way, perhaps too humanly: can the victims of Hitler and Eichmann happily spend eternity in their company? I understand this reaction, but I myself see things like this. Goodness and evil, 'heaven' and 'hell', are in the first place anthropological possibilities, in other words, decisions by men and women themselves. Not God, but human beings are the inventors of hell, precisely by the way they behave. In their situated freedom human beings are in fact in a position to do both good and evil. In this sense both heaven and hell are human possibilities. Whether there are in fact people who definitively choose evil I do not know; that is quite a different question. No man or woman can discover that; a judgment on that belongs only to God. But on the basis of human possibilities the biblical threats and perspectives of 'heaven and hell' are a therapeutic and pedagogically meaningful perspective on the future. They really point towards something. Whether this anthropological, internal possibility is also a possibility for God is another matter. The saying of Thérèse of Lisieux, 'Je crois dans l'enfer, mais je crois qu'il est vide,' I believe in hell but I think that it is empty, is anything but unbiblical!

The same problem also exists in various religious experiential traditions: some church fathers speak of a general *apokatastasis* or recapitulation, which means that in the end everyone will be saved. There is also the expression of a similar vision in the doctrine of reincarnation in non-Christian religions, that ultimately everyone will be saved. Only the way in which this is imagined is different, as there are differences in the possibility of understanding it rationally.

But I have my reservations about these somewhat too superficial solutions. To my mind they suggest too cheap a view of mercy and forgiveness; moreover, they trivialize the drama of the real course of events in the conflict between oppressed and oppressors, between the good and the evil in our human history.

Present-day preaching is silent about hell, eternal damnation and judgment; they can no longer be heard from the pulpit, only seen in modern films. After centuries of an enormous inflation of a threatening proclamation of coming doom we now maintain an uncomfortable silence: there is a universal allergy to ultimate sanctions, indeed even to the death penalty on earth.

I myself see things as follows (not so much with some hesitation, nor apodictically, but as a meaningful and plausible Christian understanding of the Bible and tradition in modern times).

Heaven and hell are asymmetrical affirmations of faith. You cannot consider them on the same level. Christian faith in eternal life in the form of 'heaven' has its foundation not in the Greek affirmation of the immortality of the human soul but in living communion with God in grace (expressed in human solidarity) during earthy life. (People used to speak of the 'state of grace'.) The bond of life with the living eternal God, sensed as being positive, cannot be destroyed by death. In Jesus God overcomes death for those who anticipate the kingdom of love and freedom in history. So there is a 'heaven'.

There can be no hell for evil men and women on the same symmetrical level. But those who are evil, oppressors, certainly punish themselves thoroughly for ever. If living communion with God is the foundation of eternal life, then the absence of this living community (not so much through theoretical denial of God as through a life-style which radically contradicts solidarity with fellow human beings and precisely in that way rejects God and living communion with God) is at the same time the foundation of non-eternal life for these people. That seems to me to be the 'second death' of the fundamental, definitive sinner (if there is such a person). That is 'hell': not sharing in eternal life nor being someone who is tortured eternally, but no longer existing at death. That is the biblical 'second death' (Rev.20.6). This sanction is the result of one's own behaviour and not a positive act of the punitive justice of God who sends sinners to an eternal hellish fire (however that may be imagined as an instrument of torture): there is just no ground for eternal life. These people have resisted God's holiness and are incapable of loving. No one in heaven will ever remember them. It is an unimaginable scenario for me as a Christian, familiar with the gospel, that while there is said to be joy among the heavenly ones, right next to heaven people are supposed to be lying for ever, gasping for breath and suffering the pains of hell for ever (however you imagine this – spiritually or physically). On the other hand, the idea of the second or definitive death respects God's holiness and his wrath at the evil that is done, to the detriment of the poor and the oppressed.

So ultimately no one is excluded from the kingdom of God; in that case there is only the 'kingdom of God', a kingdom of liberated and free people, who do not have next door to them a kingdom of those who have been definitively cast out. The evil do not have eternal life; their death is in fact the end of everything: they have excluded themselves from God and the community of the good, nor does any new heaven await them on earth. They no longer exist, and cannot sense the happiness that good men and women then enjoy. But there is no shadow kingdom of hell next to the eternally happy kingdom of God. That is inherent in the asymmetry between what we call heaven and hell. The blessed will be spared the fact that a stone's throw away from their eternal happiness, fellow human beings are being tortured for ever with whatever physical or spiritual pains.

Dante's 'sorrowful city' alongside the joyful palaces of the heavenly blessed ones is a pedagogical picture: especially destructive oppression and utter evil have no future; on the basis of their own logic they are without hope. There is nothing present in evil and wickedness which is to be marked out for eternal life. There is nothing here that can be integrated into a kingdom of freedom and love. Through its own emptiness and weightlessness the wicked world which was formerly so powerful and evil disappears by its own logic into absolutely nothing, without the blessed having to feel offended by some barracks next to heaven where their former oppressors are tortured for ever. They already had precisely this experience in their earthly life; to have it a second time, for ever, would be sheer blasphemy for them. This seems to me to be the most plausible Christian solution, in contrast to the model by which the Christian tradition has usually proclaimed this insight in the past. But in the past no distinction was made between the rights of God's holiness, which were rightly defended, and the exercising of them in the concrete and definitive fate of stubborn sinners. In other words, people put good and evil on the same level; they forgot the asymmetry of the two. They also overlooked the grotesque finitude in the megalo-mania of evil!

Of course the good also has its own intrinsic logic. But it does not follow from this that we should demythologize heaven in the same way as 'hell' and moreover look for heaven in the joy of virtue on earth without any perspective on an eternal life. Here too there is asymmetry in the relationship of God to evil and to good. As far as evil is concerned, there is no need for a transcendent factor; Thomas Aquinas himself dared to apply the term *causa prima* (first cause) to creatures where there was any question of negativity.[12] By contrast, the good finds its ultimate source (or *causa prima*) in God. The internal logic of evil therefore *terminates* in the finite mortality of human beings, while the internal logic of the good *culminates* in the eternal love of God who sustains the good man and woman (despite their many failings) in death and draws them to him over the boundary which is inherent in humanity.

So there is no future for evil and oppression, while goodness still knows a future beyond the boundary of death, thanks to the outstretched hand of God which receives us. God does not take vengeance; he leaves evil to its own, limited logic! So there is in fact an eternal difference between good and evil, between the pious and the wicked (the deepest intent of the distinction between heaven and hell), but the pious continue to be spared having to rejoice over the torture of eternal doom being inflicted on their fellow human beings. God's unassailable holiness consists, rather, in the fact that he will not compel anyone to enter the kingdom of heaven as the unique kingdom of liberated and free people. The 'eschaton' or the ultimate is exclusively positive. There is no negative eschaton. Good, not evil, has the last word. That is the message and the distinctive human praxis of Jesus of Nazareth, whom Christians therefore confess as the Christ.

## 3. The kingdom of God: universal creation and salvation from God in a particular person, Jesus Christ

I   Men and women as God's story on the model of the Davidic king

### Introduction

I can reformulate what I have been analysing in the previous section once again by means of Old Testament-Jewish models, so as finally to arrive at a universal human question on the basis of these particular models.

In the first or Old Testament we find two great divergent views of human history in its relationship to God. Both the Deuteronomic and the Yahwistic view of Israel's monarchy which was introduced in the tenth century BC under Samuel and Saul are important for our understanding of the Jewish-Christian concept of the rule or kingdom of God. Here we must also remember that the idea of a 'kingdom of God' later takes on all kinds of new connotations, above all in the period of intertestamental apocalyptic, and that these also influenced the New Testament.

When about four hundred years after the introduction of the monarchy in Israel the Deuteronomic theology reflected on the earlier events in a large-scale historical survey, this kingship had already gone completely wrong. The view of this theology is, moreover, that only YHWH the Lord is 'ruler in Israel', and that where God rules, all human rule of human beings over other human beings cease to exist. There is thus no worldly kingship. For when I Sam.8.11-18 describes 'human' rule, we hear only of exploitation and burdens, military service and confiscation of possessions: slavery. Therefore the people who want a king like other nations are solemnly told: 'In that day you will cry out because of your king, whom you have chosen for yourselves; but the Lord will not answer

you in that day' (I Sam.8.18). Precisely because only the Lord is king
of Israel (I Sam.12.12), the introduction of kingship can only mean
slavery and exploitation of the people. In that case Israel will perish just
like other worldly kingdoms.

But the monarchy still came in Israel. The Deuteronomic theology
could not deny this fact and solved the problem with a compromise: all
right, if you insist, but let there be a king in Israel! But this means: 'If
you will fear the Lord and serve him and hearken to his voice and not
rebel against the commandment of the Lord' (I Sam.12.14), then in the
end only God will rule: then there will be salvation and peace for men
and women in Israel. For this theology, the rule of God is human
liberation, not a theocracy that brings oppression. Moreover, in the
legal terms of the time, the historical fact of God's 'leading Israel out of
Egypt' is the legal basis of YHWH's lordship over Israel. Precisely for
that reason Israel must 'go after' its liberator, i.e. serve only the Lord
and not tolerate any other bonds: service to the Lord is liberation from
all other oppressions. One serves only one Lord.

So the kingdom of God may indeed also be called a rule, but as the
rule of God, for Israel it is at the same time the abolition of any alienating
lordship, a farewell to the rule of human beings over other human
beings, a farewell to the ties they themselves impose. To abandon all
'for the sake of the kingdom of God' is the only rule that brings freedom.
For this represents the rule of righteousness and love, a rule which raises
up the little ones (Deut.7.6-9). Recalling this Deuteronomic experiential
tradition, we must abandon our objection to what the word rule
conjures up, an objection which is understandable because of modern
experiences, not in favour of a theocracy or the equally misused concept
of God's omnipotence, but in favour of God's offer of salvation which
shows itself to be in solidarity with human helplessness and seeks to
raise up the oppressed. For this is the rule of God, the kingdom of God.

The older Yahwistic theology, with a different orientation, was equally
aware of the failing of Israel's kings. This trend had already worked out
quite a different theology of kingship long before the Deuteronomic
theology we have just analysed. For this tradition, the installation of
Israel's own king in the tenth century with all its syncretism is the
completely new, as it were secularizing, event of this century, which
broke with Israel's sacral past in a very definite way. As Jesus was to
do later, David could freely transgress the sacral and ritual precepts.
When he was hungry he took the sacred shewbread (I Sam.21.1-6; see
Mark 2.23-28). He transgressed the laws of purity over the death of his
own son (II Sam 12.16-23). And just as Jesus generously tolerated the
excessive use of spikenard at the anointing in Bethany, so David, when

he was thirsty, poured the precious water from Bethlehem 'senselessly' on the ground out of solidarity with his men, though he was rescued from besieged Bethlehem by three of his brave men, who risked their lives in the action (II Sam.23.13-17; cf. John 12.1-8). This wise man, king and at the same time son of man, does all this because he knows that God puts unconditional trust in him, the king.

But even the free David holds the Lord to his word (II Sam.7.25). The king who is faithful to Yahweh is God's free governor who – following God's creation as the ordering of chaotic primal powers – is now himself to recreate actual human history from chaos to order or *shalom*, in accordance with his own wise insights. David, 'the little man', 'from behind the flock' (II Sam.7.18b: 7.8c), 'taken from the dust' (I Kings 16.1-3; see I Sam.2.6-8; Ps.113.7; Gen.2.7) and himself not worthy of trust, is raised up from the dust and trusted unconditionally by God (II Sam.7.8-12); raised up from the dust, or nothing, to be king (this is evidently an ancient stereotyped inauguration formula for someone's appointment as king). He, David, on the basis of this divine trust, must work things out through his own wisdom, make free and responsible history for the benefit of his people. The welfare of this people is dependent on the wisdom of the king, the source of all life.

The Yahwistic tradition is well aware that David's descendants failed in this charge. It knows that God reproached him for this and therefore punished him for it (II Sam.7.14). But this tradition still confesses : 'But he, God, will never take his *hesed* (or good favour) from David' (II Sam.7.15). Trust in the king is never revoked by God.

The distinctive feature of this Yahwistic tradition (which influences the New Testament) lies in the fact that it tries to understand human history, from Adam, on the basis of experiences of the Davidic royal house (which before the final redaction of the Old Testament was already past history, a closed chapter). However, the message of these texts is that what happened in the Davidic history is typical of our humanity. What happened to David is the key to understanding, which discloses the human condition of all of us; it is the mirror of each person's own history.

In fact, in the Yahwistic tradition the Adam of the so-called second creation story is 'the royal man' or 'son of man', i.e. everyman, but conceived of on the model of king David: from the dust, or nothing, appointed by God as his vassal king or vizier on earth (see Gen.2.7).[13] The creator puts his fullest trust in this man of nothing, like David, 'taken from the dust'. He, a human being, as God's delegate, is entrusted with the garden, the earthly dwelling place. He must be responsible for it honourably and conscientiously, and freely work out what he is to do in it, though within limits laid down by God ('not to eat of the one tree':

an old myth is reworked within this royal theology). Human beings are themselves responsible for earthly history and will have to make order and *shalom* out of chaos, as did King David. The world and history are entrusted to human beings within their creaturely limits, and YHWH trusts them here.

But just as David fails, so too 'man' falls short, any Adam, any son of man, everyman. God punishes them, but always mercifully. For he does not take back his trust in human beings. Despite everything, God does not despair in humankind: that is the Yahwistic message of creation – not a doctrine from somewhere but a precise historical experience; an interpreted experience of real facts within the 'Davidic model'. God entrusts human beings with recreating the chaos of our human history as *shalom* and order, as salvation of and for human beings. By God's sovereign and royal decree that is what human beings are given the blessing of creation for. God's faithfulness is greater than all human failure. God's kingdom is coming, and will be inaugurated and consummated. He, God, continues to trust human beings.

## II  God's trust in human beings is finally not put to shame in Jesus

For the second or New Testament the man Jesus – Son of man, son of David, second Adam – is the final key to understanding human life, in which Israel's old dream takes firm form: the final realization of God's unconditional trust in humankind and the perfect human expression of this divine trust. In Jesus, God's trust in human beings and their reciprocal trust in God are given their historically definitive foundation, while history nevertheless continues to pursue its open and as yet undecided way.

During his life, the disciples had asked Jesus, *Lord, what shall we be when that final kingdom dawns?* But in the later, New Testament, churches the situation had meanwhile become very different. This question then becomes: *Lord, how shall we live as Christians in the midst of this world?*, since after the death of Jesus, history went on as usual. In recollection of Jesus' inspiration and in many directions, the Gospel according to Matthew answers this question in particular in the Sermon on the Mount. And this Sermon on the Mount stands in the context of the Beatitudes on those who are poor, who weep and are oppressed (Matt.5.3-12) and in the context of the great Old Testament 'Isaianic' prophecy which Jesus had made his own: 'The Lord has anointed me to bring good tidings to the afflicted; he has sent me to proclaim the opening of the prison to those who are bound... to grant to those who mourn a garland instead of ashes, the oil of gladness instead of mourning' (Isa.61.1-3).[14] A message for the poor, the weeping and the oppressed: that is the heart of the Beatitudes and the basic law of being a Christian in this world. What is the content of this message to the poor? 'The news of your salvation, the message that your God reigns' (Isa.52.7): i.e., justice and love are now going to dwell among men and women. For that, 'I, the Lord have called you... as a light to the world' (Isa.42.6). All kinds of Old Testament traditions come together here.

Jesus so identified himself with this message that for the New Testament this gospel of Jesus cannot be detached from his person, as I demonstrated earlier. The gospel, the good news, is not just 'Jesus of Nazareth' but essentially also Jesus confessed as the Coming One, 'the Christ, his only beloved Son, our Lord'. There can be no gospel without Jesus, but also no gospel without the coming Christ, confessed through and in the churches.

So Jesus' message and person are bound up through a long history with the great Jewish expectations of salvation, of the approaching kingdom of God, and also with Israel's royal messianic expectations as a model for universal human expectations. Moreover, finally, they are bound up with the creation as the starting point both of all history, in which God entrusts to human beings his struggle against the powers of chaos, and the coming final consummation of creation in a new heaven and a new earth. 'Man', or 'the son of man' – first the king, then every human being – is ultimately 'Jesus of Nazareth' (see also in Heb.2.8-9 this shift from 'man' to 'Jesus Christ'). In Jesus, God's risky trust in human beings is not put to shame. Despite everything – despite even the execution of the eschatological prophet – God's kingdom does come. Jesus' person, his life, death and resurrection, are its inauguration. The promise of creation is repeatedly thwarted by the actual course of human history, but it continues to give men and women the power and the courage not to fail. Jesus is the man in whom the task of creation – and thus history and the covenant - is fulfilled, though within the conditions of our history of suffering. The consequence of this is that trust in this man is the concrete form of faith in God, creator of heaven and earth, who through his act of creation puts unconditional trust in men and women: 'He loved us while we were still sinners' (Rom.5.8).

This already makes the New Testament message universal, since as a result it is anchored – through, in, and finally above the particular Jewish and Christian history – in the universal act of creation: faith in God, creator of heaven and earth, who will therefore judge 'the living and the dead'. We must go on to analyse further in abiding historical particularity precisely this universality of the particular phenomenon of Jesus, founded on God's creation.

## 4. The unique and definitive character of the mission of Jesus Christ as a historical task and basis for the church and its mission in the world

### Introduction

The New Testament concept of the 'eschatological prophet' implies that this prophet has a significance for world history. This is a conviction of Christian faith, which finds its basis in Jesus himself. This last emerges above all from an ancient source, used by Matthew and Luke, in which there is every guarantee that here a historical echo of Jesus' own self-understanding can be heard: 'Blessed are those to whom I am not a stumbling block' (Luke 7.23 = Matt.11.6), developed in another text from the same source: 'I tell you that anyone who takes my side before men, the Son of Man will take his side before God's angels. But anyone who denies me before men shall be denied before God's angels' (Luke 12.8-9 = Matt.10.32-33, cf. Luke 7.18-22 = Matt.11.2-6; Luke 11.20 = Matt.12.28), traditions which subsequently were developed and extended further in the Synoptic Gospels (Matt.12.32; Luke 12.10; Mark.3.28-29). The affirmation of a real relationship between the decision which people make about Jesus and the ultimate determination of their fate (which is stressed even more strongly by the Gospel of John) certainly goes back in nucleus to the historical self-understanding of Jesus: there is a connection between the coming of the kingdom of God and the person of Jesus of Nazareth.

According to the witness of the New Testament, for Christians Jesus has a normative or essential relationship to the universal kingdom of God for all men and women. For Christians it is the case that 'there is one God, and there is one mediator between God and men' (I Tim.2.5), Jesus Christ: 'And there is salvation in no one else, for there is no other name given among men by which we must be saved' (Acts 4.12). And the Johannine Jesus says: 'I am the way, the truth and the life. No one comes to the Father but by me' (John 14.6). 'For the Lord has commanded us, saying, "I have set you to be a light for the Gentiles, that you may bring salvation to the uttermost parts of the earth." And when the Gentiles heard this, they were glad' (Acts 13.47). Paulinism, too, which takes another direction but is just as Christian, says: 'As by one man came death, so too by one man came also the resurrection of

the dead. As in Adam all die, so also in Christ shall all be made alive'
(I Cor.15.21-22). What happened in Jesus is a fact 'once and for all'
(Heb.9.12); the event is true for all nations, peoples and cultures; it is
universally relevant in space and time. The post-Pauline tradition also
says: 'He is the image of the invisible God' (Col.1.15). So we hear the
same voice in all the Gospel traditions. 'He who sees him sees the Father'
(John 14.19).

Of course all these statements are statements of *faith*. They use a
language of confession, in no way a scientific language which objectifies
or makes statements and in this respect is verifiable. But this latter kind
of language by no means has an exclusive claim on the truth. However,
we cannot hermeneutically interpret away these absolute statements in
the New Testament or make them innocuous by reducing them to the
rhetoric of faith or hyperbolic style, as when lovers say to each other,
'You are the most beautiful and unique person in the world.'

Yet confessing language also has something to do with such an
expression of someone's complete dedication to the beloved. It is
relational language; it in fact says something about a person's subjective
attitude to a complete surrender to another person. But confessing
language is in no way exhausted by that. It also has an objective (though
not an objectifying) side. A particular confessing language aims to say
something real about the person who evokes this complete and radical
dedication from another and is also worth it. If the immediate basis of
such language lies in a personal or collective experience, this experience
also communicates something deeper. The ultimate ground of the
uniqueness of Jesus, of which the scriptural quotations speak, is 'In him
the fullness of the Godhead dwells' (Col.1.19), or, according to the so-
called Apostles' Creed, 'He is the Christ, God's only Son, our Lord.'

The quotations from scripture point clearly to the Christian awareness
that in Jesus of Nazareth God has revealed himself in such a form as to
manifest his will for the salvation of all humankind in a decisive and
definitive way. The God and Father of Jesus 'wills that all shall be saved
and come to the knowledge of the truth' (I Tim.2.4), even if they have
not come to learn Jesus Christ. Whether this revelation is also normative
for other religions is another matter. Here at any rate all kinds of
ambiguity can arise if we use the word 'normative' or 'criterion', because
these words are generally used at the level of 'scientific objectivity',
while the assertion that God's definitive and decisive revelation takes
place in Jesus is an affirmation of faith, not a statement, and thus is
incapable of verification beyond one's own faith.

I began this book with a quotation from the council of Florence-
Ferrara which on the basis of these New Testament texts damns all non-
Christians to hell, though this was in fact firmly contradicted by the

Second Vatican Council. This already indicates that people can in fact also understand the confession of Jesus as the Christ in a wrongly exclusivist or inclusivist sense, and indeed have often done so in the past. Christians confess what in their experience God has done for them in Jesus of Nazareth. In itself, this does not imply any judgment on how those of other religions experience salvation from God.

Precisely as a consequence of this echatological or definitive confession of Jesus' life's work, witnessed by the New Testament, we are confronted in our history with the phenomenon of the church.

# I   The church: in the power of the Spirit, the witness to the career of Jesus

## A. *The* ekklesia *of God: community of God*

The English word 'church' (like the Scottish 'kirk', German *Kirche*, Dutch *kerk* and so on) comes from the Greek *kyriake*, i.e. 'belonging to the Lord', as does *kyriakon*, the Lord's Day or Sunday. The Greek and Latin term *ekklesia/ecclesia* has a different origin. The New Testament use of the term *ekklesia* – the gathered community which calls itself church – is connected with the Jewish Deut.23.2-9. That gives conditions for entering 'the Lord's community', the *qehal YHWH*, in Greek *ekklesia tou theou*.[15] In the Jewish translation of the Septuagint into Greek, the Hebrew word *qahal* (assembly, gathering) is sometimes translated *ekklesia* and sometimes *synagoge*. With the exception of James 2.2, however, Jewish Christians exclusively opted for *ekklesia* – though not, as is often asserted,[16] to distinguish themselves from Jews who did not believe in Jesus, by avoiding the word synagogue. They opted for *ekklesia*, taking up the secular use of the term, to denote a quite specific gathering of a Jewish brotherhood of those who believed in Jesus in a particular city. In the secular Greek of the time, *ekklesia* denoted the assembly of free (male) citizens of a polis or city in order to hold elections or make important decisions. The Christians adopted this term, and that gave particular connotations to the expression from Deuteronomy. To talk of a community as an *ekklesia* is to talk of a particular group of religious people who assemble for worship: a cultic assembly in which people thank God and praise God in the Spirit, engage in prophecy and ethical admonitions, and discuss the interests of the assembly. Hence there are expressions in the New Testament like 'the church which is in Corinth', 'the church which is in Rome'. The meaning is rather different in the expression 'the church of God', 'the church of Christ', 'the church of God in Jesus', 'the church in Jesus'.[17] These last instances relate to the universal church: in contrast to what was thought earlier, this usage is not a later development of the term church, but is original from the beginning (see already Gal.1.13; I Cor.15.9; Phil.3.6). Precisely this consciousness of the church among the earliest Christians is important for understanding the relationship between the Christian communities, the earthly Jesus and Israel. This concept does not of itself imply a church repudiated or rejected by the Jewish synagogue. 'The church of God' points to a very specific, historical community, for example the church of Jerusalem or Antioch, but it transcends the boundaries of any particular or local community.

The New Testament expression *he kat'oikon ekklesia*, or house community, itself indicates that the early Christians' consciousness of the church in no way involved a break with Jewish Israel. The early church took the *oikos*, the Graeco-Roman city family house, as the pastoral basis for the whole of the Christian movement, since as well as gathering in houses in this way, the first Christians remained faithful to the temple or the synagogue. So we hear of 'the *ekklesia* which meets in the house of Aquila and Prisca' in Ephesus (I Cor.16.19) or 'in Rome' (Rom.16.5); 'the *ekklesia* which meets in the house of Philemon' in Colossae (Philemon 2); 'the *ekklesia* which meets in the house of Nympha' in Laodicea (Col.4.15), etc. It also emerges from this that the first Christians saw themselves within Judaism as a 'free organization' (*collegium*) that gathered 'at the house of', in the Graeco-Roman usage of the time, *collegium quod est in domu Sergiae Paulinae*, the free community or the free association which meets at the house of X. Precisely this idea of free community and house communities makes it clear that the first Christians remained aware of the fact that as a brotherhood, as a movement (or, according to the terminology of the pro-Roman, Jewish historian Flavius Josephus, as a 'philosophical school'), stayed within the Jewish religious community.

### B. *The Jewish roots of the church's Christianity*

By 'Judaism', scholars and commentators usually mean the community of faith which had formed since Ezra after the exile and was strengthened during the Maccabean period in the middle of the second century BC, up to and including the Jewish War (66-70/72).[18] Others call this period 'early Judaism'. It was a community of faith which stood in continuity with Israel's earlier history, but was nevertheless distinct from it in that it saw the covenant history as the roots of its own history and already recognized particular works as a biblical canon. One can say that the history of Israel up to the second century BC is the constitutive phase, while afterwards the interpretative phase begins. Though from different hermeneutical perspectives, both Jews and

Christians refer to these canonical scriptures. Christians do so in terms
of the way in which the Bible is illuminated by the event of Jesus Christ,
and Jews in the light of the later Talmudic tradition. As a result, the
term 'Jewish' becomes ambiguous.

Jesus himself was a Jew, not only by descent but also in his heart. His
disciples were also Jews, including those among them who spoke Greek.
Finally, the whole of the early church was Jewish. The association of
the Christian community or church with Judaism was only lost towards
the end of the first century. The unity of God (one might think of the
'*Shema yisrael*', a prayer that the Jews prayed three times a day, see
Deut.6.4) was also the basic confession of the first Christians. This only
God had revealed himself in a special way in Israel. Faith in the one
God, the creator and the one who acts in history, was the heart of Jesus'
message and is common to Jews and Christians. In Jewish Christianity
this action of God in Israel had its central focus in God's action in the
Jew Jesus of Nazareth: 'One is God... One is the Lord, Jesus Christ' (I
Cor.8.6). In the later great Christian creeds the '*Shema yisrael*' remains
the all-embracing background and horizon both of christology and of
Christian pneumatology: 'I believe in one God, almighty, creator of
heaven and earth.' God's unique reality and his concern for human
beings in history dominate the message of Jesus and the faith of Jews
and Christians. Jews and Christians live by the old promises, which
were entrusted to Israel. Israel's Bible was also the only canonical Bible
for the first Christians. There was no recognized 'New Testament' until
the end of the second century. But there was the living proclamation of
the salvation that Jews, followers of Jesus, had experienced in this Jesus.
The Christians also initially continued to go to the synagogue or temple;
they also supplemented this religious practice with gatherings in houses
on the basis of their experiences with Jesus confessed as the Christ.

Despite a whole variety of common forms, there were particular
elements which now and then led to tensions, just as people had known
more internal tensions within Judaism and continue to do so. For the
first Christians, who were all Jews, it was clear that the death of Jesus
was the consequence of the action of a particular group, not of the Jewish
people as such. It was Jews who, on the basis of the crucifixion of Jesus
and their faith in the resurrection, were converted and accepted the
message of the gospel. But gradually there were more disputes between
Jews who rejected Jesus and Jews who recognized Jesus as their saviour.
Initially, however, this was basically a controversy within Judaism.

In Jesus' time, Judaism had a high reputation among many citizens
in the Roman empire. Jewish monotheism and the morality that went
with it attracted many people who had lost their certainty. Many
Gentiles sympathized with Judaism: the so-called 'Godfearers' (who

were uncircumcised), and above all the 'proselytes' (who were). Moreover, it seems that out of the population of the Roman empire one person in ten was a Jew (either Jewish-born or Godfearer or proselyte).[19] From the third century BC there were also many people among the Jews who were called 'Hellenists'; these were Jews, both in the Diaspora and in Palestine and Jerusalem, who remained faithful to the Jewish community of faith but spoke Greek. This was also the case among the first Jewish Christians. Christianity did not remain limited to Palestine. Above all in Jerusalem, even within the Christian community the relations between the Jewish Christians who spoke Hebrew (Aramaic) and the Jewish Christians who spoke Greek were not too good. The Greek-speaking Jews (and the Christians among them) were critical of the temple cult and were supporters of a freer interpretation of the law: they were mistrusted by the non-Christian Aramaic-speaking Jews and also neglected by the Christian Jews in Jerusalem who spoke Aramaic. These Hellenists had eventually to leave Jerusalem. Above all after the execution of the Christian Hellenist Stephen by the (Aramaic-speaking) Jews, it was impossible for the Hellenistic Jewish Christians to remain in Jerusalem. They fled through Samaria and Phoenicia above all to Antioch, where a lively Christian community came into being. It was these Hellenists who brought the gospel to the Gentiles for the first time.

On the basis of this, and also through the prospering of the mission among the Gentiles, a degree of estrangement developed between the Palestinian Jewish Christians and the Hellenistic-Jewish Christians. So Barnabas was sent by the Christian leaders of Jerusalem to Antioch in order to bind this primarily Hellenistic-Jewish Christian community more closely to the mother church in Jerusalem. Finally the increasing tension was temporarily reduced in an gathering of the apostles in Jerusalem (Acts 11.22,25f.; 15.1-5; Gal.2.1-10, though in Acts 15.6-33 we can recognize many redactional elements from Luke). Yet again, even for the Hellenistic Jewish Christians, despite their freedom from specific precepts of the law, the basic Jewish confession of Israel and the tradition of promise in Israel remained in force. Moreover the law, the basic intention of which was expressed in the command to love God and one's neighbour (Matt.23.37-40; see 5.43-48 par; 9.13; 12.7; 23.23), also remained the expression of God's will for Jesus and his followers. However, in Jesus' time the Jewish community of faith was by no means as uniform as in the later Talmudic period. So the latter may not be taken as the norm for New Testament situations, a fact which tends to be forgotten.

The Christian mission among the Gentiles was particularly successful among the so-called 'Godfearers', who remained uncircumcised and had a looser connection with the Jewish communities. Their integration into the Christian communities meant that very quickly there were many Christians in Christian communities who had had virtually no contact with Jewish communities. Very soon these were to form the majority among Christians, as a result of the success of the Gentile mission. This is unmistakeably one of the many factors which led to the alienation between the synagogue and the church. But it should not be forgotten that in the first century of the Christian era the majority of the Gentiles who became Christians did so via Jewish faith and so were still familiar with Jewish traditions. The Jewish roots of the New Testament are fundamental, and perhaps have still not been brought out sufficiently.

Initially all Christians were Jews: Christians from paganism formed a small minority. Gradually, however, already by the middle and above all towards the end of the first century, this balance changed in favour of the Gentile Christians. These new Christian communities often had no connection at all with Jewish communities, as already seems clear from the letters to the Christians of Colossae and Ephesus. However, the alienation of many Christian churches from the Jewish faith community in no way meant a break with Judaism, nor was it a deliberate effort. The break only came about towards the end of the first century as the result of a reciprocal rejection, in which the synagogue took the initiative.

After the destruction of the temple and city in the Jewish War (AD 70), which was a great disaster for the Jews, within about twenty or thirty years the Jewish community reorganized itself. That was the work of the Pharisees, who in the process to some degree reduced Jewish faith to their own Pharisaic tradition and silenced other equally old and authentically Jewish elements. In the 90s they also definitively laid down the biblical canon (the Tenach), in so doing putting much emphasis on orthodoxy (a tendency which we then see developing everywhere, even among Christians, as we can observe in the New Testament and also in pagan religion at this time). The Pharisees at that time made a distinction between orthodox and *minim*, i.e. false teachers, among whom were the Jewish followers of Jesus. There is evidence of this in the so-called sayings against heretics, which were probably inserted into the ancient Eighteen Benedictions at this time. These are a series of eighteen blessings (*berakhot*), recited daily in the synagogue. What is presumably the oldest version of the inserted blessing reads: 'For the apostates there is no hope... Let the Christians (*nosrim*, Nazaraeans) and the heretics (*minim*) perish in a moment; may they be blotted out of the book of life and not be counted among the righteous. Blessed are you, Lord, who bring down the arrogant.'[20] This blessing, to which Christians could not possibly assent, made their exclusion from the synagogue final. This cut a quite vital link between Judaism and Christianity, first of all on the initiative of the Jews themselves. The Christians were then still in the minority.

However, this break did not come about one-sidedly and exclusively from the side of the Jews. Above all the theory of substitution, which is cherished in one form or another by some Christians, implies Christians reactingagainst the Jews: through the rejection of Jesus, this view goes, Judaism has forfeited its function of salvation. Now no longer Israel but the church is the new people of God. The church is the new Israel. Paul did not hold this view: on the contrary, he rejected it. But its beginnings can be found, for example, in Matt.21.43 (although here there is still polemic between Jews and Jewish Christians and not between Jews and Gentile Christians).[21] In a non-Christian but heretical trend, in the middle of the second century Marcion even introduced a break between the fundamental Jewish confession of faith and that of Christianity: he rejected the whole of the Old Testament, including its God. By contrast, orthodox Christianity continued to recognize the fundamental Jewish confession of faith as its own and accepted the Old Testament as the book of promises, although this book was often related as a whole to Christ in a forced way. Christianity condemned Marcion.

Without doubt there are texts in the New Testament in which early Christian criticism can be found of the Jewish law and Jewish traditions (*halachah*).[22] But no anti-Judaism can be found in them. We must not forget that here the Jewish Christians took over a pattern of criticism within Judaism. Later, these texts were certainly interpreted in an anti-Jewish sense, but within the New Testament they function in a very different way, and the polemic remains within Judaism. We must not make a hermeneutical mistake here, as sometimes happens, since criticism of a particular thesis or a particular text can be necessary because of the historical influence of this thesis, of an idea or a particular text, but this criticism does not coincide with the rejection of the original intention of the thesis, idea or text. For in the New Testament we are listening to Jews, Jewish Christians.

Only from the second century did a Christianity and a Christian theology come into being which were no longer familiar with the faith and traditions of Diaspora Judaism. So Christianity came to be increasingly alienated from its Jewish roots in its self-understanding. The Hellenistic picture of the world and humankind also became the new horizon of understanding and experience for Christians. Christianity was gradually shaped more by its dialogue with pagan religions and philosophy than by reflection on its own Jewish origin.

As long as Christians were part of Judaism, they enjoyed all the privileges of a 'lawful or permitted religion' recognized by the Roman empire, which is what Jewish religion was at the time. But from the end of the first century, when a break came about between Christianity and Judaism, until the fourth century, Christians were exposed to many persecutions. As an independent church detached from Judaism, Christianity was no longer a *religio licita*. This was the other social and historical side to the expulsion from Judaism and the break with it. However, with the well-known Constantinian shift, a completely new situation arose for Judaism and Christianity. Christianity became a state religion, and from the fifth century on the freedom of the Jews was increasingly limited and they suffered severe oppression. A Christian literature also came into being with a very bad theological character: an apologetic polemic against the Jews, above all written by the Syrian and Cappadocian church fathers, about the 'murder of God' by the Jews and suchlike (antisemitism already had long pre-Christian roots, particularly in Syria). The Middle Ages continued this new tradition; it was characterized by inquisition, persecution of the Jews and forced conversions, with occasional periods of milder 'toleration'.[23] For the Jews and for all humankind the 'holocaust' especially of Jews in the twentieth century is a tragic and absurd nadir in a long history of persecution and torture, dishonour and human shame. Christians have contributed to this absurd evil.

Christians would have done better to listen to the apostle Paul. For in a very emotional argument in Rom.9-11 Paul, the Jewish Christian and former Pharisee, gives his view of the relationship between Judaism and Christianity.[24]

For Paul the gospel is 'a power of God which saves all who believe' (Rom.1.16); 'the Jews first, and then the Greeks (or non-Jews)'. In the sight of God all human beings, Jews as well as Gentiles, are guilty. That raises the question: why then do the Jews have priority over the Gentiles (Rom.3.1)? To this Paul replies: God's promises are entrusted to the Jews (Rom.3.2b). These promises remain in power. That some of the Jewish people were unfaithful does not affect God's abiding trust in his people; their lack of trust does not do away with God's trust (Rom.3.3). Paul had already said all this at the beginning of his letter, but from chapter 9 on he goes on to discuss the problem explicitly.

In talking of the children of Abraham it is necessary to make a distinction between the children 'after the flesh' and the 'children of the promise' (9.6-13). By free choice God also makes his people those who did not belong to his people (9.14-29). So people who were Gentiles have achieved the salvation that many Israelites have not achieved (9.30-10.4). To be saved, to share in salvation, presupposes listening obediently to the message of salvation; it presupposes faith. Many from Israel certainly heard the message of salvation, but did not accept it (10.5-21). But Paul stresses that a remnant from Israel to which he himself also belongs has accepted the message in faith, and that indicates that God has not left his people in the lurch or cast them out (11.1-10).

But the non-belief of many has led Gentiles in large numbers to enter into communion with Jesus Christ (11.11-16). And from that Paul argues, first that the community of those who believe in Christ remains indissolubly tied to its Jewish roots (11.17-24). This bond is not fortuitous, and is not simply the history of the origin of Christianity. It points to a permanent and essential connection which must, moreover, be made a theme of theology. Secondly, because the word of God never becomes powerless or invalid, the promised salvation to and for Israel remains in force for ever. This is clear to Paul from the fact that a remnant of Israel began to believe in Jesus (11.25-32). Moreover, Paul outlines a perspective in which he boldly emerges as a prophet. At the end of the times, he says, 'all Israel' will be saved. Now there is certainly a dispute among modern interpreters over the correct interpretation of this text. Some say that 'all Israel' is contrasted with 'the remnant of Israel' and that corresponds to the 'full number of the Gentiles' (11.12).

But in chapter 9 Paul has put the stress above all on a distinction between children of Abraham, namely between children after the flesh and children according to the promise. Now in his simile of grafting the Gentiles on to the original Jewish olive tree he says that twigs are broken off because of their 'non-belief', but are grafted on again by God, 'in so far as they do not persevere in unbelief' (11.20-23).[25] As a Christian Paul remains confident in God's promise to Israel. He concludes his emotional argument with thanks and praise for God's wise and unfathomable system of salvation (11.33-36): for Jews and non-Jews salvation is finally open. Paul says that God's salvation in Jesus is for all humankind, but for Jews first.

So we can say that according to Paul, Judaism and Christianity do not just have a common past: Christianity is rooted in Judaism. But Jews and Christians also have a common future. Judaism and Christianity hold fast to the promises of the Tenach (for Christians, the Old Testament): the Jews are still waiting for eschatological liberation, as Christians are waiting for the promised final consummation of the salvation that dawned in Jesus Christ and is already present. For both, the eschatological future promised in the Old Testament is identical. The second covenant did not do away with the first.

Moreover, all this already finds expression in the pre-Christian baptismal catechesis of John the Baptist. John, the pre-Christian Jew, breaks with the praise and pride at that time associated with the children of Abraham, at least when this descent was regarded as an ethnic privilege which was thought to have validity with God. In the sight of God, fleshly descent gives no guarantee of salvation whatsoever. Already according to John the Baptist, a Jew by blood, God also knows other ways of making men and women children of Abraham. The privilege of Israel, to be the children of the promise given to Abraham, also remains in force for John, but this Jewish Baptist anticipates what Paul, the Jew who became a Christian, was to say about Israel as the original olive tree and about the Gentiles as the shoot grafted on to it. There is salvation for anyone who is willing to be open to God's offer of salvation. Before this became a Christian confession, it was already a Jewish confession on the lips of John the Baptist.

## C. *The church: a witness to Jesus' way towards the kingdom of God*

Over the last decades exegetes have begun to ask whether Jesus founded a church during his earthly lifetime and whether one can call him the founder of a new religion. These critical questions have been raised not only out of purely historical interest, but often also out of particular ideological interests, for example the charge made by some Jews and Christians that the Christian church left the Jewish synagogue, while Jesus had limited his mission to Israel; or as part of a specifically Christian and sometimes radical criticism of the fact that the empirical 'church of Christ' had little or nothing to do with the mission of Jesus, with his message of the kingdom of God and praxis in accordance with that, but historically is completely alien to it.

Historically, it is quite clear that Jesus did not have the intention of founding a new religious community; moreover, the earliest Christian community was specifically aware of living within the Jewish religious association. Jesus addressed the whole of Israel; his aim was the gathering, renewal and equipping of all Israel for the kingdom of God. In contrast to, for example, the Essenes, Jesus did not have any intention of founding a holy remnant within Israel either. The call of the Twelve is a symbol of the kingdom of Israel with its twelve tribes. The earliest Christian community, which spoke Aramaic, also believed itself to be sent only to Israel, although this is by no means the last word as far as the historical effect that it had is concerned. At all events, all the New Testament texts bear witness to a universality which transcends the limits of Israel (and even in this, these texts are on the same lines as a particular Jewish tradition).

However, that Jesus' mission was limited to the twelve tribes of Israel does not mean that the Christian church is not the result of Jesus' life's work. To suppose that it was not would testify to a limited view of what a historical event is, assuming that history only has to do with explicit human purposes, and neglecting sociological structures and what one might call the history of their influence, which cannot be reduced in an idealist way to human intentions. Or there can be confusion of the religious message with social and cultural presuppositions of a given time in which the message is embedded. At all events, Christianity does not appear in a social and cultural vacuum. Some say that the expectation of an approaching end to the world originally formed part of the implicit presuppositions of a large segment of Jewish culture in the time of Jesus.[26] In that case, however, the question is whether Jesus also made these presuppositions the object of his message or whether he proclaimed the message of the kingdom of God coming in and through him on the basis of a religious and cultural presupposition which he too took for granted, that of an approaching end of the world in which any future, even a future for the church, become impossible.

However, history is more than the result of human intentions. For it is certain that Jesus was one hundred per cent behind his message and meant this message to be accepted by men and women in faith. Jesus' conviction that there is an essential link between the coming of the kingdom of God which he proclaimed and his praxis of the kingdom of God, and the consequent faith conviction of his followers that the mission of Jesus has a definitive, eschatological and universal significance (as is clearly confessed by the New Testament) necessitates a continuation of Jesus' earthly mission by his disciples beyond the limited time of his earthly life – if time has any ordinary continuation after the death of Jesus (which is unmistakably the case). It is as simple as that. The mission of the apostles and the mission of the post-apostolic church are thus necessary on the basis of the eschatological and definitive character of the whole of Jesus' appearance and career, and the whole meaning of his life, founded in Jesus and recognized by Christians. The unique, 'one-off' mission of Jesus among the Jews remains untouched by this, because the content of the church's mission remains Jesus' proclamation of the kingdom of God and Jesus' own Jewish career.

The fact is that becoming a disciple of Jesus is an essential element of his message. So regardless of how we go on to fill out its shape historically at a later time, the 'church' is essentially discipleship of Jesus: following in the footsteps of Jesus to turn many people into a community which bears witness both to the kingdom of God and to Jesus' own career.

Thus the historical Jesus stands at the origin of the historical church – that does not mean to say that the forms of the church, as they have become structured and have developed historically, go back to Jesus, nor that in its actual historical and contingent growth the church underwent a necessary development willed by God, nor that as church it must inevitably come to stand alongside Israel or the synagogue. Christians nevertheless assert this; I claim that it is historically untenable. It is simply a sign of ideological fundamentalism.

If this faith in Jesus' message and this communal discipleship of Jesus were in fact intended by him – and historically this is difficult to deny – then the anthropological and sociologial implication is that with the continuation of our secular history, Christian faith and discipleship of Jesus will take on institutional aspects and in fact do so, precisely in order to be and to remain Christian faith and Christian community. The communal and institutional aspects of the church cannot be separated, just as ecclesiology and sociology cannot be separated in the concrete phenomenon of the church. Whether Jesus directly or indirectly founded a church or even a new world religion is therefore the wrong question in this connection. What is important is this: on the basis of what Jesus was, said and did, we can, may and must say without further ado that the historical phenomenon which calls itself the church of Christ is a divine foundation by Jesus for humankind. Once again, since our human time continues after Jesus' death, the need for church proclamation derives directly from the universal and definitive significance of Jesus' message and way of life. Within our historical horizon of understanding and experiencing a history which continues after the death of Jesus, the biblical eschatological meaning of the history and career of Jesus calls into being a new, 'church' history of Christian proclamation, with the implication that the church (ministers and believing community together) has a task to preserve the community of faith in the faith that is proclaimed, to be concerned for every member of the community of faith, to give guidance to communal Christian life in both liturgical worship and in the building up of the church and to be with men and women in the world in active liberation and furthering of the good.

From the beginning, the earliest Christian community, the *ekklesia* or community of God, understood itself as the eschatological people of God, into which all Israel is being gathered in faith in Jesus Christ and his gospel message. That does not mean that the church as an eschatological people of God must *per se* become a separate religion, apart from Israel. But on the other hand it cannot be denied that the appearance of Jesus confronted Israel with a choice: 'Blessed are those

to whom I am not a stumbling block' (Luke 7.23). 'This child shall be
for the falling and rising of many in Israel, he shall be a sign that is
disputed' (Luke 2.34). The origin of the church was a very complicated
process, but nevertheless of such a kind that it may be seen by believers
as the work of God, who in Jesus through the Spirit is establishing his
eschatological people. The church is not the kingdom of God, but it
bears symbolic witness to that kingdom through its word and sacrament,
and in its praxis effectively anticipates that kingdom. It does so by doing
for men and women here and now, in new situations (different from
those in Jesus' time), what Jesus did in his time: raising them up for the
coming of the kingdom of God, opening up communication among
them, caring for the poor and outcast, establishing communal ties within
the houshold of faith and serving all men and women in solidarity.

*D. The past: living recollection of Jesus (the church tradition), and the present:
the Holy Spirit*

What Jesus left us – simply through what he was, did and had said,
purely by his appearance as this particular man – was a movement, a
living community of believers which became aware of being the new
people of God: the eschatological 'assembly' of God. It was not a holy
remnant, but the first members of the assembly of all Israel, and finally
of all humankind. In other words, it was an eschatological freedom
movement, the aim of which was to bring together all men and women
in unity and peace: together, with one another and all peoples, and with
nature. And all this on the basis of unity with the living God.

The experience of God's care for human beings which had emerged
from the message and career of Jesus of Nazareth against the background
of Israel's history of faith was the origin of the first wave of the Jesus
movement, which was above all supported by Hebrew (Aramaic)-
speaking Jews who had become Christians. We find an echo of this
above all in the earliest writing of the second Testament, I Thess.1.9-
10 (see also Acts 14.15; 17.22-31; Heb.6.1-2). The first paragraph of this
letter is a pre-Pauline kerygma to Gentiles, going back to a Jewish model
of a mission sermon or instruction for Gentiles wanting to enter the
synagogue: in confessing the uniqueness of God, Gentiles abjure their
polytheism and are grafted on to Judaism. In the early Jewish model
we can recognize a three-member creed for proselytes: (*a*) belief in the
one God, the creator; (*b*) belief in judgment on those who do not repent;
(*c*) eschatological hope for converts. Creation, judgment, salvation. The
first Christians then add the specifically Christian element to that by
changing the pre-existing text: 'To look for his Son from heaven... Jesus,

who saves us from the wrath to come.' That was one of the earliest Christian confessions of faith.

But the New Testament in fact primarily came to contain the words of spokesmen from those segments of the early Christian Jesus movement who were supported by Greek-speaking Diaspora Jews turned Christians. In their milieu this Jewish movement, supported by Christians, was principally a universal mission church: a church from 'Jews *and* Gentiles'. For these Christians of the second and third generation the experience of the historical Jesus (whom they had never encountered) was not the immediate foundation of their faith, the foundation on which the church and mission were developed. This foundation was, rather, their baptism in the Spirit: their baptism in the name of Jesus, after hearing and accepting the message of Jesus proclaimed to them by the church. The God of these Christians was and is above all the God who did not leave Jesus in the lurch at his death, but made him 'life-giving Spirit' (I Cor.15.45). Moreover Christians who were baptized in him were themselves also called *pneumatikoi.*

The structure of this community experience – the self-understanding of this community of faith – is transparent in the New Testament: the new life of the community present from the power of the pneuma or Holy Spirit puts this community of faith into contact with the life-work and death of Jesus of Nazareth. *Pneuma* and *anamnesis,* both the living recollection of the story, conduct and career of Jesus of Nazareth, handed down through the church, and the active presence of the Spirit of Christ in the church community of faith, form two sides of one and the same coin. In different ways this becomes a theme in the New Testament; the original form is: 'No one can say "Jesus is Lord" except through the Holy Spirit' (I Cor.12.3). Faith in the Lord, in the risen Jesus - the origin and existence of the 'church' – is the receiving of the Spirit. 'Being in Christ' and 'life in the Spirit', individually and collectively, are with very subtle nuances synonymous in the New Testament.

## E. 'Communion' and institution

The church as 'communion' does not stand over against the church as 'institution': each calls forth the other and needs the other. But the communal and institutional church – the church embedded in concrete reality – does stand over against a bureaucratic and centralist management if it allows a cramping church policy, built on criteria which are not those of the gospel, with arbitrary and injurious attitudes towards men and women. In its empirical manifestation, the 'church of God and of Jesus the Christ' indeed is and remains an ambiguous historical phenomenon; that is part of the historical state of the church as the work of believers. Every time that the church points to the kingdom of God, within its own ranks it will also constantly have to point to the term *metanoia* or renewal of life which is bound up with that key biblical concept. And *metanoia* is never completed. Without this renewal of life which has constantly to be embarked on anew, the church, instead of being the liberation movement that it was in its origin, becomes a power structure that oppresses men and women, diminishes them and makes them suffer. Therefore the church itself, head and members, constantly remains under the gospel criticism deriving from the kingdom of God as a kingdom of freedom: non-violence and defenceless vulnerability.

Despite and in its standpoint under the gospel summons of the conversion which is never complete – *ecclesia semper purificanda*[27] – the empirical church, Christianity as a world religion, is the authentic fruit of Jesus' message and way of life. It is an essential part of the history of the influence of the historical phenomenon of Jesus of Nazareth. Yet this does not mean that in the life of Jesus you could as it were point to one particular action or one situation through which or in which he formally 'founds' *his* church. Nor is that necessary. Put in that way, the formal question whether the earthly Jesus founded the church is a mistaken one.

According to the biblical admonition, 'God's judgment begins at the house of God' (I Peter 4.17-18), and this house is the church as the eschatological people of God. The divine promise which rests on the church, 'the gates of hell shall not prevail against it' (Matt.16.18), and more positively, 'I shall be with you to the end of time' (Matt.28.20b), means that as Christians we may hope that the content of the good news that is called the gospel is so powerful, surprising and definitive that there will always be enough people, men and women, to stand in the church movement-around-the-gospel and to be willing to hand on the torch of Christian belief and in so doing build up the church. That in no way means the automatic assurance of salvation and truth.

## II  Good and bad questions in connection with the uniqueness of the Christian church

In the history of Christianity, until recently it was generally accepted that Christianity was the vehicle of absolute truth. In fact, over the course of time the Christian churches have also behaved in this way. A justified claim to liberating uniqueness and universality was imperialistically twisted into a church claim to absoluteness.

Over against such absoluteness stand hard historical facts. The history of humankind shows us a collection of differing ways of life, a multi-coloured offer of 'ways of salvation': Judaism, Christianity and Islam; Hinduism and Buddhism; Taoism, Confucianism and Shintoism; animism, African and Indian ways to salvation and blessing. We call them all 'religions'; in other words we are convinced that there are essential resemblances between all these divergent phenomena. Therefore they are referred to by one term: religion.

*Nostra Aetate*, a declaration of Vatican II, also says that men and women 'look to their different religions for an answer to the unsolved problems of human existence. The problems that weigh heavily on the hearts of men are the same today as in ages past' (no.1).In other words, through the offer of a message of salvation and the opening of a way of salvation, religions answer a fundamental question which men and women ask about their lives. Modern sociologists (e.g. H.Lübbe) speak in the same tone (but they do so functionalistically, and this does not correspond to the true nature of religion as gratuitousness), in very general terms, but correctly, about religions as 'systems of ultimate orientation' or 'systems for learning to live with contingency':[28] all-embracing systems which give meaning or systems which help us spiritually, emotionally and above all existentially to cope with our vulnerable, changeable existence in an ambivalent society.

But there are misunderstandings here about what we call 'religion' among cultural scholars and philosophers of religion. These go in two directions, taking either an essentialist approach or a nominalistic approach via 'general terms' ('universals') to what is called 'religion'.

Using a term of Wittgenstein's, we would therefore in my view do better to say that there are 'family likenesses' between the many religions. In that case we are really not talking of one or more 'common characteristics' nor speaking of 'ideal types'. Then, phenomena which show similarities and on the basis of this are denoted by one and the same term (religion) are (Wittgenstein would say, as members of a particular family), item for item, unique in their specific combination or figuration of characteristics. But on the basis of 'family likenesses', despite their uniqueness, they can be compared with one another (semiotics also thinks in a similar direction).

As a social and cultural phenomenon and system providing meaning, Christianity, too, is one religion alongside other religions: one of many. However, Christians find salvation for themselves only in Jesus confessed as the Christ. Therefore in the course of history (on the basis of their own view and attitude to life) they begin to ask how pagans, non-Christians, can achieve salvation. For their confession of the uniqueness of Jesus was not simply an expression of a subjective conviction. According to the Christian confession this view refers to reality: in other words, it is true (although that is an affirmation of faith and not a truth that can be demonstrated and verified scientifically; so one can never use it as a weapon against non-Christians).

On the basis of this conviction of abiding in the truth, sooner or later Christians raise the question of the possibility of salvation for non-Christians. Indirectly this already happened from the beginning of Christianity: the second (or New) Testament says that God wills the salvation of 'all' men and women (I Tim.2.4); moreover he wills it in an effective way, adapted to the human situation (even if people do not know Christ). And in a sermon of Peter's Luke says this even more clearly: 'Now I know that with God there is no respect for persons, but that out of every people anyone who fears him and does good is well-pleasing to him' (Acts 10.34-35). However, the real theme of this problem, how men 'can be blessed' if they have never learned to know Jesus Christ, began above all in modern times, and only in our time is it becoming a fundamental, central and even crucial theological problem.[29] Here Christianity does not drop its claim to universality – Jesus' message of universal liberation – but its exclusivist and inclusivist claim to absoluteness.

Broadly speaking, that was clearly a new way in comparison with the previous tradition extending over centuries. But it was not a break, because both the first and the second Testaments and church traditions (though these never spoke out loudly or from the heart) also recognized good things in the other religions.

In recent times Karl Rahner went even further. He not only recognized the individual possibility of salvation for the adherents of other religions, but also attached saving worth to these religions as such; they too are 'ways of salvation' to God.[30] Daniélou and de Lubac have also made comments to this effect. But the already open statements of the Second Vatican Council in *Lumen Gentium, Nostra Aetate* and *Ad Gentes* (texts to which the works of Rahner and Ratzinger, Daniélou and de Lubac were not foreign) do not go as far as this, at least in what they actually say. Implicitly H.Waldenfels seems to think that this modern position (inspired by Rahner) goes too far when he writes that if non-Christians also find salvation, 'then that does not take place "despite" but at all events "in" their religion'. And he explicitly adds: 'Christians should avoid the formula "through" their religion.'[31] I myself do not find this reserve towards a religion as social system very satisfactory: evidently there is a fear here that a grain of truth in the old absolute claim of 'imperialistic' Christianity is being attacked.

But we must concede to M.Seckler that the saving value of all religions cannot be posited abstractly and globally.[32] Item by item we will have to examine each religion in a very specific way to discover its own values and the picture of human beings and the world that it implies. There is one question here on which everyone has something to say: how do you want and see your own humanity? Inevitably in a very schematic way, Vatican II nevertheless tries to describe the specific value of Judaism and Hinduism, Buddhism and Islam; moreover, finally in *Lumen Gentium* ch.16 the council speaks of the possibility of salvation even for agnostics and atheists. Here we are already close to the position which I defended in the first chapter: 'outside the world there is no salvation'. In world history God brings about salvation through human mediation, and human beings also do disastrous things. This is the struggle with which we are involved.

In recent years some writers have gone even further than Rahner. So H.-R.Schlette reverses the categories used previously: for him Christianity is not the 'normal' or 'usual saving way' to God; that is true of the other religions. Christianity is the 'extraordinary' or 'exceptional' way to God.[33] This could even be confirmed by world statistics. According to 1982 surveys there are 1.4 billion official Christians in the world (a third of the world's population); there are 723 million Muslims, 583 million Hindus and 274 million Buddhists.[34] The number of non-Christians exceeds the number of Christians; and almost two-thirds of all Christians live outside the Western world. Although statistics are not the last word, they nevertheless warn Christians to be modest: there are more of other beliefs than there are Christians in the world. And these others are not dumb or blind.

And we still have not finished with the shift in the self-understanding of modern Christians. Recently the Catholic Paul Knitter went one stage further than Schlette: he denies any form of claim to universality on the part of Christianity, but without lapsing into religious indifference.[35] Among Christians in our time there is indeed a particular new form of modern 'indifferentism': the view that all religions are equal. Of course they are not, since even their views of what it is to be human are different, and a religion which, for instance, condemns the firstborn son to death as a sacrifice to God is certainly not of equal value to a religion which explicitly forbids it. Here too criteria of humanity apply.

If their own religion is also involved in any comparison of religions, in the end men and women cannot avoid the question of truth. But this question of truth is in fact raised within a 'hermeneutical circle', and the definitive answer to it can only be eschatological. The question is thus whether in the meanwhile there are not many open questions here which cannot be solved speculatively, and moreover whether we are asking the right questions and not the wrong ones (which can never be answered). Moreover the outcome of the question of truth with relation to one's own religion need in no way entail discrimination against other religions. No single religion exhausts the question of truth. Therefore we must leave both absolutism and relativism behind us in religious matters.

Our age has 'liberated' itself in many ways from the distinctive post-Enlightenment modern claim to truth and universality. Logically and practically, multiplicity now takes priority over unity. The old and Neoplatonic Greek ideal of unity is in no sense still a norm for modern or post-modern men and women. The monotheism of Judaism, Christianity and Islam which lays claim to all humankind is regarded by many people (or some) as totalitarian.[36] Some see it as one of the causes of the shift of many Western men and women to Asian religions. The statement 'All religions are equal' is understandable in terms of this modern spirit of the time, although this expression is cheap and basically wrong.

The question, however, is whether monotheism with its claim to universality cannot also be a criticism and provocation of this spirit of the time. The spirit of the time is certainly not a norm in itself! The universal claim of salvation in Jesus and the human reason which recalls the suffering of humanity can also provide a criticism of the liberal pluralism of the spirit of our time. There is also a cheap form of tolerance.

Christianity has, of course, often interpreted its own truth and uniqueness (which are not to be denied) as a claim to absoluteness through which all other religions are seen as having less value, while the good that is to be found in them is already thought to be present in an eminent way in Christianity itself. Here 'Christian values' are discovered in other religions, but by the same token these are deprived of their own identity. The consequence of this religious and cultural 'imperialism' was that the modern history of colonialism and mission was to a large extent also a time of oppression by foreign cultures and religions, not just in the sixteenth-century missions but also from the time of and during the Enlightenment.[37]

However, Asia and practically all countries in which Islam is dominant shut themselves off from Christianity; these universal religions also discovered their own claim to uniqueness.[38] Therefore in the open world of the West, Christianity is increasingly regarded as one religion among many and, moreover, historically as a religion under which many non-Christian cultures and other religions have suffered heavily. This change of climate in Western thought was almost automatically coupled with a privatization of Christianity as a religion: in their hearts people could happily respect Christianity as the one true religion, if only this had no consequences for others and for the public, bourgeois world.

So given this history, we shall have to look in a direction in which both absolutism and relativism are avoided in connection with what is called 'religion'. The question of the truth of Christianity is by no means the same as the question of the superiority of Christianity, as was often thought earlier. The issue is one of Christian identity, which recognizes and respects the other person's religious identity, which allows itself to be challenged by other religions and which, on the basis of its own message, also challenges other religions. In short, we are confronted with other questions than those raised earlier, with more productive questions which are more fruitful for all sides.

So we now ask other questions, though it continues to be true for Christian believers that they find salvation 'only in the name of Jesus of Nazareth'. And in this Christian perspective questions then emerge as to whether and how, for example, one can be a Christian as a Hindu, in other words whether there can be a Hindu version of Christianity. There is no question of this being a speculative approach to one another's religions; it is a perhaps centuries-long attempt to arrive at a 'common experience', for only a common experience can lead to a compatible hermeneutical interpretation. At present we are still far from having a 'common experience'. Therefore in my view the question for us is whether the pluralism of religions is a matter of fact or a matter of principle. How we answer this question of course has important consequences for our own view of the ecumene of world religions and finally for world peace, which over the centuries has been and at present still is being sorely put to the test through religious intolerance and thus on the basis of the claim to absoluteness, whether inclusive or exclusive, which is sometimes made.

In this book I shall not be saying anything about what for some years people have begun to call 'a theology of world religions' (although some of my comments indeed coincide with such a theology of world religions). Here I am directly concerned only with the identity and thus the correct self-definition of Christianity, through which this religion can also find its right place in relation to religions: on the one hand without absolutism or relativism, and on the other without discrimination or a sense of superiority.

## III   The universality and historical contingency of Jesus' career

In contrast to the earlier Christian claim to absoluteness, which was also governed by the dominant spirit of the time, in my view the positive acceptance of the difference between religions is implicit in the nature of Christianity.[39] The problem is no longer the one formulated at the level of the earlier awareness of the problem: is Christianity the one true religion, or is it (in a milder version) a better religion than all the rest? In these comparisons the term 'religion' is analysed by the one making the comparison (from whatever religion) in terms of his or her own religion, and thus by Christians in terms of Christianity. The problem is, rather, how can Christianity maintain its own identity and uniqueness and at the same time attach a positive value to the difference of religions in a non-discriminatory sense? Put in this way, what is relevant to Christianity is not what is common to many religions, but precisely that difference between them which forms their uniqueness and distinctiveness. If this is the case, then we must be able to point to a foundation within Christianity itself for this new, Christian, open and not-intolerant attitude to the other religions of the world.

In my view this foundation lies in Jesus' message and praxis of the kingdom of God, with all its consequences. At any rate in its uniqueness and distinctiveness as a religion, Christianity is essentially bound up with an unavoidable 'historical peculiarity' and thus is regional and limited. Therefore (like all religions), Christianity too is limited: limited in means of expression, perspective and specific praxis. Christians sometimes find it difficult to see this reality plainly. But this limitation is part of the nature of Christianity (and is indeed expressed above all when Christians use the 'incarnational model' in their tradition – which is regarded in this tradition as the dominant paradigm).

The special, distinctive and unique feature of Christianity is that it finds the life and being of God specifically in this historical and thus limited particularity of 'Jesus of Nazareth' – confessed as the personally human manifestation of God. In it there is a confession that Jesus is indeed a 'unique', but nevertheless 'contingent', i.e. historical and thus limited, manifestation of the gift of salvation from God for all men and women. Anyone who overlooks this fact of the specific concrete humanity of Jesus, precisely in his quality as a human being, which is geographically defined and socially and culturally recognizable and therefore limited, makes the man Jesus a 'necessary' divine emanation as a result of which all other religions are volatilized into nothingness. This then seems essentially to conflict with the deepest sense of all christological councils and confessions and ultimately with the very being of God as absolute freedom. In this view, Jesus' humanity is reduced to a docetic pseudo-humanity, while on the other hand the identity of all non-Christian religions is trivialized. Nevertheless, in the course of time Christians have absolutized precisely this historical and thus limited character of Christianity. This has led to the historical wretchedness of empirical Christianity in contrast to the original authenticity of the gospel.

But the revelation of God in Jesus, as the Christian gospel preaches this to us, in no way means that God absolutizes a historical particularity (even Jesus of Nazareth). We learn from the revelation of God in Jesus that no individual historical particularity can be said to be absolute, and that therefore through the relativity present in Jesus anyone can encounter God even outside Jesus, especially in our worldly history and in the many religions which have arisen in it. The risen Jesus of Nazareth also continues to point to God beyond himself. One could say: God points via Jesus Christ in the Spirit to himself as creator and redeemer, as a God of men and women, of *all* men and women. God is absolute, but no single religion is absolute.

The particularity of Jesus, by which the origin, character and unique-ness of Christianity are defined, thus implies that we should leave the differences between the particular religions and do not do away with them. The manifestation of God in Jesus does not fence off 'religious history', as emerges for example from the origin of Islam as a post-Christian world religion. And no one, not even Islam, can fail to recognize that further new world religions can and will arise after Islam. For all the critical questions here, particular present-day neo-religious movements are support for this hypothesis.

It is clear that there are in fact points of both convergence and divergence between all religions. However, differences must not be judged *per se* as deviations, which have to be remedied by ecumenical action; they must be regarded in a positive light. (On the basis of what criteria could we judge such deviations anyway?) However, God is too rich and too over-defined for it to be possible to exhaust him in his fullness through a particular and thus limited religious experiential tradition. Certainly, according to the Christian perspective, 'the fullness of God dwells bodily in Jesus'. New Testament texts bear witness to this for Christians (Col.2.9; see Col.1.15; Heb.1.3; II Cor.4.4). But this 'corporeality' – or 'this dwelling (of the fullness of God) in Jesus' humanity' – denotes precisely the contingent and limited form of Jesus' appearance in our history. (Otherwise we would be practising the docetism condemned by all Christian churches, i.e. the view that the divine appeared in Jesus only in phantom form.)

As a consequence of all this we can, may and must say that there is more religious truth in all the religions together than in one particular religion, and that this also applies to Christianity. There are therefore 'true', 'good', and 'beautiful' – surprising – aspects in the manifold forms of relationship with God (present in humankind), forms which have not found any place in the specific experience of Christianity and are not finding one now. There are differences in people's experience of their relationship to God, differences which cannot be smoothed over, for all the inherent similarities to other experiences. There are different authentically religious experiences which Christianity, precisely because of its historical particularity, has never thematized or put into practice. Moreover, *perhaps* (I say that cautiously, but assertively), it is the case that because of the specific and distinct accents which Jesus brought, Christianity cannot thematize such aspects without robbing these distinctive accents of the sharpness which Jesus gave them and ultimately of their specific Christian character.

From all this I learn that (even in the Christian self-understanding) the multiplicity of religions is not an evil which needs to be removed, but rather a wealth which is to be welcomed and enjoyed by all. That is in no way to deny that the historical plurality of religions which in principle is not to be removed is inwardly nurtured and supported by a unity which cannot be made an explicit theme within our history and cannot be practised: i.e. the unity of God (the trinitarian God confessed by Christians) in so far as this transcendent unity is reflected in the immanent family likenesses between these religions and allows us to give the one name 'religion' to all these different religious phenomena.[40]

The unity, identity and uniqueness of Christianity over against these other religions then lies in the fact that Christianity is a religion which associates a relationship to God with a historical and thus a very specific and therefore limited particularity: Jesus of Nazareth. This is the uniqueness and identity of Christianity, but at the same time its unavoidable historical limitation. It becomes clear here that (on the basis of Jesus' parables and praxis of the kingdom of God) the God of Jesus is a symbol of openness, not of closedness. Here Christianity has a positive relationship to other religions, but at the same time its uniqueness is nevertheless maintained, and ultimately at the same time the loyal Christian affirmation of the positive nature of the other world religions is honoured.

This in no way rules out the question of truth, but the truth here is that no one has a monopoly of the truth and that no one can ask for the fullness of God's riches for himself or herself alone. This insight, which for Christians is to some extent new, derives from the fact that we are now also asking questions which people could not ask earlier, purged as we are by past (and constantly new) meaningless wars of religion and fruitless discrimination. In entertaining it we are not advocating the cheap liberal modern principle that all religions are equal, or all equally relative, or all equally wrong (as some atheists claim).

Christology is an interpretation of Jesus of Nazareth: it explains that the God of Jesus is the redeemer of all men and in this sense is the exclusive redeemer. But what redeems, what brings liberation and redemption, is not the interpretation but the means of redemption itself.

The Sri Lankan theologian Aloysius Pieris in particular has pointed out, more strongly than I did in my *Jesus* book, that we are not redeemed by the honorific titles of Jesus but by the means of redemption itself, regardless of the linguistic framework within which that means is experienced and expressed.[41] 'Jesus' redeems us, not 'Christ'. Honorific titles emerge from a particular culture and often cannot be used in others. Moreover redemption through Jesus is unique and universal only in so far as what happened in Jesus is continued in his disciples. Without any relationship to a redeeming and liberating practice of Christians, redemption, brought by Jesus, remains in a purely speculative, empty vacuum. It is not the confession 'Jesus is Lord' (Rom.10.9) which in itself brings redemption, but 'he who does the will of my Father' (Matt.7.2). One has to go the way of Jesus himself; then Jesus' career concretely takes on a universal significance (Matt.25.37-39, 44-46). In fact a fragmentary but real making whole of humankind is the best indication of liberation.

The claim that Jesus is the universal redeemer entails that Christians in our history should begin to bring forth the fruits of the kingdom of God. So christology derives its authenticity from the concrete praxis of the kingdom of God: the history of Jesus' career must be continued in his disciples; only then is it meaningful to talk of the uniqueness and distinctiveness of Christianity. Moreover Pieris also speaks rightly of 'a co-redemptive function of the corporative Christ',[42] the community of God. As I said above, this way of life, following Jesus, has two essential characteristics: it is the way of the rejection of any power on the basis of a sovereign inner human freedom (the bold human commitment to the poor and oppressed, the solidarity of love, lies in this opposition to oppressive powers), and this way of life implies the *via crucis*, the cross. This is where uniqueness of Jesus lies. The 'proof' of this is that down the centuries Christians bear witness by going along this way of life through him, even to the point of martyrdom. 'In my body I fulfil what is still lacking in the sufferings of Christ' (Col.1.24), as it was put in antiquity. Opposition and surrender. This leads me to offer the following more specific account.


## IV   Specific present-day forms of Christian universality or catholicity

The universality of Christian faith means that the Christian community of faith is an open community. Sadly, however, the institutional church has had a tendency to universalize precisely its non-universal, historically inherited, particular features tied up with a particular culture and time, and to apply them uniformly to the whole of the Catholic world: in catechesis (think of the 'world catechism'), in liturgy and in church order, also in theology and until recently even in a uniform language (Latin). However, universality – which in Greek is 'catholicity' – means that the Christian faith is open (critically) to all, to every people and to every culture. 'Universal' means that which is equally valid for all. This universal must, moreover, be incarnate in each and every one without all the potentialities and virtualities of the universal being exhausted in these particular incarnations. Now within the present context of grinding structural world poverty, the universal openness and universal challenge of the message of the gospel takes on a very specific social dimension and as it were a new context. I am inspired to say this above all by Latin American, Asian and African forms of liberation theology, and for a long time this has also been a theme of my own theological quest.

What we have here is a 'concrete universality' through which Christian believers take upon themselves the aspirations of the wronged of this world and are in solidarity with the call for justice of poor and voiceless people. The cause of justice is a cause for all. Freedom and human rights are matters for all men and women; and if this is not the case (in other words, if these are only rights which privileged individuals demand for themselves), then there are no human rights. If rights hold only for a part of humankind, injustice would be legitimated by this part of humankind and discrimination would be sanctioned. To the degree that the church opts for the poor and those without rights and shows solidarity with the basic rights of the non-person who has not been allowed to come of age (G.Gutiérrez), it takes this universality up into itself in a concrete way, for 'catholic universality' is not only given from the beginning with the very nature of Christian faith, but is also a task to be realized in context.

In the present social, political and economic conjuncture of structural injustice for the majority of human beings, the Christian gospel is therefore not solely nor even primarily universalized by caritative diakonia (as practised incomparably by Mother Teresa), but above all by political diakonia, which seeks to remove the causes of this structural injustice and in so doing recognizes the universality of human rights and human worth. The active presence of the Christian churches among the poor and those without rights, to give voice to the cries of anguish and need from the oppressed, therefore has a universal significance: a significance for all – including the rich and the powerful. The option for the poor and the outcast is an intrinsic consequence of the specific and Christian universal love for humankind. For the promise of the kingdom of God to poor and oppressed people at the same time judges (not so much the rich as such, but) those who use oppressive force and are thus summoned to conversion and redemption. The transformation of the world to a higher humanity, to justice and peace, is therefore an essential part of the 'catholicity' or universality of Christian faith; and this is *par excellence* a non-discriminatory universality.

The important thing for Christians is through Christian praxis, in the footsteps of Jesus, to bear witness to him as the one whom they confess their God: the God of Israel, Father of Jesus Christ, who calls himself a defender of the poor, creator of heaven and earth, who cannot be claimed exclusively by any religion. But in that case, if we are to retain the accents of the gospel, we must keep clearly in mind Jesus' own accents on the concept of God. And so the question arises again: what is the essence of Christian uniqueness, the distinctive contribution of Jesus of Nazareth, to which Christians still seek to give shape, in other circumstances than those of Jesus' time? By a digression and in another context I want to point once again to what has already become clear in the first half of this third chapter.

The European Enlightenment was a reaction of Reason against the so-called 'positive religions' (in particular Christianity), in so far as they set themselves up as the enemies of all change, progress and emancipation and attached absolute value to regional and particular values and norms, applying them directly as norms for all men and women, even for the world. The Enlightenment was a protest against the *de facto* imperialism of positive religions.

Thus the Enlightenment gave a rational foundation to the struggle for emancipation; it was rightly a criticism of images of God which threaten human beings. Here, however, God is removed from any contact with our history. Precisely because God is put outside our history, the Enlightenment is only a semi-emancipation and liberation. Thus even the Enlightenment led to a new slavery for other peoples. And so even the nineteenth-century missions became part and parcel of Western neo-imperialism.

I said above that the criticism of particular images of God, especially images of God which threaten our humanity, is also an essential aspect of the gospel message of Jesus of Nazareth; it is even a focus in this message. So Christianity, on the basis of a religious source, and therefore (in contrast to the Enlightenment) on the basis of the insight of Christian faith that God is personally involved with men and women and their history, was from a theological source originally at the same time an impulse to liberation and emancipation. On the basis of the parables of Jesus and his praxis of the kingdom of God we have also seen an analysis of the way in which the biblical concept of God is essentially bound up with a praxis by which human beings free their fellows, as Jesus showed us. Precisely because in the course of church history this link was weakened and even forgotten, and God was 'objectified' so that he became the cornerstone and guarantee of all human knowledge, human order and action, the one who was appealed to for legitimation of the existing order, and therefore the enemy of all change, liberation and emancipation, the crisis of the Enlightenment was historically not only possible, but even 'inevitable'.

The consequence of all this, on the other hand, was that in Enlightened deism (and in its direct and subsidiary effects) the biblical 'appeal to God' disappeared and all that was left was a secularized process of semi-liberation and emancipation – a semi-liberation movement. From a Christian perspective, however, what is important is the unbreakable bond between worship of God (let us say prayer and mysticism) and liberation in the fullest and most comprehensive sense of this word. To proclaim this mystical and liberating message (accompanied by a praxis in accordance with the gospel, following Jesus) is the privilege of Christians. But here they must recall the saying of Amos which I quoted at the very beginning of this book: 'As I brought Israel out of Egypt, so I brought the Philistines from Caphtor, and Aram from Kir' (Amos 9.7)!

## V The universality of Jesus in connection with the question of the universal meaning of history

### A. *Experience of meaning and truth*

I think it untenable in terms both of historical criticism and of ideology (in a negative sense) to suppose that the question of meaning arose only with a modern Western bourgeois society. Historically, the myths of antiquity are quite simply answers to questions of meaning, and they are older than any philosophy and science. Both philosophy and the sciences came into being precisely on the basis of myths as interpretations of meaning. Historians of religion and culture and historians of the social development of human knowledge have made it clear to us that no matter where men and women live, in one way or another the question of the meaning of human existence is raised. People seek the all-supporting and all-embracing meaning which binds together the different sectors of human, individual and social life into a meaningful whole. The specific content of this question of meaning constantly takes new form, from and within the quite specific cultural-historical and socio-economical context of human social groups. Initially the question was simply that of the meaning of the clan community: outsiders were 'non-persons', i.e. not members of the clan. Gradually, through the joining together of different clans, people began to come together in larger social organizations, and the concept of the *humanum*, humanity, was also developed. The question of meaning thus also took on other contours, until it developed into the question of the meaning of all human life, and ultimately of the whole of human history. However, the question of a meaningful whole has always been there. But there is a clear development in what has been regarded as a whole and thus as human. Initially this 'whole' was in fact one's own clan over against all the rest. Now, however, the question is that of the meaning of all human life, including the life of 'the other', and ultimately the meaning of the history of all humankind. So what has explicitly emerged only in modern times is the question of a universal meaning which embraces the whole of human history, the whole of humankind. The human horizon has been extended, but the same question of meaning still remains.

Moreover, as a result of internal differentiation, in the long run every society gets its own specialists, who have applied themselves to questions of meaning. This initially developed into *mythologein* or the telling of many mythical stories, and later into theologizing. Still later, people began to look for the *logos*, the deep power of meaning and truth in all myths and theologies, which can also be expressed in rational human terms. Only in the time of nominalism, in the fourteenth century, did this give rise to two independent autonomous disciplines in search of the truth, philosophy and theology. Originally anti-positivist, philosophers and theologians have constantly seen themselves as defenders not of analytical-Enlightenment disciplines, but of disciplines concerned with meaning. In more recent Western history (following Aristotle), this meaning is sought above all in what is 'meta' or above physics, i.e. what lies beyond the bounds of physics, 'metaphysics'. The science of meaning becomes the metaphysical science of being. To grasp the different views of life (arising from questions about meaning), in seeking a horizon in modern times people also looked for a 'meta' or upper side to everyday life, namely meta-theories. Finally, in our present age, above all the significance of human praxis was discovered, so that the need is now felt for a 'meta-praxis', a close connection between thought and action. Thus this problem, already centuries old, has at present ended up in the dialectic of theory and praxis.

All this indicates that as a result of the meaninglessness and threat in which human life is in fact set, the question of meaning is bound up with our concrete, historical humanity itself, and is not an arbitrary or bourgeois construction. Certainly people must remain aware that the question of meaning can be put too soon, without a prior analytical investigation of where, how and when 'meaninglessness' comes about in our history. The ineradicable human need for meaning and under-standing is never detached from the historically and socially situated history in which 'humanity' and 'inhumanity', often intermingled, show themselves in time and space. But this does not mean that the question of meaning can be brushed aside.

I have already said above that particularly since the Enlightenment the concept of 'universal truth' has been detached from its essential historicity, and from men and women as personal subjects. As in the Greek conception of truth, albeit in another way, truth here equally becomes a truth-in-itself, without a subject. However, universal truth holds for all human subjects and not just for socially and economically, and consequently also intellectually, privileged men and women. Reality is expressed only by subjects who experience it, so that truth does not just have a primary relationship to reality, but also a relationship to subjects: truth is also ordered by a universal consensus, if it is in fact to be called universal, i.e. the truth. This has fundamental consequences for the concept of truth.

Of course we must follow analytical philosophy in saying that only a meaningful statement is a candidate for truth or untruth. So we have to distinguish between meaning and truth. But this analytical view of that difference needs to be corrected. Pannenberg affirms this difference on the basis of his own theological project, but he rightly adds that the question of truth is not ultimately related to the question of 'meaning' and 'significance' simply by way of being a purely external addition.[43] A totality of meaning embracing all experience does indeed at the same time coincide with the revelation of truth. For by definition such a totality of meaning does not allow any experience outside itself which could make the truth of this experienced meaning problematical.[44] In the all-embracing totality of meaning (if there is such a thing), experience of meaning and experience of truth coincide. That is beyond question. But without wanting to contradict this ultimate coincidence of meaning, relevance and truth, at this point I want to introduce a subtle qualifi-cation.

The question of universal meaning is a question which is rationally both inevitable and insoluble, not just on the basis of human thought but also on the basis of human reality itself.[45] Real history is made wherever meaning and meaninglessness lie alongside and over each other, are mixed up with each other; it is where joy and suffering, laughing and weeping are; it is finitude. Therefore because of the constant obstinacy of all meaningless suffering, we cannot rationalize the combination of meaning and meaninglessness – the very warp of history (as it has already been analysed above) – into a coherent theoretical project.

We can certainly say that particular experiences are possible only on the basis of the question of total meaning which is inevitably implied in them logically. On the one hand, this logically implied question in no way means that universal history must in reality *per se* have a definitively positive meaning. And on the other hand it cannot argue away theoretically and logically the remained of meaninglessness and disaster. Moreover, Logos, meaning, and facticity, the occurrence of meaninglessness, injustice and suffering, are interrelated in a tension which cannot be resolved theoretically. Therefore theoretical reason cannot rationally reach forward to a universal, total meaning of history. Moreover, given that the historical process of development is not yet complete, any particular experience of meaning is also subject to a theoretically insoluble, fundamental doubt. If totality may be meaningless, this has an effect on any specific experience of meaning, which then goes on to share in this infinite lack of meaning. So in the end theoretical reason cannot in itself decide on meaning. Can practical reason help here, and if so, how?

If history has an ultimate, total meaning, then this meaning cannot be subject to a logical pressure towards totality, at least if it deserves the name of human history: history of freedom, made in conditions of chance, pressure and violence. This universal meaning cannot be established either idealistically or materialistically in a 'logic of development'. For in that case we would not ultimately include the specific histories of human suffering. An excessively large piece of real history would then be regarded as rubbish, the sweepings of history, which no one cares about. This so-called surplus of suffering, injustice and meaninglessness escapes the *logos* of theoretical reason. Theoretically it cannot be placed, and rationally it cannot be interpreted meaningfully. Theoretical talk about the infinite, total meaning of history is therefore not meaningful: in specific terms it would amount to a lack of sensitivity to world-historical and personal dramas, the unavoidable and also the avoidable catastrophes in our history. Here at least (even if we may not approve of his neopositivism), Hans Albert seems to be right when he talks of the 'myth of total reason' (meant as theoretical reason).[46] But in contrast to what he claims, this in no way means that the concept of totality is itself meaningless. The relationship between the part and the whole, regarded by a long hermeneutical tradition as logically unavoidable, is, as a problem given rationally, difficult to deny in any particular experience of meaning.[47] However, the inescapable difficulty in a purely theoretical thematization of the universal meaning of history, of the totality of meaning as logically implied in any particular experience of meaning, finds its basis in the historical process of experience itself.

This is on the one hand incomplete and on the other hand also confronts us with intolerable meaninglessness.

The conclusion is then that the thematization of universal meaning can be accomplished meaningfully only with a practical-critical intention, i.e. in a perspective in which a bit of meaninglessness is done away with, step by step, through human action. The thematization or reflection must thus be supported by a praxis of gradual liberation which will prepare and free the way for total meaning. In other words, total meaning can only come about through historical experiences and commitment; it cannot be speculatively thought out in a theoretical anticipation, precisely because concrete history is a mixture of sense and nonsense. This indicates that talk about a total and universal meaning of history is impossible if one leaves out of account a particular praxis which seeks to make all men and women the free subjects of a living history, without detriment to any of them. However, as memory, the meaningless residue of history which theoretical reason cannot grasp (think of Hegel) remains a power, a cognitive stimulus to practical reason which – if it is to remain reason – is as a result prompted to liberating action which seeks to remove the meaninglessness from history. But historical reality teaches that within history this liberating action in essence remains limited, fragmentary; the history of sinfulness and meaniglessness continues to weigh heavy. That does not alter the fact that the protest of the history of suffering as a result of injustice and torture, which is never silenced in our human history, remains a spur towards realizing the meaning which is never to be given up in history and thus a challenge to injustice and meaninglessness. All this raises the question: is not the purely secular history of freedom itself only semi-emancipation and a history of semi-freedom?

*B. The Christian experiential tradition as a practical anticipation of universal meaning*

In its praxis of prayer and liberation (in faithfulness and in unfaithfulness) the Christian, biblical experiential tradition, as living recollection of the message, the life and the death of the risen Jesus, can be an inspiration and give a very definite orientation to human practical reason. This Christian experiential tradition does not say that human beings are the masters of reality; only God is the Lord of history. God can still give future to the fragmentary liberating action of men and women. This religious experiential tradition sees the praxis of the kingdom of God as future for all men and women, as this already becomes present in Jesus' words and deeds, a practical anticipation of a universal kingdom of justice, peace and love, of all and for all, with

God as the living centre and binding factor of this community in
solidarity. In the Christian religious experiential tradition, that which
is sought, hoped-for and still unexpected – expressed in the New
Testament by powerful pictures like kingdom of God, universal brotherhood and sisterhood, a heavenly banquet, the freedom of the children
of God, the universal kingdom of justice and peace – is not a vague
utopia which is completely in the future, nor a theoretical anticipation
of a total meaning of history. What is hoped for is, rather, vividly
anticipated in a career and praxis: that of Jesus, whose person, message
and praxis, despite historical failure on the cross, is confirmed by his
resurrection from the dead by God as in fact a praxis of the kingdom of
God: salvation for all men and women. In this life-story, being a
historical victim, i.e. suffering, takes on its own cognitive significance
and power (though this cannot be given a place in theory) for humankind
on its long way in search of truth and goodness, justice and meaning.

According to the Christian confession of faith, a non-theoretical but
practical prolepsis or anticipation of the new world is given in Jesus, in
which salvation is also promised to people without salvation, to those
who are suffering and overwhelmed, even to the dead. Over against the
praxis of earth and the criticism of heaven – already topical in Jesus'
time – Jesus sets the praxis of the kingdom of God. So the world that is
sought, the world that is a 'good world' for all, already takes on meaning,
albeit in the conditions of the 'old world', in the praxis and execution of
Jesus. Therefore this career not only causes irritation because of the
injustice which constantly arises anew, but also provides inspiration for
an alternative liberating action which realizes meaning. Finally, by its
content, this way of life, which is above all pragmatism, gives orientation
and direction to the action of Christians in the world.

The universality of Christian salvation is an offer of salvation from
God to all men and women, as I said above – an offer of salvation with
the aim of actually realizing salvation and liberation for all, in freedom,
through a praxis in accordance with the gospel, in the steps of Jesus.
The salvation that is founded in Christ as a promise for all becomes
universal, not through the mediation of an abstract, universal idea, but
by the power of its cognitive, critical and liberating character in and
through a consistent praxis of the kingdom of God. So this is not a purely
speculative, theoretical universality, but a universality which can be
realized in the fragmentary forms of our history only through the
spreading of the story of Jesus confessed by Christians as the Christ,
and through Christian praxis.

But, without fragments there is also no total salvation! So we cannot
regard the salvation or total meaning, founded in Jesus and given to us
as promise, as a 'transcendental' omnipresence of the Christian gospel.

It is a historical presence of the Christian inspiration and orientation through the story of Jesus and his specific historical praxis of liberation (and ours, in his footsteps), which experiences living communion with God as the source and foundation of total human freedom: as salvation not only for a particular privileged class, nor just for the living or the survivors, but for all, including those who are written off, oppressed and ultimately dead.

## C. Orthodoxy is at stake in orthopraxis

The conclusion from what has just been said is that truly liberating truth which is relevant to life, and therefore the ultimate coincidence of the experience of meaning and the experience of truth, also stands under the primacy of the cognitive, critical and liberating power of memories of histories of suffering. If practical reason takes these recollections seriously, they prompt this reason to quite particular liberating action. Only through this action is truth in fact made universal, applying not only to some privileged men and women but to each and all. 'What is true' must be relevant to all men and women, including those who are dead and overwhelmed.[48] This universal liberating praxis is not a secondary superstructure upon, or merely a consequence of, a theoretical truth already recognized as universal, but it is the historical mediation of the manifestation of truth as universal truth, applying to all men and women.

In this perspective it can be said that in right action, orthopraxis, at the same time the historical manifestation of right thinking, or orthodoxy, is at risk. If truth is to be universal, and thus truth, then it is also mediated practically, even politically and socially. Although the Christian content of faith has its own cognitive power, which is manifested historically in the way in which Jesus is followed in the life of the churches (though with ups and downs), this cognitive critical and liberating power is not to be identified with the cognitive power of a theory or a theoretical anticipation of universal meaning. The basic Christian story about Jesus, as the story of the life and death of the risen Jesus, and as the story of the church's following of Jesus, is not a theoretical anticipation of universal meaning; it is a story founded in the history of Jesus as the Christ, of trust and hope, which historically, as with Jesus, manifest themselves in a message of universal justice and peace of and for one another in a praxis of solidarity which hopes to bring about for all men and women inner freedom and a society freed from compulsion. Moreover this faith – the content of which is ultimately a hope, not a theory: 'Faith is a firm ground of what we hope' (Heb.11.1) – is specifically a praxis of faith, unless we reduce Christian faith to a purely intellectual acceptance of particular contents of faith. For on this last level (which traditionally is usually called that of the *fides quae*), one can hardly assert that the truth-value of these expressions of faith is decided on by a praxis which is either consistent or inconsistent with this content of faith. Theoretical ideologies also have their followers with a faithful and consistent praxis, but this coherent praxis in no way settles the truth value of the theory which is defended. In that case, for example, the stubborn loyalty with which some people followed the Nazi ideology would prove the truth of Nazism!

The question which arises here (in connection with the *fides qua*) is that of the primacy of the Christian story and Christian praxis over all theological theory. Liberating action in faith does not call for less but more critical-theoretical analysis.[49] The reciprocal critical correlation which was disucssed at the end of the first chapter therefore implies a truly critical unity of theory and praxis. The correlation between Christian faith (with its own narrative-practical structure and the distinctive cognitive, critical and liberating power given in it) on the one hand and contemporary experiences within a modern society on the other can ultimately be carried through in a productive way only on the basis of a praxis which seeks to realize salvation for all and as a result seeks to allow truth to come into its own as universal truth.

That is to say at the same time that the aporias in which the present problems of theory and praxis become involved, whether in an idealistic or in a materialistic sense, have their origin in the failure to recognize the distinctive cognitive, critical and liberating power which is not peculiar to, and therefore cannot be reduced to, the cognitive power of theoretical contemplative knowledge, and is also not peculiar to, and cannot be reduced to, the similar cognitive power of manipulative or domineering praxis. Belief is concerned with the cognitive power which is peculiar to the story of a 'pathic' praxis, above all the 'pathic' power of stories of the suffering of quite specific men and women.[50] For anyone who does not think in idealistic terms must make an intrinsic connection between the universal human love proclaimed by Christianity, and partisan solidarity with all human existence that is damaged or injured. If that does not happen, we have an abstract Enlightenment universalism which in fact always makes an alliance with the powerful of this earth. Because of its universality, which does not exclude anyone, Christian love, seen in social and political terms, is in practice partisan – otherwise it is not universal!

# VI   The God who escapes all our identifications

In Chapter 2 I mentioned the threefold way of life to be found in mystical talk of God: the *via affirmativa, negativa et eminentiae*. God is ultimately the invisible and unnameable One. And I said that in this Chapter 3 we would discuss this further in connection with the uniqueness of Jesus, which would be analysed in the meantime. The time for that has now come.

In two books, *An Asian Theology of Liberation* and *Love meets Wisdom. A Christian Experience of Buddhism*,[51] Aloysius Pieris has pointed out that with its absolutizing of the love command (the unity of love of humankind and love of God), Christianity has to begin a dialogue with wisdom (*gnosis*) as the basic principle of Asian spirituality. This Eastern wisdom relativizes the creaturely world in a radical way, and also our human efforts for a better and juster world. From its perspective, at the same time it can point to the one-sidedness of the Christian principle of universal love of neighbour (in both its caritative and its socio-political dimensions). Asian men and women are more resigned to injustice and suffering. Gnosis does not seek any identification of what or who God is. God is unimaginable, he is totally other even than as he has appeared in Jesus. Nevertheless, despite the 'negative theology' which is also present in Christianity, by contrast New Testament Christianity stresses the fact that God has shown us his face in the man Jesus; it is the theme and also the basic notion of the whole of this book. In this chapter I am saying that this is the distinctive feature of Christianity: the God of all men and women shows in Jesus of Nazareth who he is, namely universal love for men and women. Jesus Christ is the historical, culturally located expression of this universal message of the gospel.

Thus Christianity does have the intention of identifying God: that is its distinctiveness. For Christians, Jesus is the definition of God; otherwise their christology makes no sense. At the same time, for Christians too, this is a definition of God in non-divine terms, namely in and through the historical contingent humanity of Jesus. The definition of God which appears in Jesus finally points to an elusive, invisible God who escapes all identifications; otherwise 'mysticism' makes no sense. That is why I said that the multiplicity of religions is not just a historical fact that must be transcended, but a matter of principle. There are authentic-religious experiences in other religions which are never realized or thematized in Christianity and, I added, perhaps cannot be without robbing Jesus' identification of God of its distinctiveness. Must christology then give way to mysticism or mysticism to christology? All Christian mystics wrestle with this problem and (in my view apart from Hadewych and Teresa of Avila) tend to relativize christology; they do not know where to put christology within their mysticism (this applies particularly at least to Eckhart and John of the Cross). That produces the danger that Christianity may be seen as a special historical form of an unchangeable, supra-historical, metaphysical and religious nucleus, of which all religions are simply chance expressions.

But a Christian cannot let go of the human appearance of Jesus which identifies God in favour of a transcendence which escapes all identification. In that case we are giving up our Christian faith. Moreover we are losing sight of the fact that God's being is absolute freedom, absolute initiative, albeit from eternity, and not a metaphysical mystery resting on and in itself. It is not we Christians who identify God. It is a free initiative of the living God towards us. What I said above continues to hold for Christians: all *our* images of God must ultimately be shattered again. But in Jesus, the Christ, do we not have a human project or product. There we have an image of God that we have not produced; we are simply deciphering the image of God that is given to us, according to the Christian confession, by God in Jesus Christ. According to this confession it is God himself who allows himself to be identified in and through the career of Jesus of Nazareth. For Christians to let this go means turning their backs on Christianity. But this Christian affirmation of faith, as I have already said, does not deny that in basic and source experiences of other religions, religious men and women are – and rightly – cautious in identifying God from images which they have constructed themselves. And this also applies to Christians: all images of God among Christians which deviate from the basic intention of the gospel fall under the demolition hammer of the image of God that is Jesus of Nazareth himself.

The critical question is: is the identification which Jesus himself gives us of God an open or a closed one?

I see mysticism which relativizes the world, both Eastern and Western (alongside the factuality of a non-religious mysticism), as going in two different and irreconcilable directions. In one direction the mystic leaves the world behind for good by turning inwards and by interiorization. One can call this the mysticism of 'God and only God': the radical negation of all that is finite. By contrast, in the other direction, while as in the first trend one initially also arrives at an inner void, resignation and inner freedom, by this self-abandonment and detachment from all ties to the finite, one finally arrives at the God who cannot be identified, but of whom one nevertheless experiences 'in patches' that he is the inexpressible source of all that is creaturely. The procedure of the radical negation of the finite is an attempt to find God in his Godness, in himself. And righly so. But there one notes that God's being is not a negation of the creature: he creates the creature in its finite but own autonomy and value.

In God one experiences that in absolute freedom he is essentially creator, the lover of the finite, loving with the absoluteness of a divine love which is unfathomable to us. In this mystical view he then wills to be the beloved of all creation. Anyone who wants to find God as God in his innermost authenticity cannot then exclude the creatures. And precisely within this view we can have a consistent understanding of the distinctive, even unique, place of the man Jesus of Nazareth within world history, which can at least be vividly understood even by non-Christian forms of mysticism, without any discrimination against other religions. This form of mystic abandonment (Eckhart, John of the Cross, Francis and also many Buddhist forms of mysticism) can coincide completely with prophetic Christianity. For Jesus, his mystical 'Abba' experience is the source of his prophetic activity. In such mysticism, love for all men and women and all-embracing love for fellow creatures as an expression of love of God can come fully into its own. Within this mysticism there is plenty of room for the struggle for justice and love, for making the creation whole, for all that lives in this finite world. Within this mysticism a Buddhist cannot even deliberately kill a bug that may bite him, but must open the window to let the creature escape. By contrast, with the first form of mysticism – the radical negation of all that is finite as a last mystical response – Christianity can never arrive at one synthesis, but only enter into dialogue, in a conversation of two religions which cannot be reduced to either of them.

When I spoke in the previous chapter of the autonomous ethic which is experienced by Christians within a mystical context, it already emerged that universal human love – bodily, spiritual and social liberation and affirmation of one's fellow men and women – cannot ultimately be expressed in purely ethical terms. This is a Christian universal love of neighbour which is one with love of God, and which is thus essentially theologal and mystical. Anyone who has experienced a eucharist of Latin American believers can almost physically empathize with the mystical movement of their social and political urge for liberation. In negative terms there is something absolute in the injustice that is specifically done in history to fellow men and women, and therefore one cannot clear up this injustice or describe it in or with exclusively ethical terms and categories (although non-religious men and women can experience substantially the same radical quality as believers. The critical point does not lie there. Of course what is at stake is not a Christian apologetic, but believers' own understanding of their faith).

That the Christian love of neighbour, as inspired by a theologal, mystical concern for God, is an open and not a closed concept, emerges fully from Jesus' resignation and inner freedom on the cross. For Jesus this mystical resignation was the supreme consequence of trust in his message of universal love for men and women, and here above all for the poor, the oppressed, and those without a voice. Precisely on the cross, the God identified by Jesus nevertheless showed himself to be the elusive and unnameable God whose divine properties can never be identified. Therefore even on the cross Jesus was silent about the mystery, despite the cry 'Why? Why?' which he is said to have uttered through psalms. Therefore a Christian can say: on the basis of the gospel of Jesus Christ I confess that the name of God is rightly associated with the gospel utopia of justice and love, with the dream of a liberation to a constantly better humanity, and that it is wrong to associate this name of God with active or passive justification of a social and economic situation which injures and enslaves many men and women (no matter how mystical the motives may be).

As a Christian I cannot tolerate the immeasurable torturing of men and women in our history. To me as a Christian, the 'resignation' (with regard to all possible evil and suffering) which is often a principle in some non-Christian religions, without any prior opposition (although in fact we also find a similar premature resignation among individual Christians), seems to be too hasty a capitulation to evil, suffering and injustice, and thus a kind of complicity in evil. Jesus' resignation on the cross was, in the conditions of the evil world, the consequence of his opposition to this evil world. If the resignation comes too early, and the cross which is wrongly inflicted is accepted too early, then evidently the holy wrath of indignation at the fact that each cross is unworthy of men and women is absent. In this sense, flight from the world and passive resignation are not, in my view, Christian; they cannot be reconciled with the religious experience of Christians. Nevertheless I have to concede that the living God is in fact greater than this view of Christianity. Theologically in a somewhat childish and naive way, but pungently and more sharply than with measured theological categories, one might perhaps best put it like this: God is not 'the same' before and after his creation. All mystics have to take account of this.

## VII   Consequences for the church's mission

All religions have and are something unique, although that does not make them all equal. I already said above that according to the New Testament gospel, Christianity proclaims the definitive lordship of God as being founded on the message, career and death of the crucified but risen Jesus of Nazareth. This is the 'God of all men and women', the creator, the foundation, source and horizon of the eschatological or final unity of world history. This divine creator is no private possession of the Christian churches, although he is identical with the God of Israel and the Jew Jesus, and also – and this should not be forgotten – with the creator and leader of all peoples.

The mission which was previously aimed above all at the salvation of souls and the communication of salvation (because then the church was seen as the only means of salvation) finds itself confused over the changes in the view of the claim to universality. Here and there mission even suffers under the suspicion of being *passé*, or one hears the charge that mission has been narrowed down to a form of collaboration in development.

A theology of mission must take account not only of what I have called the uniqueness and at the same time the historical limitations of Christianity, but also of what I mentioned already in Chapter 1, namely that God himself brings about salvation in human history and that the church and its mission should therefore be given second place, though this is not an insignificant one. Such a theology must also be connected with what in Chapter 1 I called the relationship of the gospel to the present context: the present day enters into the content of the understanding of the gospel.

It is not the case that mission is possible only if one begins from the conviction that one's message that is brought is superior to the religious culture of those whom the missionary addresses. Rather, mission spirituality is a matter of being grasped by the event and the value of the kingdom of God in order to realize the praxis of this kingdom in the steps of Jesus: inner *metanoia* and reform of society and one's own person in the direction of that kingdom, in the direction of greater humanity and universal liberation. Christians are led to bear witness to Jesus Christ and thus to spread the gospel, because they want to further God's kingdom of justice and love throughout the world.

I was very moved on reading Jean-Marc Ela's book *Le cri de l'homme Africain*.[52] The author sees the first task of mission as being not the liturgical, catechetical and theological inculturation of Christianity, but the quest for the kingdom of God in the form of a human society characterized by solidarity. That agrees with what I said some pages earlier about the universality of the churches which are in solidarity with the freedom and human rights of the poor and those without rights. In general, mission occupies itself above all in 'oeuvres de suppléance' – activities which supplement those of the state. It is precisely that which keeps the existing injustice in place. In that case the correct approach of true mission is to make people aware of the unacceptable character of the oppression under which they live. That was also the perspective of Jesus' proclamation of the kingdom of God: his experience of the blatant contrast between this world of injustice and suffering and his 'Abba' experience of God as at the same time the fatherly and motherly principle of life.

As prophet, the missioner must go and stand alongside the oppressed in the struggle which in fact is being carried on for more humanity and salvation, for a better future. It is in this very struggle (which need not necessarily be a violent one) that the possibility of a proper understanding of the gospel and thus of the indigenization, i.e. the inculturation, of that gospel in local culture, lies. The conflict that is provoked by structural poverty also defines the content of the Christian gospel witness. In place of the earlier contrast – the 'light' of Christianity as opposed to the 'darkness' of the pagan religions – we are now aware of the conflict between the kingdom of God and what the Bible calls 'this world', i.e. the world created good by God but into which men and women have introduced injustice and sin. This is the perspective for all mission. The active presence of the Christian church at the forefront of these conflicts is the primary action of mission. The gospel is shown to men and women by its liberating fruits.

In Chapter 1 I said that the churches are not salvation, but a sign of salvation. The church is an actual minority which is there to serve a majority and is not concerned with winning as many souls as possible for itself. In the active presence of Christians in the struggle against oppression and structural poverty, witness is borne to the gospel, witness which also takes shape, for example, in the concrete African situation. This includes on the one hand patient listening to the non-secularized, religious culture of many nations, admitting the possibility of being taught by 'the other', and on the other hand, the telling of the story of the ancient Christian experiential tradition from which we Christians ourselves live and from which we derive the power to take the side of the oppressed and dishonoured on this earth. Only in this active presence does true inculturation have a chance.

Mission comprises evangelization and collaboration in development and the work of liberation: caritative and political diakonia. The gospel mission seeks a connection with those layers of the population where the call of men and women for freedom and human worth, justice and peace, rings out loudly, for Christian hope and expectation for the future become concrete only when they link up with the human tragedy of poverty, injustice and oppression. That was also the perspective of Jesus' own mission. In concrete terms this calls for a prophetic-critical and even political diakonia to men and women in need.

Because in their colonial past the Christian churches stood more on the side of the rich and powerful (with some good exceptions) and not on the side of the people, in what are called 'mission countries' (in fact the Third World), the state and the ruling classes feel betrayed by a church which now stands up for the human rights of the poor and the oppressed. Where churches support the powerful, they are protected and privileged, but alienated from the people. Where they are in solidarity with the people's call for justice, as a result of the ideology of 'national security' (which serves the interests of national and international capital), they are under police control and there are martyrs among their members. In that case they face the dramatic dilemma whether to integrate thenselves or become the object of repression. This is the primary problem of mission in the last decade of this century. The guideline here is that it is right to associate the name of God with a utopia in the light of Jesus' proclamation of the kingdom of God as a kingdom of justice and love among men and among women, and this name may not therefore be used to justify our existing economic system which exploits men and women structurally. Christians need to use the name of God only where it belongs: in solidarity with the victims of our economic situation, in the struggle for the furtherance and redistribution of work, income and spiritual goods, and so on.

To bring the gospel to all the needy in the world, not only through words but through solidarity in action and thus through a praxis of liberation, is the very nature of Christianity. Mission is therefore connected with questions of justice and peace, of the distribution of material and spiritual values, of the distribution of work and juster conditions of trade. Precisely because these problems can in fact be solved only in a world context, mission in our time takes on a more comprehensive dimension. By bearing witness to the gospel of and for the poor, Christians constantly create new groups which also themselves hand on the torch and, in the footsteps of Jesus, share in God's saving initiative. This means that Christianity with its message and own way of life is not a categorical imperative for men and women but an 'offer', and in this way, in its distinctiveness, is also dialogue with and possible criticism and provocation of other religions, which in their turn put equally critical and provocative questions to Christianity in the dialogue.

The Christian message of the kingdom of God with its potential for liberation remains in its distinctive character an offer to all men and women, and at the same time also a confrontation with other religions as such (and not simply with their members). Human culture, even religious cultures, can be evangelized without these cultures having to give up their specific peculiarity and identity.[53] And in turn Christianity, too, can find a new Christian 'inculturation' from and in other religious cultures.

The ecumene of world religions cannot be called peace among religions if one tones down the religious accents of the particular, diverging, religions in favour of an abstract and also eclectic universality which joins all religions together and in so doing in fact becomes unreal. Anyone who, for example, seeks to make Christianity a mystical religion from which at least all the liberating accents of Jesus' distinctive image of God have disappeared – and that implies the partisan choice for the poor and oppressed – damages the originality of Christianity. In this view we then no longer have the Christian gospel. (The same is true of course, conversely, of the distinctive accents of the identity of religions like Buddhism or Islam.) Precisely in its own option for the gospel, Christianity (often along with criticism of its own historical past and even present) is, in origin and in its deepest irritation, inspiration and orientation, a religious enterprise which truly brings freedom to men and women.

## CHAPTER 4

# Towards Democratic Rule of the Church as a Community of God

## Introduction

It is self-evident to everyone, Christians and non-Christians, that the community which calls itself the church of Christ never lives in a social, cultural or political vacuum. We know from history that the church, after an original first period of separate ghetto life apart from its pagan Roman or Hellenistic surroundings, mostly adapted itself to the structures of the society around it, though not without some critical distancing. And these structures in turn influenced church structures.[1] That was already the case at an early stage. But this process of assimilation, above all the structuring of church organization and the arrangements for local churches, became even clearer when the church became a state church, partially after Constantine and completely after Theodosius. It happily took over the splendid insignia and distinguishing marks of the imperial Byzantine court in attitude, clothing and pomp. After that, it took over the feudal order, the customs and status symbols of the nobility, both in church structures and in the order and rites of its liturgy. Bishops became feudal princes of the church.

The church then later got into trouble with the rising guilds of the mediaeval bourgeoisie, with their views about the collective participation and shared responsibility of all members. Moreover, a result of the Reformation, above all Calvinism, which at that time had already taken a more democratic turn (which it also showed in its church order), was that in reaction,the Catholic Counter-Reformation began to put even more emphasis on hierarchical authority from above. In the Ancien Régime this church hierarchy flourished with worldly triumph, until by the time of absolute rulers in Europe, within the church, too, the pope began to be seen as an absolute monarch with all the privileges of such a figure, a supreme authority against which nothing could be said. This was a kind of climax to a particular ecclesiology.

But if the democratic structures of our modern state system are becoming common property, the church would seem to have quite insuperable difficulties in adapting its structures to demands for the contribution and involvement of all believers in the government of the church (however this must or can be organized in specific terms). To express this caution about the contribution to and involvement of believers the church constantly refers to what it calls its 'divinely willed hierarchical structure'. This hierarchical articulation of the church is supposed, in accordance with a divine plan, not to allow any democratic structures within the church.

This historical misunderstanding (subsequent analysis will demonstrate that this in fact is what it is) is one of the most painful points of dispute between Catholic faithful and their leaders in our democratic age. And in a time which is wary of any monarchical absolutism, above all a goverment with a single head or an élitist oligarchy which soon degenerate and show signs of arbitrariness, this is a particuarly sensitive point and is really felt to be intolerable. So I shall end this book with an investigation of the specific historical face of the church.

# 1. The specific historical face of the church

I   Abstract and historically coloured ecclesiologies

Even by referring to the proclamation which emerges from the Bible, the Old and New Testaments, we can in fact speak in abstract or speculative terms about the church. Moreover we can speak 'performatively' about the phenomenon of the 'church', i.e. say what the specific nature of the church must be (after a critical analysis of Old and New Testaments and the history of the church's belief which is accepted unanimously). However, in neither case can we by-pass the empirical, specific historical manifestations of the church. For alongside all the gifts and favours of a material and spiritual kind which it has brought to many people down the ages, at the same time, in the past, it has tended to exclude people, cultures, other religions, and, I might say, 'alternative Christians', even devastating, destroying and overwhelming them. All this has happened, not on the basis of the church's own gospel which it has preached (although that is how it has been presented), but in fact with reference to its own, ideological and imperialistic claim to be right.

These are facts which we must recognize and concede before we can and must, also as Christians, go on to make our requisitions. In many ecclesiologies, both older and more modern ones, no mention is made of the negative side of the empirical churches, which in the language of faith are called the 'community of God', or at any rate this side is not made a theme in the theology of the church. That can no longer happen in our present situation. Things must change, not for fear that we Christians will be confronted with our own past by others, historians, but because as Christians – not in pathological self-accusation (of which there is also a danger here), but simply by being 'honest to God' and acting in accordance with human worth – we cannot live out our own Christian identity here and now except by at the same time explicitly dissociating ourselves from what an ideological kind of Christianity has done to people up to the present time and still continues to do.

## II    The mystery of the church according to Vatican II

### A. *The kingdom of God and the Christian churches*

In the previous chapter, which dealt with ecclesiology, as a theologian I adopted as it were already a post-ecumenical standpoint, as for the most part I had also deliberately done in the first two books of this trilogy. This was in no way because of a lack of interest in ecumenical matters. On the contrary. At that point, as earlier in this book, I deliberately did not go into church and confessional differences, at least explicitly (though the awareness of confessional differences implicitly plays a part in all my theological reflections), because I did not want at any point to make these differences a specific theme. In my view this is also a legitimate form of theological ecumenism.

Not least because of all kinds of cultural and social circumstances, the standpoint 'from which' we, as Christians – or to put it perhaps more modestly, at least I as a Christian – begin to think is increasingly the ecumene of the world religions and the ecumene of humankind, to which agnostics and atheists also belong. In all that I have said so far (and also throughout my theological quest) I have adopted that standpoint. Really and finally, my main concern is with the 'ecumene of suffering humankind' (to use a phrase of J.B.Metz). Although in my view this human interest in 'humankind' must not be underestimated in Christian theologizing, I realize that in fact from a Christian perspective Christians, including myself in my post-ecumenical theological thought, certainly do not live in a post-ecumenical period. Furthermore, precisely in our time Christians live in a period in which the Christian ecumenical approach is encountering greater difficulties and frustrations (at least at the official level of the different Christian and confessional churches) than were present at a recent earlier stage of the ecumenical movement, above all in the base communities and under church authorities which were loyally tolerant. Now things are different.

For these reasons it would be unreal for me not to look now at what was presented in Chapter 3 from a broader, as it were 'methodologically supra-Christian post-ecumenical' standpoint, in the light of the present crisis in the more limited, intra-Christian ecumene, which is not to be underestimated (for all kinds of reasons and interests in church politics). Here the Second Vatican Council initially plays an important role.

In the text of the Preparatory Commission it was said that the biblical 'mystery of the church' is *ipso facto* the 'Roman Catholic Church'.[2] When this preparatory draft was discussed in plenary assemblies during the first session of the Council, there was sharp opposition from bishops all over the world to this simplistic approach. The result was that a new draft had to be made.

Just as in New Delhi in 1961 the confession of the Triune God was set up as the basis and condition of membership of the World Council of Churches, so the second, new outline of the constitution saw the mystery of the church against the background of the proclamation of the saving action of the Father through the Son in the Holy Spirit.[3] Through the sending of the Son and the distinct sending of the Holy Spirit, the church was connected with the sovereign-free initiative of the Father.

Whereas in defining the church more closely the first outline sought to make a direct link with the encyclical *Mystici Corporis*, which stressed the social, juridical and corporate aspect of the church (with some reference to Romans and I Corinthians), this second preliminary outline sought inspiration above all in the concept of the 'body' in the captivity letters of Paul: the believers are 'the body of Christ' through their personal union with the humiliated and exalted body of the Lord, by the power of the saving acts of God. Through baptism and eucharist, this union is brought about in faith, in the body of Christ, *in corpore Christi*. Only from there was the transition made to the location of the social and juridical aspect of the concept of the body: the church as the differentiated and organized totality of gifts and services. In this way the narrow perspective of the encyclical *Mystici Corporis* is already transcended, especially since the aspect stressed in this encyclical is taken up more broadly and with a more biblical orientation. Thus emphasis came to be laid on the saving acts of the exalted Christ who, at work through the Spirit in visible forms of the church, incorporates believers personally into his body. As a result the church is simply and at least 'in nucleus and approach' the kingdom of God.[4]

The affirmations from the first outline scheme are taken up in this new perspective: 'The visible community (of the church) and the mystical body of Christ are not two things but one reality, integrated from a human and a divine element', not without some analogy with the Word incarnate.[5]

Then follows: 'This church, grounded in this world and ordered as a community, is the Ecclesia Catholica, governed by the Pope and the bishops in union with him', to which is added: 'although outside its structure various elements of sanctification can be found which, as realities peculiar to the church of Christ, contribute towards Catholic unity'.[6] Thus the church and the mystical body are one and the same reality, although they point to two aspects of one reality. So the church is a sacrament, an effective sign of God's redemptive presence of grace in Jesus Christ.

Nevertheless, this second revised draft constitution was also thoroughly criticized by the world episcopate. They continued to oppose an unqualified identification of the mystical body with the Roman Catholic Church. This identification continues to deny the eschatological tension in the church, and as a result there is a tendency to see the heavenly consummation of the church already realized in the church which is still a pilgrim on earth. So many bishops asked for the idea of the kingdom of God to be given a central place instead of the concept of the church. This, they said, would give sharper definition to the church on the way, in a sober and realistic awareness that it too needs God's redemptive grace. Cardinal König and Abbot Butler from England stressed that only if this were done could the Dogmatic Constitution on the Church itself be said to help ecumenism. This would open up the way to a loyal confession of the ecclesial reality of the other non-Catholic churches, which was what the debate was really about.

The third revised draft, which eventually (at least on this point) also emerged as the final redaction in the Dogmatic Constitution on the Church, took account of these last amendments (at least to a considerable degree, because a minority continued to exercise their veto). For all its openness, the final redaction is nevertheless a compromise. Within the trinitarian perspective of the earlier, second outline, the new version above all stresses the 'kyrial' status of Jesus, i.e. Jesus as the 'Lord' (Kyrios) who inaugurated on earth the veiled beginning of the kingdom of God in his life, work and person. It is from this that the church movement is said to have arisen historically.[7]

Therefore this last version of the draft constitution put the kerygma of the kingdom or kingly rule of God between the express confession of the Trinity and the affirmative proclamation of the mystery of the church. This divine kingdom becomes manifest and visible in the words, actions and miracles of Jesus, and finally in his whole person. The exalted Jesus sends his Spirit and gives his church the task of proclaiming the kingdom of God and in so doing announcing itself as the 'nucleus and beginning' of this kingdom, though intent in pilgrimage to the eschatological consummation.[8] The kingdom of God and the church are thus not identified with each other, but they are not separated either. The church proclaims the eschatological kingdom, but first of all in and through its own being, since it is the beginning of this kingdom.

After a brief account of the various biblical images and metaphors by which the church is denoted, this third and last draft of the Dogmatic Constitution concentrates on the biblical image of 'the body of Christ'. Even more transparently than in the previous draft this image is developed in the biblical context of the dead and glorified body of the Lord and the eucharistic bread, which guarantees communion with the body of Christ, without, however, losing sight of the idea of the structured, social body.[9]

Within this totality with its new accents, the meaning shifts again (at least in substance) towards that of the very first outline scheme, in connection with the visible and pneumatic character of the church: 'One cannot regard the community, built up from hierarchically structured elements, and the mystical body of Christ, the visible assembly (*coetus*) and the spiritual community (*communitas*), the earthly church and the church which is endowed with heavenly gifts, as two things, but they form one complex reality, made up of a human and a divine element.'[10] The explanatory memorandum explains this further: 'There are not two churches, but only one, which at the same time is both heavenly and earthly.'[11]

According to this third draft of the Constitution it is this church of which the creed confesses that it is 'one, holy, catholic and apostolic'. It is then said of this same church: 'This church, constituted and ordered in the world as a community, exists in the Catholic Church, which is governed by the successor of Peter and the bishops in communion with him, although many elements of holiness and truth are found outside its framework (*compago*), which as the distinctive gifts of the church of Christ contribute towards Catholic unity.'[12]

The 'identification' of the biblical mystery of the church with the Catholic Church was formulated carefully, diplomatically and as a result somewhat ambiguously, in a way worthy of a senator politician (it was also an invention of the Flemish priest, senator and theologian,

Mgr Prof. G.Philips of Louvain), as follows: '*Haec Ecclesia* subsistit in *Ecclesia Catholica*'. Philips in no way gave this *subsistere in* a specifically scholastic significance (although the minority swallowed the formula precisely because of the scholastic aura surrounding it. *Subsistere, substantia*: in Scholasticism these two words were heavily ontological, which is why the minority yielded). However, it emerges from the Acts of the council that *subsistere in* was chosen as a weaker version of the first, stronger expression '*Haec Ecclesia* est *Ecclesia Catholica*'.[13] The weakened expression is used precisely so as not to blot out the reality of elements of the church in the other Christian churches. The reasons given for the acceptance or rejection of relevant amendments to this *subsistit in* make it clear that the aim of the commission was to indicate that 'the church, of which the inner and concealed being was described as "the mystery of the church", has been concretely found here on earth in the Catholic church',[14] but in its explanatory memorandum the commission betrays its second intention, which is hidden behind the main aim by the choice of the terms *subsistit in*: 'This empirical church reveals the mystery (of the church), but not without shadows, and it does so until it is brought into the full light, as Christ also reached glory through humiliation.'[15] This is all put very carefully; people were as it were anxious to indicate to outsiders that there is sin even in the church. At all events, in this final redaction it becomes clear that (in contrast to post-Vatican attempts subsequently to give the word '*subsistere*' a heavily ontological significance) this word is used because of its suggestive power, in which the *sub* is not without its explosive significance: '*sistit sub...*'. In other words, what the New Testament envisages with its biblical mystery of the church is present in the Ecclesia Catholica under all kinds of historical veils and distortions: the mystery is present, but...! It is also present elsewhere, in other churches, but...! In this formula the uncritical, almost exclusive, identification of the mystery of the church with the Catholic Church is put aside.

The Commission's justification for refusing to accept particular amendments in this connection went like this: the church is unique, 'although ecclesial elements are also found outside it'.[16]

   In the same Council's Decree on Ecumenism it is stated not only that many ecclesial values are present 'outside the visible limits of the Catholic Church', but at the same time that this can be for our edification – Catholics can learn from it – and moreover that through the existence of different Christian churches it becomes more difficult for 'the church to express the fullness of its catholicity in all its aspects in the reality of life'.[17] The process by which 'the mystery of the church in the catholic church' becomes transparent takes place in a concrete way 'both in power and in weakness', 'in sin and in purification'.[18]

This amended last preliminary sketch was approved by 2,144 votes out of 2,189. The last possibility of improving this text or shifting it in a conservative direction by introducing *modi* or final amendments as it were at the eleventh hour (a situation in which in the last instance the official commission could decide on a free and autonomous basis whether or not it would accept the final proposals for amendments – unless a veto intervened 'from above', as had been the case with other themes), did not bring any changes (at least in connection with this theme). The text I have just analysed then in fact became the final text and thus the authentic rendering of the Dogmatic Constitution itself.

But it is interesting to note that in the last instance there were still some bishops who wanted to add further qualifications to the formula which had already been broken open ecumenically (*subsistit in*), in order to put yet more stress on the ecclesial character of the non-Catholic Christian churches.[19]

The purpose of this Dogmatic Constitution is clear: the mystery of the church of Christ, 'the community of God', as the Constitution had sketched this out in broad outline in its first chapter, is not an idealistic or unreal vision, nor a coming reality which is not in fact present in any way now. No, according to this constitution that mystery is really present in our history, in a very concrete community, in the Catholic Church, though that presents this mystery in shadows, distortions and deficiencies, and through this distortion sometimes or often makes it almost unrecognizable. However, these blemishes do not make it downright impossible for that mystery to be manifested or made transparent in this church. That was the view of Vatican II, and also the spirit of this council. The council here wanted to go a long way towards the other Christian churches without being unfaithful to the centuries-old self-understanding of the Catholic Church.

It cannot be denied that the Dogmatic Constitution on the Church stands in a notably different climate from that of Catholic church theology prior to the council. The rejection by Vatican II of the pre-conciliar draft in particular was a specific reaction against the one-sided and indeed triumphalistic accents of the encyclical *Mystici Corporis*. Here I would like to indicate three clear differences.

1. The clearly marked distinction between the church on earth and the kingdom of God is striking, though the intrinsic bond and connection between them is maintained.

2. Equally striking in comparison with pre-conciliar ecclesiology is

the carefully qualified identification of the biblical mystery of the church, the mystical body, with the Roman Catholic church (though this is formulated with almost prudish care). But this conciliar declaration implies (though this is said only in a minor key) that the same biblical mystery of the church, albeit under yet another veil and distortion than the empirical distortions within the Catholic church, is also present in other Christian churches in a varied way.

3. Finally, it emerges from the whole of this Dogmatic Constitution on the Church, although it is not said in so many words, that this Constitution accepts a distinction between the church as a 'saving institution', and the church 'as the fruit of divine redemption', in other words between the institutional element in the church and the eschatological community of faith and grace, although this distinction remains inadequate.[20]

In Chapter 2 of this Constitution, which deals with the people of God, it is said of this people of God: 'All those, who in faith look towards Jesus, the author of salvation and the principle of unity and peace, God has gathered together and established as the church, that it may be for each and everyone the visible sacrament of this saving unity.'[21]

## B. 'Ecclesia sancta' *(one, holy, catholic and apostolic)*, 'sed semper purificanda'

According to the bibical admonition, 'judgment begins at the house of God', in Israel and the church (I Peter 4.17-18). Therefore Vatican II took over the Reformation concern for the *Ecclesia semper reformanda* almost literally, *Ecclesia semper purificanda*.[22] For of the church on the way, the mystery of which is described in the first chapter of *Lumen Gentium*, the same council says: 'Advancing through trials and tribulations the church is comforted (in the biblical sense, strengthened) by God's grace, promised to her by the Lord so that she may not waver from perfect fidelity, but remain the worthy bride of the Lord, ceaselessly renewing herself through the action of the Holy Spirit until, through the cross, she may attain to that light which knows no setting.'[23] The conquest of weakness takes place only 'through the power of Christ and love'.[24] Here in its own way the council is accepting a Reformation view when it says that the church is *sancta simul et purificanda*: it is holy, but must constantly be purified; it must arrive at *metanoia*, repentance and renewal.[25]

This promise does not rest only on the church as a whole but on a particular, i.e. ministerial, way on ministerial service in the church,[26] especially – in both its function as proclamatory teaching – [27] of cultic and sacramental healing through presiding in prayer and sacrament[28] – and finally in its function of pastoral guidance.[29]

However, given that the biblical admonition constantly to renew oneself in the Spirit in the weakness of the flesh is addressed to the people of God as a whole, even before there is any mention (in this Dogmatic Constitution) of the functional or ministerial or official differences between believers and ministers, both the hierarchy and believers stand under the constant admonition to incessant renewal and a Christian 'return to the sources'.

From this it may be concluded that the church as the community of salvation and as a saving institution stands under the powerful promise of the Lord, who will not tolerate its becoming unfaithful. Nevertheless this church must constantly renew itself in the power of the Spirit.

The synchronic affirmation of the *Ecclesia indefectibilis* (i.e. a church which cannot fall away from its basic inspiration or cannot come loose from its original roots) and the *Ecclesia semper purificanda* (the church which must always purify itself) poses serious and delicate problems. Precisely on the basis of the support promised it by the Lord, 'The gates of hell shall not prevail against it' (Matt.16.18), and thus on the basis of the Lord's powerful promise, the firm stand of the church on its indefectibility takes the historical form of a constantly renewed *metanoia*, renewal and self-correction. It already emerges from this that this is an indefectibility not in triumphalism, but in weakness in which God's grace triumphs. This implies that there is no indefectibility *despite* weakness, i.e. automatic indefectibility, but in and through constant renewal in faith, hope and love.

The indefectibility of the church is therefore not a static, as it were fixed, essentialist property of the church which could by-pass the constantly precarious, existential faith of the church in obedience to God's promise. The promised indefectibility becomes effective only in the faith, trust and constant self-correction of the church. The term 'divine guarantee' does not fit in with this. It is at least misleading, though it can be used as an extrapolation of the overwhelming power of grace into the juridical sphere, grace so powerful that it is at work *in* the reponse of the church in faith. But a juridical objectification of this indefectiblity at work in faith and in believing self-correction is impossible, because the nature of the church called to life through the career of Jesus Christ implies the existential experience of the community of salvation, precisely as the fruit of redemption.

We must also see the so-called four marks of the church in this perspective. With the creed of the Council of Constantinople in 381 (often wrongly called the Nicene Creed), all Christian churches confess: 'I believe the one, holy, catholic and apostolic *ecclesia* or community of faith'. In the Second Vatican Council this is said of each local church in which, also living in community with the other local churches, the universal church is present. But we know that this unity does not exist: the Christian churches are divided. We all suffer under our own sinfulness and that of our churches. So the four marks do not describe our real churches in their historical forms, while on the other hand no church can achieve a mystical distillation of the essence 'church': churches exist only in historical forms.

This does not mean on the other hand that the four marks of the church are purely eschatological, a reality of the final kingdom. It means that all the Christian churches now already contain elements which call for this unity, particularly the church's belief in one God and one Lord, one baptism and one table. Because these four marks are present in all churches defectively and in a mediocre way, in particular or restrictive compartmentalization, they are nevertheless internal imperatives of change within all the churches: a summons really to go on the way to the final ecumenical fulfilment. The dynamic of these structural elements in all the churches does not call for this break. The gospel does not legitimize mediocrity. And the message that is proclaimed is in no way the basis for shutting oneself off in different hiding places to provide protective security from 'the other'! The four 'properties' of the church issue a summons for conversion to all Christian churches. One cannot just ask for the conversion of other Christian churches. All local and confessional churches are 'church' to the degree that they can affirm, encourage and further *communio*, communication, with other local churches.

The scandal is not that there are differences but that these differences are used as an obstacle to communion (though on the other hand people rightly do not want to make a comedy of unity; they take the differences seriously). But richly diverse unity-in-communion in no way calls for a formal, institutional and administrative unity, nor a super-church. Even for the Roman Catholic church the four 'properties' confessed are not a description of the specific form of the church but an imperative for it, as they are for other churches. The ecumene is not a private annexation of the gospel by any confessional church, but the 'self-dispossession' of each and every Christian church. Although there is historical plurality as a system of exclusion, there is also multiplicity which need not arouse opposition and can be experienced within communion and mutual recognition. Difference is positive only within communion with the other: in respect of the other who is other and yet not alien to us.

There can be no authentic ecumene without the attempt to understand and experience the plurality of churches theologically: we must be able to experience and understand it... in mutual difference. There is no eternally valid model of unity to which all churches must convert themselves. We need all Christian churches for the ecumene as the true church of Jesus, the Christ. All Christians must strive for a unity the model for which does not fully exist in any single church. Unity is future for all the Christian churches, not a return to any old situation. Moreover there is no community without internal conflicts except in utopia (i.e. nowhere, except in wishful thinking) and eschatologically, in heaven. But this final consummation judges our present by the human and Christian revolt against the unredeemed present of the churches and the world.

## III   The so-called 'classical' face of the church and the other face (with a more biblical profile)

In this connection, at present there is not only an ecumenical standstill and polarization between the churches but also malaise and polarization within the Roman Catholic church.

### A. *The church as a pyramidal hierarchy*

In the Neoplatonic-hierarchical conception of the church, the church forms a pyramid, a multi-stage system: God, Christ, the Pope, the bishops, priests and deacons; below these the religious and then the 'laity': first the men and finally the women and children. This picture of the church developed in the second half of the first millennium and from the eleventh century led to an intensive centralization of ecclesiastical power in Rome. After Trent this picture of the church took on juridical features, above all in the works of the Jesuit Bellarmine and the Dominican Torquemada. Afterwards it was accepted everywhere, and since the nineteenth century has been further strengthened in the struggle against the modern world. The church was described as a community organized around the Pope of Rome, whose prefects are the bishops in every diocese, while the priests are the local representatives of these prefects to look after the flock, far away in the field.

The ideological legitimation of this picture of the church is based on two foundations: 1. the predominance of a christology which forgot the blowing of the Spirit over the lowermost levels of the church and in practice annexed the role of the Holy Spirit through the minsterial succession exclusively for the hierarchy; and 2. the social significance of papal infallibility. In this view the Pope becomes the 'representative of Christ' in this world, just as the governors were the representatives of the Roman emperor in distant places. So the gift of the Holy Spirit was reduced to obedience at a lower level, that of the believers, to what was said or decided at the top of the hierarchy. This picture of the church completely excluded believers from the level on which decisions were made. The laity, above all the women, in it are no longer subjects, those who carry on and make church history; they become the objects of the priestly, hierarchical and male proclamation and pastorate.

The ominous element in all this is above all the practical shift in the authority that particular papal acts could have in legally controlled, well-defined circumstances, to the person of the Pope himself, who is then said to be infallible as a person. It is then said that the Pope is personally infallible – which from a Roman Catholic perspective is a heresy, though one of the few heresies which has never been condemned from the official side. Particular papal or conciliar decisions taken in the name of the whole church community at the level of challenges which are vital for the gospel faith can indeed be 'infallible', i.e. in a more or less happy way they nevertheless give historical expression to Christian truth. For Christians, this bears witness to the support of the Holy Spirit, which safeguards the unabbreviated gospel; but it does not elevate the person of the Pope. The person of the Pope here remains what he is: a personality who may be brilliant or mediocre, democratic or authoritarian.

Even to move from this infallibility circumscribed by the law of the church to the person of the Pope in fact robs all the other institutional authorities in the church, both the bishops and the community of faith, of their original Christian authority and authenticity. A personality cult of the Pope as a consequence of this mysticism of infallibility overlooks the fact that the Peter function or the Petrine function of providing unity or communication involves only one office in the church, and is thus one ministerial service among many other ministries in the church.

*B. The intensification of the hierarchical character of the church: its anti-democratic face between the French Revolution and the period before Vatican II*

For a century and a half, the church hierarchy and its official theology fiercely rejected the fundamental inspiration of bourgeois religion. We could describe this situation as follows: the First Vatican Council was a church gathering of a feudal hierarchy which had survived into the modern world, while the Second Vatican Council was a church gathering within the horizons of the bourgeois world, a council in which the Roman Catholic church caught up on its social and cultural backwardness in terms of bourgeois freedom, though it did this (and here is a historical irony) at a moment when the Western world was beginning to become highly critical of the social and political shadow sides of the bourgeois liberal approach.

Although this same church had still rejected the protest of the Jansenists against the rise of self-conscious modernity as an anachronism in the seventeenth and eighteenth centuries (and as a result got in difficulties with the letter of its centuries-old Augustinian Western past), after the French Revolution it became the tardy but resolute champion of anti-modern feudal ideas, which it then began stubbornly to maintain almost as a truth of faith precisely at the point where positions were involved which ran directly counter to the basic bourgeois principles of what was now called 'modernity'.

Against the 'bourgeois Christ' revered by Enlightenment believers, who in modern society from now was extending his rule only in the inner meaning he was given by believers (religion is a private affair) and in a view of the church according to which the church had to make itself functionally true if it was to have any credibility, the official church set the all-embracing 'supreme Imperium of Christ', under whose sphere of power the whole human race comes.[30] We can see this in connection with the devotion to the Sacred Heart: while it grew up from the grass roots, it was only approved by Clement III in 1765, when this devotion fitted the papal church politics of the time and was seen by the church hierarchy as an instrument against the Enlightenment. Subsequently it came to an institutional climax when Pope Leo XIII dedicated the world to the Sacred Heart.

According to all the Popes who were against the Enlightenment, the rule of Christ over all the world is put in the hands of the church hierarchy to the exclusion of anyone else, even the people of God. This was a reaction by the hierarchy against the Enlightenment position of 'the will of the people'. Moroever, when this will of the people welcomed by the bourgeois did not remain bound to the ordinances of the church hierarchy and natural law (which legally were interpreted by this same hierarchy), then according to Pius IX, nothing could flow from this but 'the unrestrained covetousness of the soul, which serves its own lusts and advantages'.[31] The saving action of God proclaimed by the church cannot be limited to a sub-system of the great bourgeois society, as the bourgeois saw it. For, Pius IX argues, in that case the spheres of science and legislation, declared to be autonomous, would in principle be withdrawn from the so-called particular religious competence of the Roman Catholic hierarchy, which represents the all-embracing rule of Christ over all the world. Therefore this Pope sharply condemned the assertion that 'the science of philosophical and moral matters, like the bourgeois laws, should be able to, indeed should have to, deviate from divine and church authority'.[32]

The bourgeois idea of the social contract is also rejected. In other words, only that social form is legitimate which on rational grounds does justice to the needs of all individuals, who have equal rights. For his part a subsequent Pope, Pius X, said on the same lines against the modernists that the church did not come into being out of a need to communicate to believers and that its church order and official structure is similarly not derived from the development of social structures. The church emerges directly from the will of Christ in such a way that the form which it has received from its divine founder cannot be changed even by the Pope.[33]

According to this church-hierarchical view, being the church cannot be reconciled with the modern history of freedom and with its process of democratization. In this connection the church reaction to the notorious 'Bismarck Letter' of 14 May 1872 is very interesting because within one and the same feudal and hierarchical view, it nevertheless displays differences of accent between the German Catholic episcopate and the narrower Vatican view. In his circular letter Bismarck, who, prompted by the forthcoming papal election, had addressed the ambassadors of the German Empire to the foreign great powers, attacked the Pope in connection with the declaration of infallibility and above all the claim to absolute leadership associated with it. This address demonstrates that the bishops of the local churches must inevitably function as pawns of the Pope. This in turn implies that in the eyes of other governments, bishops are really officials of an alien sovereign, a strange sovereign who, moreover, is alone among modern sovereign states, in regarding himself as absolute ruler.

Defending Rome, the German bishops rejected this intervention of Bismarck's. Here above all the reasoning of these bishops is important. Against Bismarck's charge that the Pope is setting himself up as an absolutist monarch, it is specifically said: 'The Pope is subject to divine right and is bound by the commands given by Christ to his church';[34] he is 'bound by the content of Holy Scripture to the tradition and to the official decisions already taken'.[35] The tone of this episcopal reaction is different from that of the Vatican documents. Apart from the First Vatican Council, which in fact associates the infallibility of quite particular papal statements with the indefectibility of the whole church and thus with the belief of the people of God, and therefore does not make this infallibility independent of, or detach it from, 'the faith of all the church', the papal anti-Enlightenment documents nowhere put any stress on it. They even constantly kept quiet about this fundamentally anti-authoritarian fact (until above all Vatican II began to lay stress on it). The letter of the German bishops deliberately stresses that the Pope cannot even promulgate dogmas as he wills.[36] Rome puts the stress on the obedience of all to the Pope, while the German episcopate, not denying this authority, emphasizes the way in which the Pope is bound by scripture and its biblical exposition in the tradition of the church.

From this position of the German bishops and the papal approval of it, it becomes clearer that Vatican I in no way had any intention of bestowing any absolute power on the Pope. To the extent that Vatican I associates papal infallibility with the indefectibility with which 'the divine redeemer wanted to equip his church in the definition of faith and morals',[37] the Constitution on the Church in Vatican I at the same time recognizes that God's saving action in Jesus Christ is not at work simply as the invisible action of grace, but also in the visible forms of the historical government of the church. From this the church hierarchy drew the conclusion, which was to have major historical consequences, that according to Vatican I the Pope is subject to no one's judgment. That is even the main tenor of the dogmatic declaration by this nineteenth-century council. This lack of any demand for a degree of control over the church hierarchy, over the so-called 'holy rule' of the church, was an utter scandal to every conscious human being, including Christians. In contemporary democratic bourgeois society there was no longer room for this.

Alongside the contrast between modern democracy and church hierarchy at that time, there was also the contrast between bourgeois belief in progress and the Catholic Church. In the bourgeois world there developed the idea of the historicity of human beings and belief in the historical progress of humankind. At this time 'the citizen' was the 'new man', *homo novus*. But for the church hierarchy this new man was the 'old Adam', the sinner who has 'secularized' himself, i.e. removed and emancipated himself from divine authority – in concrete terms, that of the church hierarchy. According to the church of the time that was a damnable, sinful pretention. In his social encyclical Leo XIII consistently calls the value-creating work so lauded by the bourgeois a necessary penance: a burden and suffering only for the sustenance of life.[38]

The church hierarchy did not call socialized individuals, as the bourgeois world saw them, the germ of society, but the pre-industrial family of the Ancien Régime. Apart from the many ignominious atrocities perpetrated during the French Revolution, which Kant (who in no way concealed his sympathies for this Revolution) castigated severely, on the other hand the church's condemnation of all the good that the Revolution has brought our society and those valuable achievements of bourgeois society that we still continue to praise (as did also Vatican II) is still documented most strongly at the end of the *Syllabus*. Here the position is condemned which claims that 'the Roman Pontifex can and must come to terms with progress, with liberalism and the new bourgeois world'.[39] Over against all progress, evolution or development, the revealed dogmas are presented as 'truths fallen from heaven'.[40] As a result of this the use of the ideological-critical method in exegesis and theology was put in a bad light and in fact condemned. In its turn, the church authority cannot be legitimately judged or condemned by anyone. That authority is immune, because it shares in God's authority. So says the church.

Another (and in my view perhaps the only decisive) point of dispute between the bourgeois world and ministerial authority in the church (the other issues in dispute can be solved more flexibly by both parties) is the contrast between the Enlightenment concept of truth and the non-historical concept of truth held by the church hierarchy.

First of all, we must note that at this point the official theology of the church has taken over some fundamental elements of the Enlightenment (which are even older than the Enlightenment): the interest and importance of 'natural reason', human freedom of choice, and finally the natural knowledge of God (this last really means that in the question of God every rational person has the right to a say, since the matter relates to his or own human nature, although that was perhaps in no way the main intent of Vatican I). Apart from these insights which were endorsed by the church hierarchy, even if they did derive from the Enlightenment, that authority nevertheless withdrew all truth from time and space, eternalized it in an abstract way and put it beyond any time or any place,[41] here clearly taking the side of the folk church which had not come of age, which did not want anything to do with what is now called 'responsible Christianity'.

In the context of this belief of the folk church it is evident that the official church will automatically reject the assertion that 'the truth is not unchanging, any more than man himself, because it develops with this man, in this man and through this man'.[42] Thus Pius XII interprets the truth which knows no history. According to his reasoning, change-able history must direct itself by the truth as this has been revealed in Jesus Christ and handed on to the church through the Holy Spirit. This truth does not in any way have to satisfy the present needs of men and women and thus adapt itself to modern language.[43] This hierarchical view goes so far that one might claim that the truth can be found only in the linguistic form of Scholastic metaphysics as an objective expression of the will of God. History is thus removed from the meaning which human beings seek to give it as historical subjects. The whole human mediation, in which human beings are subjects in their own history, with much determinism and chance, falls away, and here God becomes as it were the direct subject of history.[44] I concede that this document of Pius XII pays homage to God as the subject of history, but it cannot be denied that the way in which this Pope puts it deprives men and women of their awakened consciousness of bourgeois freedom.

In a quotation from Gregory XVI, at one point Pope Pius IX could even incomprehensibly say: 'From this repulsive source of indifferentism springs the absurd and foolish claim or, more exactly, the folly that every man should have freedom of conscience and should be able to demand it. The way to this pernicious delusion has been prepared for by the demand for complete and unlimited freedom of opinion which seeks to go on to the annihilation of the holy and the revealed.'[45] In later editions of church documents this papal document (which in fact had said precisely the opposite to Vatican II) was gently pushed aside, scrapped from Denzinger,[46] as though no one might know that the official church had ever made such a statement which passes all human understanding.

The first statements of the church in which a Pope spoke with any sympathy about a democratic state were made by Pius XII on Christmas Eve 1944, at the end of the Second World War.[47] In his address he condemned state absolutism, which is still carefully distinguished from 'absolute monarchy' ('though I do not want to talk about this now,' the Pope added). But the date of this statement coincides with the fall of Nazism and Fascism. Had it been made some years earlier, the comments about a democratic state would have sounded more credible. At that time they were interpreted on all sides as church-political, ecclesiocentric opportunism. In 1945 the choice of bourgeois democracy was at the same time a matter of the church opting for the Western camp against Communism. Bourgeois democracy was, moreover, not taken on its merits, but as a new weapon against Communist countries. Finally, it remained a piece of self-defence on the part of the church. That becomes all the more clear from the fact that the hierarchy does not tolerate any form of democracy in its own church circles. It is an option against the people. Only gradually, under subsequent Popes, would the civil ambiguity of the hierarchical preference for democracy in the world disappear. Therefore the abiding opposition to democratic claims and the co-responsibility of the 'people of God' for decisions by the church authorities which are important for all the church is all the more incomprehensible – or all too comprehensible!

Historically, it is impossible to deny that the church had reluctantly resigned itself to the modern division between church and state, and later for the most part limited what from its hierarchical perspective appeared as detrimental consequences, by the concluding of concordats.

In church politics the correct affirmation of faith, i.e. that faith must penetrate the whole of human life, including social life, was at that time (in a right-wing political perspective) taken to mean that the church as an institution must have a place in all sectors of social life. An encyclical issued at the inauguration of the Feast of Christ the King completely typifies the attitude of the church in its century-and-a-half-long struggle against the new achievements of bourgeois liberalism.

The rise of Catholic Action, too, was not so much, or not primarily, meant as a promotion of the lay apostolate or an emancipation of the laity, but was also intended to give the church hierarchy, which in a liberal society was thenceforward swept out of public view, new importance in all sectors of society through the laity. Actually, for this the laity were given a 'mandate' by the church hierarchy, a kind of 'canonical mission'. This suggests that the issue was the power of the hierarchy: because of the liberal neutralization of the church hierarchy, Catholic laity might then share in this power, in order to compensate for the hierarchy's loss. For as a result of the division of church and state, the social power of the church hierarchy was indeed crippled, by contrast with its historically powerful past.

Anyone who compares these facts, given official church documentation by the authoritative documents of what is called the 'Pius tradition' – Pius IX, Pius X, Pius XI and Pius XII – and with them the century and a half of official church opposition to the good achievements of bourgeois liberalism (leaving aside the violence and force that the French Revolution brought on Europe, which are in no way to be trivialized), with texts from Vatican II about freedom of conscience, freedom of religion, belief in progress, tolerance and human rights, humanism and a far-reaching universalism of salvation, above all after a century of church Augustinianism, a kind of Thomistic acceptance of the worldliness of the world and its own autonomy in many domains, and so on, has to concede that the Second Vatican Council accepted bourgeois values with open arms as achievements of the French Revolution (in retrospect, at some points rather naively), after having opposed them for a century and a half with solemn fulminations. In retrospect we can also understand how in the century and a half of church opposition to anything that was called new and 'modern', the modern world has sometimes angrily, sometimes gently but firmly, turned its back on this church which had written high on its banner the fight against the modern world and against the conscious self-understanding of modern man. The anti-modern church could have made other criticisms of the 'modern bourgeois world' – criticisms of eighteenth- and ninetenth-century bourgeois liberalism which above all after Vatican II the world itself began to make with great seriousness and skill. From this prehistory we can equally understand the drama of a Mgr Marcel Lefebvre, who in fact has stubbornly continued to subscribe to all these conceptions of the anti-bourgeois Roman Catholic hierarchy, from Leo XIII up to and including Pius XII, even after the shift at Vatican II, which for all its compromises was nevertheless a radical one, distancing the church from what had gone before.

We must therefore unmistakably place the Roman Catholic Church's break with its feudal past in the period between 1962 and 1965: the time of Vatican II, though this was the official church expression of what had long been felt among many Catholics and their theological spokesmen. In this sense the Second Vatican Council (for many theologians who are critical of culture and society this is perhaps a somewhat compromising remark) is a belated triumph of liberal theology: it was, in fact, a liberal council. Given the anti-liberal cast of the Catholic Church we needed such a council. Vatican II in the church was the breakthrough of the achievements of the French Revolution, taking place 150 years later. And at that time quite different problems were on the agenda! In my view, for both the right and left wings, that is the drama of the great phenomenon of the Second Vatican Concil. Above all in the Pastoral Constitution *Gaudium et Spes* there are in fact formulae which recall the battle-cry of the French Revolution, 'Liberté, Égalité et Fraternité'. We must not forget that bishops (who took part in this council), along with their theological advisors, on the basis of their pastoral practice and the questions with which they were concerned, saw no salvation in the abstract, anti-modern attitude of the Vatican hierarchy. For them it was a remote scene. The questions and concerns above all of those who are called 'mission bishops' (at that time a not inconsiderable part of the world episcopate) ran quite counter to the pre-conciliar draft texts, which were still feudal and hierarchical.

But after this council, the non-feudal insights which were finally gained and approved by the council in turn came to clash with contemporary criticisms of society and ideology and later with the people's theology of the liberation theologians from various continents. Vatican II was a catching-up manoeuvre of the church which came too late (in relation to what was happening in the world). By that time the developed and critical consciousness of the world and general human consciousness had already moved on much further than the late feudal dreams that the church still cherished.

I shall go on to demonstrate that this catching-up manoeuvre on modern secular achievements, earlier disputed by the church but now enthusiatically welcomed by this council (Vatican II), i.e. the acceptance by Vatican II of the history of human freedom and its relative autonomy, causes more problems than it solves within the phenomenon of the 'church'.

## C. New post-Vatican perspectives inspired by the 'liberal' Second Vatican Council

The Second Vatican Council showed another face of the church; at least in theory it heavily corrected the previous image of the church. Sadly enough, it still did not give this new image of the church any institutional and canonical protection, but according to the wish of John XXIII here provided for a future revision of the church Codex (a revision which was indeed made, much later, but which in some fundamental points is unfaithful to the basic intuitions of Vatican II). Even before mentioning church ministries, this council defined the church as the people called together by God. In it all believers are equal, believing subjects of equal worth 'living from the Spirit', free children of God.

Only after talking about the people of God on the way to final consummation does this council speak of particular elements which give organic structure to the church or the people of God. Thus the powers of the church ministry are not put outside the church community or the people of God. The differentiations in ministry which are made in this structuring do not affect the rights of the people of God as the subjects of being-the-church. All ministers are there for that people, as a service. That these ministries, too, are also a special charisma of the Spirit does not say anything about the concrete institutional regulation of them or the possibility of the control of believers over the ministers of the church.

The way in which the church in fact organizes the ministries rules out, or at least makes very difficult, a basis for the free play of the Holy Spirit among lay believers which is safeguarded by the institution. That the ministry is a charisma of the Holy Spirit, moreover, tells us nothing about how the ministers must be appointed. 'What affects all is also a matter for all' was the old church and papal adage in these matters.

In its character as compromise, even Vatican II sometimes still points towards the pyramidal view of the church, albeit unintentionally. The Council first defines the right and duty of all believers also to be responsible for the church as *christifideles*, but from a later chapter (4) of *Lumen Gentium* it emerges that in practice a 'predetermined harmony' is postulated between the 'believed faith of the whole church community' and what the hierarchy proclaims and formulates as faith and policy, while believers are not involved in either the expression of the faith or the government of the church. The argument is that on the basis of the will of Christ there can be no opposition between what is present as the content of faith in the life of a church community and what the Pope or the hierarchy proposes. For – the argument goes – the object of the life of the people of God is the 'revealed mystery' and the object of proclamation, worship and government by the hierarchy is that same mystery, while the limits of the hierarchical authorities are the limits of revelation. So there is a smooth equilibrium, a postivistically postulated harmony (as it were a pre-established harmony, to take over a term from the philosopher Leibniz) between the life of believers and the teaching of the church hierarchy.

This idyll of internal harmony has ominous consequences for the institution. For as a result of it any actual conflict between believers and hierarchy, and any conflict between a local church community and the top of the church, is assigned to the order of sinfulness: disobedience on the part of the underlings. The conflict is thought soluble by the hierarchy, which, sometimes to the point of arrogance, appeals to the believers for obedience. This actual practice of not a few bishops identifies the mystery of the church as it were adequately with a structure of authority and obedience within the church, and is silent about the fact that church history has never been such a harmonious idyll of authority which is always right, and believers who must simply obey.

In this view, the actual history of conflicts is then seen *a priori* as the fruit of sin, in such a way that any conflict within this logic is resolved in favour of the stronger, i.e. hierarchical, position, and declared by this powerful side to be sin on the part of the grass roots. And the above all psychological consequence (of this theologically incorrect view) conjures up feelings of both helplessness or nothingness and disappointment, opposition and sometimes even antipathy. The 'laity', too, sense that there can be conflicts which have nothing to do with sinfulness but derive from differences of insight and assessment of salvation history, for example the pastoral interest of the people and the specific interests of the hierarchical organs. And in practice this viewpoint is neglected. This declaration that any conflict in the church is either non-existent or sinful puts the hierarchy in an immune or storm-free zone. The church is in fact seen as a *societas perfecta*,[48] the perfected kingdom of God under the direction of Christ's representative, while on the side of believers only loyal obedience is appropriate. To the degree that the church is faithful, in this view, moreover, it has no real history. Any actual conflicts that there ever were and still are are simply declared to be a history of the human sinfulness of believers.

It is precisely because of this view, which is not just a view but in many dioceses a practice of the hierarchy, that many believers suffer over their church. All over the world, and not just in the church province of the Netherlands, it seems clear, as has become evident after the so-called 'Cologne Declaration of Theologians', that many people are suffering for the faith: Catholics and also fellow-Christians who are sympathetic to the Roman Catholic Church. When hierarchy and believers sometimes go divergent ways, the leadership often forgets that these believers usually do so out of deep concern for the gospel, and for the sake of the church. And although we are all sinful men and women, it is a cheap joke within the ideological logic of this pyramidal picture of the church in conflicts to divide believers bluntly, and ecclesiologically incorrectly, into orthodox and freethinking. If the church hierarchy is fallible in most of its actions and nevertheless in the power of the Spirit, through ups and downs, keeps the church community firmly on a gospel course, and if, as a help in this, in some exceptional cases it can also prove 'infallible' (here, of course, showing an infallibility which, even according to the First Vatican Council, is merely the critical reflection of the firmness of the course of the whole of the church's community of faith), why, according to this picture of the church laid down by the council, should the right *a priori* lie with Pope and bishops? Even according to the spirit of the First Vatican Council, there is also something like the obedience in faith of the hierarchy to the faith of the people of God, to which John Henry Newman already drew our attention.[49]

The co-responsibility of all believers for the church on the basis of our baptism in water and the Spirit essentially includes the participation of all believers in decisions relating to church government (however this may be organized in practice). Vatican II also gave at least some institutional encouragement towards making this universal participation possible: the Roman synods, the national councils, the episcopal conferences, the councils of priests, the diocesan and parish councils of lay believers and the frameworks of many Catholic organizations. But when these institutions bore their varied fruit in practice, they were undermined from above and tamed. Moreover, most administrative decrees after the Second Vatican Council predominantly followed just one line of this council, so that the effectiveness of the other line in that same council (precisely the line which was refreshingly new) does not get any institutional support and therefore – on the basis of the law of the tension between charisma and institution – is doomed for the moment to disappear from the life of the church. One cannot in fact honestly speak of the equality of all in the church (Gal.3.28) if one does not specify, or provide institutional safeguards for, the forms which follow from this equality.

*D. Stemming the tide of the breakthrough at Vatican II, subsequently
legitimated by an ideological appeal to the term 'church as mystery'*

In recent times, use, but above all much misuse, has been made of
the deep insight that the church is a 'mystery'.[50] This misuse is supported
by a tenacious, dualistic misunderstanding.

It is obvious to all of us that the church of Jesus Christ, like any
other community, never lives in a socio-historical and political-cultural
vacuum. The community of the 'church' is either opposed to that world
environment around it or, whether for evangelical and pastoral or from
ideological motives, critically or uncritically accepts it. So in the course
of time it has taken on many faces. In its historical manifestations it has
sometimes shown very attractive and often not very sympathetic aspects,
sometimes bleak and at other times non-committal or neutral. Sometimes there was nothing in the church to feel warm about or to overwhelm
one; believers then speak of a 'lukewarm' church, as the book of
Revelation already says to the church of Laodicea: 'I know your deeds,
you are neither cold nor hot. Would that you were either cold or hot!'
(Rev.3.15). There were also times when we cannot regard the empirical
churches in their local or even their world-wide setting as having been
other than sinful, sinful above all through neglect, while their saints,
those who continued to be faithful to the gospel, at the same time led a
hidden life or underwent a martyr death.

Precisely because the concrete church is a reality which can be discussed
from many standpoints, a certain ecclesiology often proves to be alien
to reality. Many people already have a spontaneous experience of
communities in general. These can also be analysed scientifically in
more specific terms. So among other things the sociology of knowledge
has shown *how* structures of authority come into being in a community
and *why* they arise, and thus how the particular experiential wisdom of
which a particular culture is the real vehicle in the long run nevertheless
develops towards the specialization and protection (through individuals
from the community) of its own values and views which are close to the
heart of all.[51]

The specialized subject of authority in a particular cultural tradition
of experience, and thus the specialized subject of this protection, defence
and exposition of particular popular values and wisdom, can sometimes
coincide. But on the basis of the content of the specific direction of the
two, through social differentiation and the distribution of tasks the
manifold interests of this particular cultural tradition will ultimately be
encouraged within this community by various authorities. All this can
be analysed in sociological terms and also tested historically, and in this

way one can also trace the sociologial rules of developments and conflicts between different instances within a cultural community.

All this equally applies to religious communities of faith, including the church as a society which in the religious language of faith is called a 'community of God'. Moreover it will also be necessary to speak in a 'second discourse', namely in the religious language of faith, about the same secular religious and social reality. What is described in human experiential terms and sociologically analysed must ultimately also be expressed in the language of faith. This means that the religious language of faith becomes empty and meaningless unless it contains a recognizable reference to real human experiences and the autonomous structures implied in them. On the other hand, talk in the language of faith about a social, empirically accessible reality such as the church is not in fact a superfluous luxury nor (at least in itself) ideological talk about an event which could already be understood adequately on a purely secular basis. The saving revelation of God, offered to us through and in the Christian experiential tradition of the church community of faith, is indeed a grace, but a grace mediated through and in the structure of historical experiences. Anyone who forgets that begins for example to split up the mystery of the church as it were gnostically and dualistically into a 'heavenly part' (which then, in this hypothesis, falls outside all sociological approaches and ideological criticism) and an earthly part, about which (in the same hypothesis) evidently all the bad things may be said. By contrast, Vatican II says: 'The earthly Church and the Church endowed with heavenly riches are not to be thought of as two realities.'[52]

There is also an extremely urgent need to investigate these historical mediations of the grace of God scientifically (with the help of the humane, behavioural and semiotic sciences), above all at a time which (in all religions) is tending towards religious fundamentalism, dualism and flight from its own insecurity and ignorance into the arms of a guru or self-assured and omniscient leader.

However, if anywhere in theology there is any question of pseudo-problems piling up, then it is precisely in the field of the relationship to all these cases in which human reality and the reality of grace – like, for example, freedom and grace; emancipatory self-liberation and Christian redemption; the humanity and divinity of Jesus – are set side by side and alongside each other as two different realities which on this presupposition must subsequently be reconciled dialectically by all kinds of theological devices. Above all we have here the pseudo-problem that one and the same reality which can be discussed in different languages (e.g. scientific and religious) is wrongly regarded as two different opposed or parallel realities. This is to overlook the fact that this one reality, because of its riches, is fully accessible (and then still in a limited human way) only from two (or more) different perspectives, questions and language games.

Anyone who loses sight of the different perspectives either has grace working only where men and women cease to have active responsibility and then calls that the area of 'mystery' or passes over the reality that one can receive God's grace in very different ways, even to the point of actually rejecting this grace to which reference is made. Creation and redemption, christology and ecclesiology, are then proclaimed at the expense of autonomous human and historical experience and reality. Instead of grace in the structure of historically mediating human experiences and praxis, we then get a stereophony of laborious human activity on the one hand and blessings direct from heaven on the other. These latter are then called the real mystery, which can no longer be approached in scientific terms. However, the real mystery lies in the human reality itself, as a mystery of justice or faithfulness to the grace in human acts of government and decision, and as a mystery of injustice where the government and decisions leave aside the mediating organs of the Holy Spirit or interpret them in terms of their own interests.

However, what in fact stands directly over against this is, for example, human freedom *as thought* and grace *as thought*. In other words, at the level of the concepts and their linguistic expression both terms – human freedom and divine grace – are indeed thought of as being next to and alongside each other, but in truth they are one and the same thing, a text to be deciphered in different language games. God and the creature can never be added together or written on one line or captured in one proposition. Where this happens nevertheless, two language games are being jumbled up and the ace of trumps is thrown on to the board in the middle of a chess game, on the assumption that the game can be won with this card. This is often literally the case when particular bishops make an immunizing reference to the 'mystery of the church' as opposed to what social and behavioural scientists say about this same church.

The language of faith and empirical, descriptive language always relate to one and the same reality, so we do not have to reconcile two competing realities, however dialectically. There is fidelity and infidelity to grace, half-hearted trust and half-trust, good will and barely good will, or just mistrust – in many shades. Here, too, *'sancta, sed semper purificanda'* holds.

The charge that is often heard from particular episcopal and some-times also theological quarters of the Christian churches, namely that contemporary theologians go too much in their teachings by human sciences and so (the dualism is already betrayed by this 'so') think too horizontally and thus overlook the 'vertical' mystery of the church in fact goes back either to a dualistic and supranaturalistic or a fideistic view of religious realities. It bears witness to a kind of religious positivism which, either out of anxiety or short-sightedness, gives itself immunity from scientific clarification, ideological criticism or theological hermeneutics by referring to 'mystery'. In other words, it is a form of fundamentalism which is spreading everywhere at present, even in the Catholic Church, which has always thought that this is an erroneous characteristic of some Protestantism.

The church community as mystery cannot be found behind or above concrete, visible reality. The church community is to be found *in* this reality which can be demonstrated here and now. We too, along with everyone in the base communities, are part of this living mystery. What happens in these communities is at the same time part of what we call the mystery of the church. The experiments and explorations, the mistakes and perhaps even follies and the finding, are parts of the phenomenon of the one great Catholica, which is found precisely as Catholica, here and now, in greater or lesser degrees of density in many Christian communities of faith, more watered down or more strongly concentrated. It is to be found in the meetings of base communities, of some house communities, of men and women, who come together in the name of Jesus, confessed by them as the Christ. Among them are many people who suffer from and over the present-day world and their own church and oppose the suffering which God does not will. They too are part of the mystery of the church, they too celebrate and bear witness to that mystery, and they do not allow themselves to be banned from this mystery by a church government with a short-sighted policy.

Together, these men and women of God are a real and true segment of the 'people of God' – an honorific title which was given by the Second Vatican Council to 'the Catholica': *subsistit in!* We too, along with all those in the base communities, are contained in this (= *subsistit in*), even when for reasons of church politics (for this is what they are – nothing to do with the gospel and theology) bishops do not want to enter into dialogue with what for them are nuisances at the grass roots. We too are nevertheless part of 'the mystery of the church', *sancta et semper purificanda.*

## 2. Democratic government of the church through its ministers

### Introduction

At the end of my short analysis of the century and a half of narrow anti-bourgeois opposition from the hierarchical church I said that Vatican II had left all kinds of questions unanswered with the cessation of this opposition. For we cannot introduce the bourgeois values achieved into the heart of the church while in theory and practice the church continues to appeal to its feudal and hierarchical structure of authority.

We can say that a church which obscures its own truth, especially the liberating freedom of Jesus Christ, through the form of its authoritarian and hierarchical mediation, becomes an unattractive and abstract institution for believers. Moreover we see that the basis of the salvation-bringing attitude of faith among believers, day by day, is less and less the teaching authority of the church. The truth that the church has to cherish - God's eternal self-revelation in the historical form of the dead but risen Lord, Jesus Christ – itself lies embedded in a concrete historical form of proclamation and institutionalization. This implies a question of trust, mistrust or negligent nonchalance to the advances of grace. Today this raises the question what form both theological argumentation and the church's decisions on teaching and authority must take in order to be capable of reconciliation with the possibility of truth for believers in a modern world.

### I   Speaking with authority and letting oneself be told: the subjection of the whole church to the Word of God

Any human speaking with authority is in the first instance a matter of letting oneself to be told, i.e. putting oneself under authority in speaking. That is the rule for any humanly meaningful talk. No one, however highly placed, however professionally qualified, is immediately a master of his or her own language. To start with: in speaking we use language, a language which we have not invented but which is there already. Moreover everyone comes into the world in an environment in which the story of humankind, the religious and Christian story, has already long been going the rounds. Human beings can only take up the thread of the story that has been handed down and at best add a meaningful chapter to it. Language and story – the context in which men and women really live – thus have a structural priority over any speaker. Individuals do not have authority of their own to speak, since before men and women speak, even if they are put in authority, they are already spoken to. And behind or rather with all language and story there is the mystery of the reality which we have not devised but which is offered to us.

This to some degree Heideggerian dialectic of being spoken to and paying heed, of attentive listening and reactive answering so that one can oneself speak meaningfully and with authority, may be true and correct; however, it is not as innocent as it seems. It is a half-truth and therefore always a dangerous and threatening partial truth. It ignores another somewhat hidden dialectic. For language can be misused ideologically and even work as a power structure (cf. Chapter 1 above, where this is analysed). The story that is handed down (including the Christian story) underwent all kinds of distortions in the course of time, sometimes unconscious, and thus works as a power structure.

Experiences, including the transmitted story of earlier experiences, have authority to the degree that they reveal meaning and communicate meaning, a meaning which raises men and women up, heals and liberates, and creates peace. But in that case we must also take account of all kinds of conditions, from which it can become clear that we do not imagine meaning or ideologically posit meaning where there is no meaning, but that meaning reveals itself to us autonomously, as a gift. I already said above that revelation never comes directly on a fine, blank sheet: it never lands in a psychological, cultural or social vacuum. Some people hold the view that there is only authority when this is accepted by a community. The element of truth here is that this stresses the fact that without what patristic and mediaeval theology calls the *receptio* of an authoritative statement of authority by the community of faith, church authority in fact becomes historically 'ineffective'. Certainly people often do not admit that authority does not become *per se* illegitimate without such reception by believers (however barren such authority may be when it functions in the community of faith). However important reception may be in the life of the church and for the power and effectiveness of decisions by a church government, it is not the legitimation and basis of an official statement of authority in the church. Reception is simply the historically effective response to a statement of authority, the foundation of which nevertheless lies elsewhere: not in formal authority, nor in the people's reception of a decision of the authorities.[53]

## II   The Holy Spirit, foundation of all authority, including official authority, in the church, and the variety of instruments through which it works

### A. *The Holy Spirit, source of all authority in the church*

The foundation of both the authoritative life of the community of faith and ministerial authority within the community of God is the Lordship of Christ in the church through his pneuma or Spirit and the Spirit of the Father. Let me put it this way: the general teaching authority of the people of God and the ministerial teaching authority in the church have a pneuma-christological foundation: in so far as this is 'authority', it goes back to the effectiveness of the Spirit of Jesus the Christ. The functioning of ministerial authority must, moreover, be organized in such a way that the liberating authority of the Lord Jesus, which is abidingly present, can come into effect time and again in the life of the Christian community of faith. Fundamentally, therefore, the norm in the church is not the formal authority of the ministry, but the *paratheke*, i.e. 'the entrusted pledge' (I Tim.6.20; II Tim.1.14), namely the gospel (I Tim.1.11; II Tim.2.8) as the apostles interpreted it, that is to say, 'the *didaskalia* or teaching of God our Saviour'(Titus 2.10).

Essentially it is a matter of the unbroken sucession of the apostolic tradition of the gospel content of the faith. The teaching authority of the church is subject to this apostolic content as ministerial service, but the one calls for the other (the so-called 'apostolic succession' in the ministry). Moroever, this gospel content is the very life of the Christian communities in their local character and communion with one another, i.e. the life of the 'apostolic church'. As Paul says, it is imprinted as a letter, not just somewhere in canonical books, but on the hearts of believers. So the teaching authority of the ministry is also directed to the actual life of the church communities of faith, at the grass roots, locally and in their mutual recognition of one another, here and now and through the ages, and under the direction of the searchlight of the first, i.e. biblical, normative documentation of the life of the first witnesses and followers of Jesus.

On the basis of this structure there may be no master-servant relationships in the church. There may not be any structure of lordship in the church: 'You know that the rulers of the Gentiles lord it over them, and their great men exercise authority over them. It shall not be so among you' (Matt.20.25-26; Mark 10.42-43; Luke 22.25). Although there is authority and leadership in the church, there is really no *hierarchy*. Talk of church hierarchy in the sense of a pyramidal hierarchical structure of the church community is also inspired by the social status symbols of the Graeco-Roman empire (of which the post-Constantinian church took over many features when the competition fell away) and from the sixth century was very strongly influenced by the Neoplatonic works of Pseudo-Dionysius, who tried to legitimize all this in philosophical and theological terms.[54] Pastoral and sociological differentiations in the church are given theological clarification in this Neoplatonic view of the world. On this model the different services of ministry which grew up in the church over history become hierarchical: in multi-stage levels from the top down to the more inferior levels. The higher level thus has in a supreme way what the lower level has to a lesser degree and with limited power. The ministerial competences of all the 'lower' ministries were to be found in absolute completeness at the highest level: historically this plenitude of power was from an early time, the second half of the second century (say between 150 and 200), the episcopate in the current sense of the word.

This pseudo-Dionysian principle of substitution devalued the pluriform specialized ministries in the church which came into being historically as a result of church needs, being thought pastorally necessary. This hierarchical development at the top of the church devalued the laity, 'at the base of the pyramid', so that they became merely the object of episcopal and priestly pastoral care. And in this situation pastoral care could at the same time be misused as a means of control in questions of power. In principle the clergy (among which the episcopate embodied the highest *status perfectionis* or state of perfection) realized in a perfect way a religious pattern of life and a religious unity with God which 'ordinary' believers could experience only indirectly and incompletely, purely in obedience to the *maiores*, the notables or prelates in the church.

Such a hierarchy inspired by Neoplatonism, which followed in the footsteps of declining late antiquity, no longer has anything to do with the nature of the church. If one wants to apply the term 'the hierarchy' to all those who legitimately bear authority and exercise leadership at the heart of the church and here, through the mediation of the church, even do so from God, that is fine as far as I am concerned: no problem. But hierarchy conceived in this way has nothing to do with the concept which I analysed above and therefore already in no way excludes *a priori* a democratic church government. However, in all official documents of the Roman Catholic church 'hierarchy' is used specifically as an argument for rejecting any democratic exercise of authority and thus democratic participation in the government of the church by the people of God on the basis of 'divine law'.

This refusal brings us to conflicting positions of the church hierarchy. For we can regularly establish from the Acts of the Holy See that the present official church commends and prefers democracy as a kind of ideal for any historical 'civil society', but that in terms of ministry, and indeed in principle, this same Roman Catholic Church presents itself as a non-democratic community.

The argument for this exception for the church, which is said to be hierarchical and therefore already non-democratic, goes like this. The church, as founded by God, has its own specific social form. This is by divine right and therefore (the argument goes) is non-democratic. The arguments in favour amount to this: just as the Pope is not the delegate of the universal church, so the bishop is not the delegate of his see. Pope and bishops have their authority direct from Christ and not from a mandate which is given to them by the people of God or by the diocese. Of course as 'hierarchies' they are at the service of the people of God, local and world-wide, but this service is a function of truth and love, the final aim of which is that the people of God should experience God's call. And this call is not dependent on the people. It is God's own absolute initiative.

Through its appeal to what it calls the hierarchical structure of the church the ministerial church seeks to demonstrate that the church (both believers and those in authority) does not exercise any rule, is not the owner of God's call or its institutional form. From this argument, which up to a point is theologically correct, the conclusion suddenly seems to be drawn that democracy 'thus' cannot be the model for the church, because the church lives from the word of God about human beings' 'ultimate concern', and no man or woman has any say over that. And in all this the same church, clearly without any sign of hesitation, has taken over for itself the civil forms of imperial-authoritarian, feudal and later absolute monarchical government as a matter of course and as such has regarded them as legitimate.

The 'category mistake' or false reasoning which goes astray in the argument that I have just mentioned is certainly subtle, but as false reasoning it is no less real. Precisely because (apart from its very beginning) the church traditionally has almost never experienced 'democratic' forms of government, at least in the modern sense of the word, the exercise of any form of democratic authority has been rejected, while the authoritarian exercise of authority has been, and is, approved with enthusiasm.

The mistake in all this false reasoning lies in the fact that democracy (which in fact is the fruit of the American and French Revolutions, now two hundred years in the past) stands or falls by respect for human rights. To look for the foundation of human rights is very different from the model of the functioning of these rights. Just as the state and civil society are not proprietors of human rights, so the church is not the proprietor of the word of God. The nature of a church community does not lie here. 'Not lording it over' does not exclude democracy! Why then should the church not be able to democratize its model of government and rule without in so doing harming its subjection to the word of God? As if an authoritarian government went better with the subjection of the church to God's word than a democratic government, in which the voice of the whole people of God is listened to more clearly and accurately!

However, that is the nub of the argument in all the official documents of the official Roman Catholic Church: democratic government harms subjection to God's revelation. Why? Such an argument is in my view a basically false argument, which has as its tacit ideology the view that the authority in power (because guided by the Holy Spirit) is always right; it does not need to be unnecessarily hindered in its actions by contributions from below. I recall the slogan of the war years 'Il duce ha sempre ragione' (the Duce, or the Führer, is always right). In the meantime the category mistake which is made here has not been cleared up at all, for what is under discussion is not whether or not the church is subject to the word of God, but how in practice the subjection of the church and hierarchy to God's revelation can be carried out in the most appropriate way. In other words, the supposedly non-democratic structure of the church is in no way rooted in the nature of the church, but can only be defended with a straight reference to the actual and contingent history of this church, which until recently moved in non-democratic civil societies and then to a large degree took over the non-democratic forms of government of the surrounding social and cultural milieu.

The only argument that is used to defend a non-democratic church is thus in fact merely a reference to twenty centuries of non-democratic cultures, from which the church, too, took the broad outlines of its own forms of government. Here history (including ourselves and everyone else) is a witness to that fact, so that immunizing references to underlying mysteries are no longer any help. The rejection by the official church of the possibility of a democratically governed community of faith in fact has nothing to do with subjection to the Word of God, which is under no one's sovereign control (i.e. neither that of the community of faith or the hierarchy), whereas on the official side constantly renewed subjection to the word of God is and was the only argument against the democratic exercising of authority in the church.

I have learned from Peter Berger, the American sociologist and theologian,[55] that what I have just said can be called the 'positivism of tradition'. In using the phrase 'positivism of tradition' this sociologist still wants to attach some rational value to the Barthian positivism of revelation which he criticizes. But in that case we have to analyse the reasons why people opt for these particular elements in tradition. And then one arrives at the question why in the past this church government could with great self-assurance take over the civil forms of feudal government and later also those of an absolute monarchy, while being completely closed to modern forms of government and rule, especially democratic forms of authority. The reasons are not dogmatic motives! To claim that the church cannot be democratic because it is hierarchical is thus simply false reasoning and a magical and ideological use of the word 'hierarchy'.

However, that does not mean that a church authority with a democratic bent must *ipso facto* take over all the ideology of a modern democracy. So it can escape the intrinsic paradox of democracy (though it is difficult to find a better system) that the authorities which have to take decisions are dependent on the electorate, who to some degree, rightly or wrongly, can dismiss their leaders at will in the next election. However, a variety of forms of democratic participation and co-responsibility of all members in church government can be organized without the periodical elections of church leaders. But all those involved must have their own say in the choice of church leaders.

There is more. There are also intrinsic ecclesiological reasons for preferring a democratic exercise of ministerial authority in the church to oligarchical, monarchical or feudal forms of government.

## B. Intrinsic theological reasons for the democratic exercising of authority in the church

### 1. The instruments of the Holy Spirit

Christians believe in the support of the Holy Spirit, which in the end keeps the church on a correct, firm, non-ideological, biblical course, despite ups and downs. This Spirit is at work throughout the life of the church: generally and specifically in all the people of God and in a specific ministerial way in the official activity of the church leaders. In concrete terms this means that the Spirit is at work in a number of differing historical mediations in which both the believing people and the hierarchy give access in different ways to the gifts of the Spirit or shut themselves off from them. The result of the working of the Spirit cannot therefore always be said to be equally successful in its appropriation by believers and church leaders! God's grace does not work in such an automatic way. Anyone who disregards the manifold ecclesial mediations of the work of the Holy Spirit (and thinks that he or she possesses the truth, simply by referring to the Holy Spirit) shuts off the working of the Spirit of the Father, at work in Jesus, the glorified Son, through and in his church on earth.

If the ministerial teaching authority overlooks these mediations, above all the mediation of the structured people of believers themselves, here and now in the stream of time, it runs the risk of not having listened faithfully to the Holy Spirit. In that case a heavy burden is placed on the decisions or statements that it in fact makes. In terms of church theology this means that in neglecting these mediations, while at a pinch one can refer to this Spirit, which in fact also supports the church's ministry, one cannot neglect the other channels of the Holy Spirit. If that happens, such a reference is even ideological, and in any case one-sided. People close their ears, and even their eyes, to the channels along which the Spirit is also at work. The Spirit is reduced to silence, at least in the nuances that it suggests. A reference to the support of the Holy Spirit is therefore only meaningful in ecclesiological terms if the ministerial authority has taken serious account of all these ecclesial mediations and has become informed about them in order to take its own ministerial responsibility seriously. (To withdraw in solitary prayer in order to hear the whispering of the Holy Spirit is indeed necessary, but certainly not enough; it can then have an ideological effect.)

It is clear that the democratic participation of everyone (for which a form of organization has to be found) in a theologically responsible way could and, in ecclesiological terms, must play a role at precisely this level, without harming the distinctive responsibilty of the hierarchy. However, the church authorities cannot appeal to the Holy Spirit to provide subsequent defence of an official decision or claim if in fact they ignore the mediating organs of the Holy Spirit or have undermined its effective power in advance by all kinds of rules. In that case, the Spirit is stifled (I Thess.5.19).

## 2. The vulnerable rule of God as a model for ministerial authority in the church

There are yet other intrinsically ecclesiological reasons which impel the church of Jesus Christ to follow the non-authoritarian, vulnerable, even helpless, rule of God.

I have already said repeatedly that for believers, God's action in the world and the church is marked by the fact that it is never at work above or alongside human history, as it were in magical phenomena, but in this history itself, modestly and in a hidden way. It can be both in the everyday events of our history and in its dramatic events, including the crucifixion, though it is never fused with this history nor does it coincide with it. Precisely from this history, above all from the story of Israel and finally of Jesus of Nazareth, we learn *how* God rules in history: certainly not like emperors, potentates and prelates, but rather in the utmost respect for human freedom. The recognition of the reality of the risen Crucified One, as the distinctive divine way of manifest rule over all history, is possible only in the same spirit of fearfulness and compassion. By this non-powerful rule of God's eternal love over all men and women through his special love for the poor and oppressed, his church, 'the community of God', is called to life and we also come to build up the church in this world. The power of the church hierarchy or 'holy rule' does not transcend the *exousia* or authority of Jesus Christ.

I recall a splendid interpretation by Thomas Aquinas of what the 'rule of Christ' involves. He writes (the Latin text is quoted in the notes): 'The power and rule of Christ over human beings is exercised by truth, justice and above all love.'[56] In Thomas, in these Aristotelian terms we can still hear the biblical background (at least in the Vulgate version) from his biblical commentaries: faithfulness (*emet* as 'truth'), justice (*tsedaqa*) and loving mercy (*ḥesed*). Where the church of Christ lays claim to another rule, it does not simply depart from the spirit of freedom, the Spirit of Jesus Christ, but it also fails in its duty towards the world, namely to proclaim and practice the liberating power of the Christian message credibly and understandably.

Beyond doubt, the exercise of this authority borne by the glorified Jesus through the faithfulness, justice and mercy of God itself also always needs theological clarification (see the closing paragraph which follows).


I said that God's saving action becomes transparent in our history when we hold this history against the light of the biblical narrative. Of course there is another side to this. To what degree do people, believers, leave room in our history for the gracious action of God? One cannot make an automatic appeal to God's grace. There is not only the *mysterium gratiae* but also the *mysterium iniquitatis*, the unfathomable depth of faithlessness and sinfulness. Here criticism of ideology is necessary, but theologically this is not enough. The church rightly puts the stress on the unfailing faithfulness of God; that never changes.

But on the basis of a different view, both the Enlightenment and the church hierarchy acted as though what they were doing was good for all simply in the doing of it: it served the general welfare. This can be real, but it can also be an ideology. It does not have an automatic effect. The Enlightenment was concerned with *my* rights and my freedom, and not so much with the freedom and rights of *others*. Only then does hierarchy become a 'holy rule' which is no longer a rule but service: the eschatological token of the kingdom or rule of God in our history –

although this rule as service can never be found in its fullness in a historical form, either inside or outside the church.

## 3. The interplay of official teaching authority and the teaching authority of believers and their theologians (always in some tension)

Theology, too, may share in the privilege of the whole of the people of God of being a channel of the Holy Spirit. It is a possible channel – for at the same time it can also share in sinful neglect, if in the exercising of its function (which is one of the many organs which mediate the Holy Spirit) it is either unfaithful in tacit passiveness, or in self-assurance it neglects the working of the Spirit in other organs, for example those of the church's ministry.

Though the teaching authority of the ministry, in an extreme exception even infallibly, bears witness to the gospel of Jesus Christ and its implications, this witness in many ways remains 'relative', i.e. related to. In particular it is 1. related to the coming rule of God as bound up with the whole appearance and person of Jesus Christ: the heart of the message which in one way or another must also resound in any particular ministerial statement (here I am thinking of the Vatican II 'hierarchy of truths') and the mediaeval theory of the *articulus fidei*, the *cardines* or main hinges which 'articulate' the whole of the doctrine of faith in fundamental, less central and finally even peripheral truths; 2. related to scripture and all its prehistory; 3. related to history after scripture, i.e. to the particular situations in the world and the church in which during the course of church history the church and the teaching authority of the ministry has borne witness to the gospel of Jesus Christ as the message of salvation from God which brings human liberation. Even a dogma has a history of its own and cannot be understood outside the process by which it developed; 4. related to our present, which is also an essential element in the understanding of the Christian tradition of faith – the present both of the people of God and the world situation.

In connection with this last criterion (the present), here and there one often finds the misunderstanding that present-day theologians use present patterns of thought as a norm for the Christian understanding of faith. However, the fact that there is a time-difference, or diachrony, between religion and the world in no way means that we need to remove this time-difference as quickly as possible in an attempt at *aggiornamento* which will bring Christianity up to date. The critical question here is 'up to which date?' That of our bourgeois and one-sidedly technological consumer society? In that case there would be a risk of our making

Christianity into a 'civil religion' of the bourgeoisie. Alongside what is indeed an obstructive time-difference between old formulae of faith (which in their time were a successful expression of basic Christian experiences) and present-day Christian experiences, in the Christian religion there is also a time difference which is part of its being, a liberating time difference which believers must use creatively to change both our society and our bourgeois heart, our thought-patterns and our behaviour.

From all these mediations it emerges on the one hand that even the magisterial language of dogma must always be related back to the original Christian 'interpretandum', that which is to be interpreted: the appearance of Jesus of Nazareth in our history, interpreted in canonical scripture as the Christ, the anointed Son of God who wishes salvation from God and in fact also offers it to all men and women. On the other hand what the ministry says,even in dogmatic statements, about this offer of salvation in Jesus can only be understood in the totality of the whole of human history. In other words, even a so-called Christian dogma is not an immovable rock; it has undergone a very changing history. Even this milestone in the life of the Christian history of faith and dogma cannot be understood outside the history of its development, as though precisely in being in fact a legitimate and even permanent milestone, it were a supra-historical pointer which in different cultural circumstances cannot tolerate any use of other categories of understanding which were still unknown earlier.This is not what happens in the life of the church guided by God's Spirit.

Because the teaching authority of the ministry is pastoral by nature, and thus not a scientific institution for finding the truth or an academy, theology is also needed alongside the pastoral proclamation of the teaching authority: the 'theological teaching authority' as a scientific translation of the non-ministerial, general 'teaching authority' of the church's people of God. For there, in the faith of the church, lies the source of any authoritative statement even by the hierarchy, also in subjection to the Word of God. Precisely in listening to and standing critically by the specific faith which is alive at the grass roots – the people of God – the theologian is at the same time a servant of the authority of the ministry in the church, but not its cringing slave.

It is also the special task of the theologian to trace out accurately the manifold rationality of the statements of the ministry which I have just mentioned, whereas the teaching authority has to do something rather different in its direct pastoral concern. But above all in difficult times, in which emphasis is put on the binding character of formal authority in a rather desperate way and there is a certain mistrust of anything that does not come to life in the church from above, there is a danger that the pastoral teaching authority will keep to the letter of a statement made once in the past without much concern for the multiple references and thus the relativity of the statements of the *magisterium*. This could in fact have been the one and only way of expressing a truth of faith in fidelity to the gospel at that time. In later times, however, on the basis of cultural developments Christians can be offered new possibilities of clarifying the same truth of faith through other categories which were not present earlier in culture, with equal fidelity to the gospel. Not to see or even not to want to accept this possibility, basically perhaps because of a static concept of the truth, can result in tragic disruptions of communication between the teaching authority and theology.

A survey of the history of the relationship between the teaching authority of the ministry and academic-theological teaching authority can itself cast more light on this relationship of tension.[57]

The relationship between the pastoral teaching authority of the magisterium and theology (the theological magisterium) has changed a good deal in the course of time. In the first millennium we see that the teaching authority of the ministry and theology usually overlap. Although many laity and monks were theologians, the episcopate was in fact the *ordo doctorum*: the bishops proclaimed the faith both as ministers of the church and professional theologians. However, after the cathedral schools came into being in the high Middle Ages (think of Chartres, Laon and Paris), later to be followed by scholarly-academic theology in the first European universities, a new status of doctors or magisters in theology developed: the guild of master theologians. And because in feudal times the bishops came predominantly from the nobility, often with hardly enough theological training, a marked difference arose between the *magisterium episcoporum* and the *magisterium theologorum*, a field of tension which has led to much crossing of boundaries on both sides.

Thomas Aquinas drew the distinction between the teaching office as *officium praelationis* (an office which was part of the service of the church government) and the *officium magisterii* (the magisterium of the theologians).[58] Thus a third power came into being alongside *imperium* and *sacerdotium*: *studium* or the university. That was the beginning of the real tensions between the hierarchical teaching authority (the so-called *authentica*) and the magisterial authority of the theologians (the so-called *magistralia*).[59] As witness to a tradition which had already grown up by then, Magister Gratianus could say: 'The expositors of Scripture (i.e. the theologians as *expositores Sacrae paginae*) relying on *gratia*, on greater *scientia* and on more *ratio*, stand above the Pontifices (i.e. Pope and bishops), not in juridical decisions over disputed cases but in the explanation of Holy Scripture.'[60] Moreover we see that in those days there was less a conflict between theologians and the Holy See than sometimes stubborn fights between theological schools, disputing with one another and condemning one another, in which both parties even tried to turn an appeal to the Holy See to their own advantage, in one case even by manipulation, until one of the two parties was excommunicated and compelled to burn the offending theological work.

At the same time it is a fact that the mediaeval ministerial decisions of the church were hardly of any significance, either in furthering or delaying developments in theology. Bonaventure and Albert could say boldly that on this or that point the Pope was in error. By contrast, Thomas clearly thought the same thing, but also because of his noble descent 'as a gentleman' he solved questions in a rather more charming way by the method of *exponere reverenter*: in other words, out of respect for an author or the authorities, as it were imitating mediaeval courtesy in a knightly tournament, one did not attack another person's theological statement directly or head on, but interpreted his text in such a way that virtually the opposite to what the author had meant could be distilled from it. Thomas was a master at this.

In the late Middle Ages things had even gone so far that the theological faculties actually began to make doctrinal decisions about orthodoxy! Here the Council of Trent rightly drew sharp boundaries; jurisdictional authority was assigned only to bishops, not to theologians. But the bishops needed theological advice if they were not to make too great mistakes. In fact theology was omnipresent. The question sometimes is, 'What theology?' That is still the case now.

Since the nineteenth century, as well as the ongoing influence of the old model of theologians as critical partners of the bishops, a completely new type came into being that one could (somewhat maliciously) call the model of the theologians as party ideologists; or, to put it more fairly, a form of theologizing which repeats ministerial authority without sober reflection and in repeating it gives it clarificatory explanations and defends it against other views. Under Pius IX, Pius X, Pius XI and Pius XII the teaching authority of the ministry exercised a kind of totalitarian claim on the theologians which itself also became very dogmatic. The theologians had no teaching authority at all other than what was delegated to them on the basis of a *missio canonica*. In the Roman Catholic Church this was the time of a variety of forms of 'mandates' and 'canonical missions': a Christian could really do nothing by himself (i.e. on the basis of his baptism in the Spirit) unless this had been granted by the highest church authority.

This was a time dominated by an image of the church according to which all heavenly gifts came into the whole church through the Pope and in which it was forgotten that on the basis of Christian baptism the community of faith, and its leaders, is itself the subject of being the church, and thus also the subject of theological self-understanding, and not on the basis of a canonical mission from above. That there can and may be special institutions set up by church law (why not?) in which some people teach in the name of the Holy See is acceptable, but that has nothing to do with the peculiarly ecclesial status of Christian theology, which one cannot regard as a pure extension of papal or episcopal teaching authority.

That there is always a tension in the life of the church between the pastoral-legal teaching authority of the ministry and the academic 'magisterate' of the theologian is normal and healthy for church life. However, if there is a kind of witch-hunt of theologians in the church and on the other hand theologians are certainly not rebelling *en masse* against the central authority but in all earnestness have to present complaints to that central authority, then something is wrong in the normal relationships of the church. Moreover the malaise points to very widespread discontent among many, largely intellectual, believers of whom the theologians to some degree are also the spokesmen. One cannot solve this problem with a reference to the faith of simple believers, i.e. a faith of people who do not reflect on their faith and are supported in so doing by the hierarchy, so that they themselves prefer to listen blindly to the central authority – 'true or untrue' – as the popular saying now goes and as the clergy stress, not without a touch of humour. Moreover, too often, out of mistrust of theologians, who are concerned for the well-being of the church (and even appeal to it themselves), a reference is made to the old *superbia theologia*, theological pride, as though there were not also a *superbia hierarchica*. Both believers and their church leaders are human beings who on the one hand can can be petty and all too human, and on the other hand can refer to their distinct 'state of grace'. However, these last two can hardly be played off against each other. The question is, though, whether and how on either side room has been made for the working of the Holy Spirit.

The hierarchy indeed has authority in the church, but it does not have control over the Holy Spirit (any more, of course, than does the church people of God). In serious situations of conflict and thus in exceptional circumstances, definitions of church order, which are in fact necessary for the concrete and practical life of the church community of faith (a church order that believers should also themselves observe sincerely in normal circumstances which respect human worth), can never resolve the religious and theological question of the authentic place where, here and now, the concrete effectiveness of the Holy Spirit can be demonstrated. Not even the church authority has a special charisma here; it has the authority to settle unresolved questions for a time – in order to even out polarization. Otherwise this is is an unnecessary and barren game in which people pass the buck to one another.

From all that has gone before we should rather learn the lesson that the teaching authority of the ministry, church theology and the believing community are dependent on one another and are so in a new way, different from what was the case earlier. Community, ministry, theology: these three are themselves fundamentally dependent – in a process in which they are relativized – on the living God, who brings his creation in Jesus Christ, through our history, to a final consummation after history.

# CHAPTER 5

# By Way of an Epilogue

## 1. Has the church still a future?

There is a whole literature in which it is taken for granted that in the long run religion and the church will disappear from the world. The argument which is referred to is particularly the phenomenon of secularization: the accelerated process of secularization since the Second World War. For believers, however, the rather naive confidence with which this position is expounded is open to criticism from the religious belief in creation. In addition, many so-called analyses of trends in the sphere of faith and religion over the last thirty years once again have been overtaken by the facts. The revival of Islam in the world was not forecast by any sociologist or analyst of trends. The upsurge of social criticism in the 1960s was just as unexpected. Some years ago no sociologist or other analyst who had dared to use ideas like *glasnost*, openness, and *perestroika*, restructuring, would have been taken seriously. Not to mention what has happened recently in Eastern Europe. With this brief summary I simply want to stress what analysts themselves often say: we are often completely wrong in our cultural prognostications. That can equally be the case with all kinds of conclusions from the analysis of trends in the so-called process of secularization.

The Jewish-Christian belief in creation, which does not seek to be an explanation of our world and our humanity, makes us ask quite different questions from those involved in the presupposition that this belief in creation is a kind of alternative explanation of humankind and the world to the explanations given by the natural sciences and anthropology (which are also acceptable to believers). Belief in creation does not claim to give an explanation of the origin of the world. If God is said to be the *explanation* of the fact that things and events are what they are, then any attempt to change these things and situations (for better or for worse) is in fact blasphemous, or, on the other hand, it turns human beings and our whole world into a puppet-show in which God alone holds the strings in his hands behind the screen: human history as a large-scale Muppet show! In that case one's duty is simply to fit oneself into the universe which was determined from the beginning. In that case, moreover, God is the power and guarantee of the established order – not *Salvator*, Saviour, as Christians call him, but *Conservator*, as the Roman Hellenistic religions called him. The consequence of this is that if anything has gone wrong, the only meaningful transformation of the world and society is in a restoration of things to their ideal order. Whether one puts this ideal order at the beginning of time, the earthly paradise, or in a distant future at the end of times, a coming golden age, makes little structural difference. In both cases the creation faith is falsified and turned into a misplaced explanation. Instead of being good news for men and women, who are anxious about their finitude, it is narrowed down to an explanatory teaching. Whether one sees history as a fall from an original ideal state or as progressive evolutionary progress to an ideal state, makes little difference to the pattern of explanation used. In both cases there is a failure to take account of contingency as a characteristic of human beings and the world. Historicity is then reduced either to a genetic development of a pre-programmed plan or to a process which takes place by the logic of development. The essential aspect of all historicity is thus neglected, i.e. finitude: all could just as well not have been, or could have been other than it in fact is (i.e. contingent, a philosophical technical term).

This applies to everything that is manifested in our world, in nature, history and society. Institutions, concrete historical forms like languages, cultures and civilizations, even the forms of religions, are also mortal: they come and go. And in that case we need not be surprised that a day arrives when they do go. Nothing of all this is not contingent. That means that even matter, as an interplay of chance and necessity, need not have been or could have been quite different. However, the contingency of any process of development is annulled by a view of creation which understands itself as an explanation of these phenomena in nature and history. On a human level that also applies to human beings. If we are created (and for a Christian this means, if we are created in the image and likeness of God), then we must be something other than conservers, restorers or discoverers of what is already given. In that case, we ourselves become, rather, the principle of what we shall do and what we shall make of the world and society – and what could have not been and in fact is, by virtue of contingent free will.

God creates human beings as the principle of their own human lives, so that human action has to develop and effectuate the world and its future in human solidarity, within contingent situations and given boundaries, and therefore with respect for both inanimate and animate nature. For God can never be the absolute origin of our humanity, in other words, creator, if he has created human beings only to carry out his predetermined divine blueprint. On the contrary, he creates human beings with a free human will, freely to develop their own human future, to realize it in contingent, chance and also specific situations. As a result, one can choose between many alternatives, including between good and evil – a distinction which does not precede this freedom but which human beings, by their free choice, bring to light without being its source. Otherwise in a subtle way the contingency, i.e. the reality, of the world and the humanity of men and women is annulled.

The transformation of the world, the outlining of a better society and a new earth which is worthwhile for all men and women to live in, has been taken in hand by contingent human beings themselves. They therefore cannot expect God to solve their problems. Given a proper belief in creation, we cannot shift on to God what is our task in the world, because of the unsurpassable boundary (on our side) between the finite and the infinite. To overcome suffering and evil wherever we encounter them with all possible scientific and technological means, with the help of our fellow human beings and if necessary perhaps (when all other means are exhausted) by rebellion, is our task and our burden within all our finitude and contingency. It is not God's cause, except that this task of ours is within the absolute saving presence of God among us and thus as a human concern is also very close to God's heart. That the world appears as it does is, despite all coincidences and causal patterns, also to be understood in terms of the historical and social contingent free will of human beings in their dialectical relationship to nature.

This also implies that in principle there is the possibility of an overriding negation, as an element of anticipation or the outline of the future by human beings themselves. Belief in creation does not give us any information about the inner constitution of human beings, the world and society. To seek this out is the task of philosophers and scientists, of human beings. However, faith points out that the contingency of all worldly and human figures (which philosophy also knows) is supported by the absolute saving presence of God in all that is finite. The future is also contingent; it can never be interpreted or effected purely in terms of teleology, technology or the logic of development. The believer knows that God makes himself present in a saving way in this history. Indeed, only God is also the Lord of our history. He is the one who began this adventure and so it is also close to his heart. What is God going to do with his own divine life? Creation is ultimately the meaning that God has wanted to give to his divine life. He wanted, freely, also to be God for others, and expected them, with their finite free will, which was also open to other possibilities, to accept his offer. Otherwise I do not understand at all why he, God, resolved to take the final precarious decision of creating human beings. But who am I, at least in the framework of this divine adventure, incomprehensible to humanity, which is played for such high stakes?

This consideration brings me to an idea which I have already expressed several times. What formerly seemed almost only to have been the interest of religious people is now, above all in Europe and America, a matter for all kinds of human sciences, techniques and actions: they all strive for the healing, making whole or salvation of human beings and their society in a nature spared all kinds of pollution. It is hard to deny that the question of a sound human life worth living is more than ever a live one throughout humankind, and that in our time the answer to it is becoming increasingly urgent, the more on the one hand we discover that people are falling short, going short, and above all being short-changed, and on the other hand we can already experience comforting and hopeful fragments of human healing and self-liberation. The question of a human life worth living is in fact always put within conditions of alienation, disintegration and much human oppression. We see, too late, that evil has already happened. In our day the question of salvation which arises from this, at one time exclusively the theme of religions, has more than ever become the great stimulus within our whole existence, even outside all religion. In our time the question of salvation is the great motive force within our present history, not just in religious and theological but also in secular terms.

What used to be seen only as the concern of religions, including Christianity, now seems to be experienced as the common task of all men and women. But that in no way weakens the belief of both Christians and others in creation. Quite the contrary! Since when is a particular view of reality less true because it has also come to be shared by many others and universalized? Yet here and there I hear reservations. They go like this: granted, the introduction of many ideas of value, above all in the West, is also due (directly or indirectly, we need not be pedantic here) to the Christian experiential tradition. Now, however, they have become common property and therefore now, after thanking the Christian churches for the service they have done, we can say good-bye to Christian faith. However, I believe that if this happens we are thinking far too little about the inexhaustible potential of Christian creation faith for expectation and inspiration. The so-called tendency towards secularization, which is to be welcomed – understood as a gradual universalization (or the dissemination among many men and women) of an originally religious idea – seems to me to be quite inadequate as a total theory, even in rational terms. That is for two fundamental reasons.

(*a*) The first reason is the very finitude of our existence in a finite world and a finite history. For both believers and agnostics, finitude is really part of the definition of human beings and the world; it is even the definition of all secularity. Being-the-world, and therefore not-God, can never itself be secularized, for in that case the modern secularized world would have to find a means of doing away with the constitutive finitude of human beings and the world. It is precisely as a result of this abiding finitude that again and again new religious attitudes arise in history. Being-the-church continues to have a future and survives all secularization because while finitude can be experienced by men and women in a secularized way, for believers it is *par excellence* the never-failing source of all religion. This last statement is an affirmation of faith. But this conviction of faith can rationally point to the constantly recurring phenomenon of religion, in situations of the worst and most long-lasting religious persecution. Moreover – and this temptation is much more subtle – it points to the coming religious and semi-religious need which arises from the enjoyment of great wealth and consumption that in the end becomes satiating: as a result of this prosperity on the one hand the dangerous recollection of the experience of finitude is lulled to sleep, while on the other hand there is experience of the desolate void of this finitude when interpreted in secular terms.

(*b*) The second reason lies in the self-understanding of the religions, including Christianity. At least in the Christian experiential tradition, mutual humanity of equal worth, the criterion of the best that there seems to be in worldly experience, is meant not only as an ethical but also as a theological guideline (the tradition calls it *virtus theologica*). The Christian religious tradition sees cohumanity (which is incrasing over wide areas of the world's population) as a latent religious depth-dimension which is essentially bound up with the insight of faith that finitude is not left in its solitude but is supported by the absolute, saving presence of the living God. And this presence is and remains an inexhaustible source which can never be secularized.

It is precisely the critical, productive and liberating power of authentic belief in creation, above all as realized in the proclamation and praxis of Jesus of Nazareth, which makes it clear to us that the values, inspiration and orientation which keep emerging from this Christian experiential tradition, constantly universalizable and in this sense capable of secularization, emerging in the secular world for the benefit of all men and women and so as it were escaping the monopoly or particularity of the religions, can never catch up with the inexhaustible potential for expectation and inspiration that is in faith in God. Secularity means finitude, that which is not godly. And for the believer, non-divine finitude is precisely the place where the infinite and the finite come most closely into contact. From this close contact of the secular and the transcendent, the infinite and the finite, there arises, as mystics say, the spark of the soul; there all religion takes fire.[1] There lies the source of all religion, which, in an association of like-minded men and women who have shared the same experience, unavoidably leads to *communio* or the formation of the church. On this basis – and this is the sure conviction of believers whch can also be made understandable and credible on the basis of human experiences – finitude or secularity will to the end of days continue to be pointed towards the source and ground, inspiration and orientation which transcends all secularity – whom believers call the living God, the one who is not susceptible to any secularization.

The coming of the kingdom of God is a grace, but a grace which is effective in and through human action and not outside it, above it or behind it. We sometimes subsequently experience precisely the good that we ourselves do and provoke as human beings, as Christians and believers in the gospel, as the unmerited and surprising grace of God. Now from the structure of the whole event of revelation and redemption as it has been analysed in this book, it dawns on believers or readers looking for faith, almost more clearly than sunlight, that the church only has a future to the degree to which it is a saving presence in the future of human beings and their world, above all where men and women are tortured, individually or as a society. The church only has a future to the degree to which it lets go of all supernaturalism and dualism, and thus on the one hand does not reduce salvation to a purely spiritual kingdom or a simply heavenly future, and on the other hand does not become introverted and concentrate on itself as a church, but turns outside and directs itself to others, to men and women in the world. And in that case it will not think exclusively of its own historical self-preservation as a spiritual power in the world.

## 2. The worldly or cosmic aspect of the kingdom of God

In all that has been said previously the emphasis was on the solidarity of human beings with one another, with the poor, with the cultural or religious 'other', and so on, and thus on the political relevance of the Christian gospel: on justice and peace. But in that case what becomes of the cosmic aspect of Christian redemption and liberation? Above all in the urgent period of the so-called 'conciliar process', in which everyone's concern for our natural environment, the earth and even its ozone layer, is being mobilized, this appeal raises serious questions about the Christian view of the kingdom of God.[2]

Is the coming of the kingdom of God purely spiritual? According to some exegetes this cosmic aspect of the kingdom of God does not exist. For them it is imagery which is aimed at purely spiritual realities.[3] But what we can call the service or the virtue of co-humanity lies too deep in the Jewish-Christian tradition (though there, too, in its later, more recent, tradition it is often hidden to serve economic interests) to be turned into a Christian soteriology or view of salvation: human redemption and liberation is also connected with our material milieu.

In the 1950s and above all the 1960s the word 'co-humanity' became a fashionable replacement in our everyday language for the familiar term love of neighbour. At that time we were still living in a world which had emerged from the chaos of the Second World War and which had become over-bold as a result of economic progress and an international perspective on peace (even if the latter was somewhat ambiguous). As a result of the economic recovery, people became more friendly towards one another, after much selfish 'struggle for life' during a grim war.

And since the 1970s we have all been confronted with the world question of reciprocal or equal humanity while at the same time our picture of the world has become disturbingly aggressive and unjustly oppressive. In the meantime it has become an undeniable fact that only since 1965 has there been a call in our world for more democratizing of all relationships, individual and structural. Only then did major world problems with deeply human connotations come to the attention of all of us, a development also encouraged by the obvious attention paid to them by the media: nuclear energy, nuclear armament, the pollution of the environment, the exhaustion of our natural resources, the oil crisis and the shifting of the East-West conflict to the North-South conflict. Moreover the Eurocentric place of the West European churches has been weakened, and Europeans are more than ever aware of their regional and thus one-sided self-understanding. The 1970s also brought great alarm about Western prosperity. This led to mistrust, helplessness and anxiety; people saw the fragility of the political and economic world situation. Periods of crisis always provoke radicalizing, conflicting trends which lead to polarization. Many people then become apolitical, escaping into free inwardness, and others escape into external wantonness and grim vandalism – often without any soul or inwardness, without the concern to help humanity to survive in ourselves and others.

The contrast with the 1960s could not have been greater. In the meanwhile co-humanity had become a conscious value among us and the word co-humanity, which has now become jargon, was the linguistic expression of this. This was the time of a 'God of human beings'. But God is not just a God of human beings. Or rather, one dimension was forgotten; the fact that with inorganic and organic creatures we share in the one creation. For in the meantime the concrete world was busy destroying once and for all the natural living human environment, inorganic and organic, and doing so above all for motives of economic gain.

Against this background it is good to recall that in the biblical account of creation, 'the work of God's hands', in Gen.1, human beings do not get a separate day of creation. God creates human beings – male and female – on the same day as 'the cattle, the creeping things and the wild beasts'. God is concerned, we are told there, for 'man and beast'. Even after man has ruined his task of creation in the world and God wills to save humanity, God takes animals into his protection along with Noah, his wife and family, and after the flood he makes a covenant not only with Noah and his descendants but also 'with all the living beings who were with him'. God clearly wants a future for all his creation. And Ps.36.7 says explicitly; 'You, Lord, will make man and beast share in your salvation'. After Ps.103 has celebrated God's mercy towards human beings, Ps.104 is completely dominated by all the 'works of God's hand': the earth, plants and animals may rejoice in God's mercy.

But there is something special in the story about the creation of human beings. They are not created 'each after its kind', as we are told of God's creation of animals and plants. These may be what and as they are. And that is good. However, human beings are created 'in the image and likeness of God'. We can say that according to this story human beings must *take after God*. Here we are listening to something special. For in the Bible as it stands in its final redaction, with the much later creation story nevertheless prefaced to the beginning of the history of salvation from God as interpreted by the Jews and at the same time with the beginning (somewhat later) of a history of disaster brought about by human beings, readers of the Bible (within this story) know of God only that he is *creator* (those were the first pages that they read). From this these readers could hear that the story was about a God who controls chaos and makes life possible for all that moves upon the earth.

In this context (for the original reader or readers, who still did not know what was going to come after this initial story), the saying 'let us make God in our own image' (Gen.1.26) can only mean that human beings, too, must act creatively in their environment. As human beings they must control the many kinds of chaos, make life possible, and moreover show great concern for all life present on earth. They must act creatively for 'the work of God's hands'. Human beings will become truly human in creative activity with the earth. Here they come into their own. In Ps.8 it is even said that human beings may continue to be 'almost godly' if they have loving mercy for life on earth; for the life of plants, the life of animals, the life of their fellow men and women. Being creatures among many other non-human creatures and being human beings must go hand in hand. Thus 'ruling the earth' as a creative task in no way implies the demolition and pollution of this earth; it must be a constructive – almost divine – , caring creativity. No chaos, no domination, but creativity: raising up everything, aiming at justice, peace and the integrity of all creation.

As servants of creation, human beings are superior in creation. But in this respect they are simply the delegates (men and women) and stewards of God, to whom they must give account. So human beings must also look after animals: animals to all of which they have given a name, as to recognizable fellow creatures with their own unassailable rights.

One can ask: if that is Israel's story with reference to the material, physical, organic and animal environment, how is it possible that so many animal sacrifices were offered in this Israel with its compassion for creation (although the Jews abolished them after the Jewish War)? Was this not in contradiction to all this reverence for God's creation, for its life and survival? The animal provisionally has a representative function in this context. In exchange for an animal life God frees a human existence decaying in sin from destruction, for the human being who must be a blessing for fellow human beings and animals, a blessing for all life on earth, is becoming a curse to himself and all the earth.

Isaiah 24 laments: 'The earth mourns and withers, the world languishes and withers; the heavens languish together with the earth. The earth lies polluted under its inhabitants; for they have transgressed the laws, violated the statutes, broken the everlasting covenant. Therefore a curse devours the earth, and its inhabitants suffer for their guilt... Desolation is left in the city, the gates are broken into ruins... Violent men do violence, violent men do violence increasingly... The earth staggers like a drunken man.'

And later Paul is to express this just as sharply: the creation looks for the redemptive moment when human beings will finally have mercy on it as good shepherds, caring stewards, so that the cosmos too can take its breath again (Rom.8). According to the deepest conviction of Paul and many other early Christians this latter had happened in Christ Jesus. With the sacrifice of Jesus, the lamb of God, as above all Hebrews says, the old sacrificial cult of animals has been abolished for good. In Jesus the sacrifice of the cross is not only human salvation but also that of the animal world. No human sacrifice: God already said this to Abraham when Israel was led astray by the Canaanite religion to offer the firstborn Son to the deity, but spared Isaac at God's command. In the New Testament, moreover, the same God, the God of Israel and Jesus Christ, says that animal sacrifices, too, are of the evil one. This applies in only one particular realm. Evidently only in the kingdom of God; only there, according to the witness of Jesus' career, do no scapegoats seem necessary.

Here the concern is not only, nor above all, the preservation of nature to ensure self-preservation, although the limits of nature are also our limits. But with such an attitude we would again be giving human beings a central place in creation. What we need is above all self-restraint and a more sober life-style in order to protect creation. Of course we need one another, but above all the other, including nature, needs us. In my view what is now called the conciliar process, 'justice, peace and the integrity of creation', has everything to do with Jewish-Christian belief in creation and with the significance of redemption in Jesus Christ, which is also cosmic. It belongs at the heart of the Christian creed.

The parallels between human beings and nature are now also rightly stressed more than before. In biochemistry, for example, scientists have arrived at the insight that human beings, like animals and plants, are a piece of living chemistry. But on the other hand anthropology rightly stresses that there is something in human beings that cannot be reduced to nature. There is a 'surplus'. In human beings there is also an element that is not nature. Nature itself cannot pray: as material, inorganic and biologically living creatureliness it needs human beings to come to the praise of God. In contrast to animals, human beings have a somatic spiritual awareness, something transcendent, as a result of which they can recall their relationship with God.

Human beings and nature are related to each other. God's bond with the earth runs through the unique position of human beings as the image of God, through a human focus. Human beings are God's regents or representatives on earth. Therefore the earth is more than just the human world. We can see this: in Ps.104 the whole creation celebrates, and sun, moon and stars sing the praise of God. Human beings hardly enter into it. That is true, but this still is and remains a human psalm which expresses the praise of creation to God. When we say 'What a beautiful view?' we are already humanizing nature. For animals there are no landscapes, only territory for feeding and prey and room to play... although, when the darkness begins to fall and you then see a blackbird on the highest branch of a tree or on a television aerial, singing and looking round in a meditative way, you sometimes get the impression that this blackbird enjoying the landscape is musing, and praying in its own way. But there, too, we are reading something in. Without human vision and contemplation of nature there is no panorama. Thus nature transcends itself in human beings, who are themselves part of nature.

Of course we human beings must be modest about this, despite the fact that in our involvement in nature we transcend nature. The way in which human destiny is bound up with nature and nature is bound up with human beings means on the one hand that human beings must reverence nature's own structure, and on the other hand that this nature is really consummated by the fact that human beings are present in it – human beings who experience nature, contemplate it, find it attractive, and can also can do 'wonders' with it: wonders of technology and healing, to name just two. But if we objectify nature, we end up in a kind of mythology. And it follows naturally that the relationship of human beings to nature cannot be reduced one-sidedly to control and technology.

On the basis of the catastrophe to the environment we have become aware that our relationship to nature is subject to ethical values and norms. The modern ecological experiences of contrast have led us to the insight that here too, and not just at a personal and social level, ethical dimensions are present.[4] In classic handbooks of morality, this dimension is completely lacking. I once saw a cartoon: the background showed a row of factory chimneys pouring out sulphur and all kinds of poison while in the foreground, at the edge of a wood, a boy and a girl were embracing. A pastor walks by, huffing and puffing, sees the couple, and exclaims, 'Dirty pair!'. That is about the most adequate sketch one could have of traditional ethics between 1900 and 1955.

In the meantime it has become increasingly clear to us that we cannot go on endlessly with technology which exploits the earth, however legitimate technology may be as such. It is legitimate as technology, but we need not have all the technology of which we are capable: just because it is possible does not mean that it is ethically permissible. If it is good, technology serves the authentic values of true, good and truly happy humanity. The technology which is now causing pollution to a large degree serves a consumer society. It is here that criticism must begin, and not with technology as such. Criticism must begin with a technology which has no ethical priorities and sees everything in terms of the priority of belief in economic progress and a desire for gain.

The problems that we now have in our society with human beings, nature and animals is closely connected with the fact that our picture of the world of human beings and animals is going wrong. The decisive question is: what image of human beings do you opt for? I would want to say that the culture which has brought about the ecological crisis and the extinction of valuable species of animals is a culture in which science and technology have become, if not the exclusive, then the representative values of a particular civilization. The movement for a more contemplative and ludic relationship to the world of animals and nature seems to me to be a clear reaction against a one-sided technocracy intent on gain, consumption and luxury.

Moreover we can see that an unbridled consumer society does not itself produce a happy human world. Not only do many people have no chance, but there are also many who fail, who are empty and lonely. Not to mention the rising number of suicides among young people in the prosperous countries. The call for a more sober life-style clearly has a liberating dimension. And the more sober life-style which has now become necessary is not as pessimistic as it seems: there is also something attractive, well-proportioned about it; it has an element of sharing and thus something of a festal element. And why is it necessary to have to choose from 150 varieties if one goes to buy a bar of soap? Of course there is something creative about not all wearing the same kind of outfit or going round in the same kind of footwear. Colourful differences are part of our make-up, and if that should disappear, then something of the poetic, lyrical and playful dimension of our humanity would be lost. But even with a good deal less luxury there is still a good deal of room for human fantasy. We see that clearly in the Second World, and it is something that we can learn from people in these socialist countries.

Some see it as writing on the wall that we need a separate ministry for environmental hygiene. Of course this points to the fact that something is wrong with our environment, but it also indicates that we have finally become aware of this misuse. Earlier this concern did not seem necessary... although in the Middle Ages all Europe suffered under the plague and thousands upon thousands died, because there were no sewers. The plague disappeared from Europe, not thanks to the doctors but thanks to the engineers who put in sewers. At that time, J.le Goff, the great mediaevalist, tells us, the whole of Europe was one stinking cesspit. At that time there was less concern for the environment than now, but the pollution of the environment then was not yet attacking the principles of life itself, which is now the case with all our chemicals.

In some circles, the environmental catastrophe is blamed on Jewish and Christian religions on the basis of the Genesis story: 'Be fruitful and multiply, and fill the earth and subdue it; and have dominion over the fish of the sea and over the birds of the air and over every living thing that moves upon the earth' (Gen.1.28). It is indeed a fact that (not in antiquity and in the Middle Ages but) with the rise of bourgeois capitalism among Western Christians this biblical text has often been misused to legitimate the exploitation and pollution of nature. But that is a very recent, ideological legitimation which has little or nothing to do with the biblical roots and meaning of these texts.

For many Christians the Bible is the great stumbling block which prevents them from speaking with critical intent about science, technology, bio-industry and so on. It is dangerous to look in the Bible for a direct answer to specialized contemporary questions like those of environmental concern and nuclear energy, bio-technology and bio-industry. Often the quest for biblical texts is an attempt to provide biblical legitimation after the event for decisions and choices which Christians have already made and acted on for other reasons. However, confronted with the risks of this unrestrained exploitation which was not previously foreseen, at a time of greater concern for the environment, Christians have begun to read this Genesis text again, and helped by biblical scholars they are now saying that what this text means is not that human beings are lords and masters of nature, which they can exploit at will for their human projects; rather, they are the guardians of nature. In both cases the significance of this biblical text is decided beforehand: the Bible serves as a confirmation of one's own view.

Because of this frequent misuse of the Bible, yet others assert that to link world problems of ecology and politics with the Bible represents a horizontalizing of religion. However, despite all these hesitations, the creation story at the same time has something to say to us that relates to our problem. For that to happen, this creation story must then be read within its context in the 'Priestly tradition', and here we must finally also consider the whole dynamic of the Bible.[5]

The word *kabash* used in Gen.1.28 has many meanings and by itself can indeed be translated 'rule over nature', in the sense of exploiting it. However, in the context of the Priestly tradition *kabash*, literally to put one's foot on something, denotes what we would express by saying 'lay one's hand on something', i.e. take possession of something. According to the story of the Priestly tradition God, having first prepared all the environment necessary for human beings, created human beings ('male and female created he them'). These two are then given a blessing, not for all times and all places, but for the time of the consummation of creation, namely the time when the earth is filled with various peoples and their cultures.

According to the Priestly conception of things, God has devised a place on earth for all peoples. But within the context of this story there are initially only two individuals. So God gives them a blessing in order that they can multiply into a people as quickly as possible. Then at a later stage of this story each of their many descendants goes as a people on a journey to its promised land (see Gen.5, a first list of peoples, and in Gen.10, after the flood, a second list of peoples, 'according to their land, language, tribe and people'). Special attention is paid here to Israel as one of many peoples: Abraham and Jacob are given the special blessing to form their own people Israel (Gen.17.6-7, 15-20; 35.11). Thereupon this people is also promised its own land, Canaan (Gen.17.8; 35.12). Finally all the people have found their place on earth and Israel, too, has arrived in Canaan, where it 'takes possession of the land' (Josh.18.1, the same word *kabash* as in Genesis). From then on Israel's own land is itself divided into different lots or parcels according to the twelve tribes (with a separate status for the tribe of Levi, Josh.19.51). Only thus does the Priestly story of primal history in mythical terms come to an end.

What was foreseen in the mythical-temporal six-day week of God's work has thus been given historical order. In this way the creation has been completed so that there is a stable community for individuals and peoples, with its own place on earth for every people. At this moment of primal history, God's blessing on Adam, 'Be fruitful and multiply, fill the earth and take possession of it', is fulfilled (according to this Priestly version). From now on human beings live 'on the fruit of the land' (Josh.5.11-12). Just as God rested on the seventh day of his creation, now that the earth is inhabited and the division of the peoples by land, race and language has taken place, Israel too enters as it were into an eternal 'liturgical sabbath rest' after setting up a sanctuary in Shiloh (Josh.18.1). That is a Priestly view of the actual division of lands and peoples.

The purpose of this mythically developed story is to show that this is the way in which God intended the ordering of the world and this is how it must remain, i.e. as a world in which all individuals and peoples live together in peace, each in their territory, even in cosmic peace in which human beings live as tenant farmers 'on the land flowing with milk and honey', where the creator is constantly praised liturgically. And Israel too saw that it was good! This is the golden thread of the Priestly narrative in the Pentateuch. But it in no way amounts to divine approval of the way in which the peoples came to arrive at the particular part of the earth which they now inhabit: the Priestly theology really does not say anything about that.

Given the purpose of this story, we cannot draw any conclusions from it, for example in connection with the ethics of propagation or for or against rational family planning, or in connection with the ethics of ecology or the exploitation of nature, far less with reference to bioethics. The sacred writers see the fact of different cultures, lands and peoples, spread over the earth, in which each people is assigned its own land with frontiers, as a summons to all human beings and peoples to live thus, in peace with one another, for the happiness of all men and women and the praise of God. Only in connection with animals are human beings told: 'Have dominion over the fish of the sea and over the birds of the air and over every living thing that moves upon the earth' (Gen.1.28).

But in this context the Hebrew word *radah*, the root meaning of which is 'rule', but which has many meanings and in fact can also mean 'beat down', cannot mean kill, because in Gen.1.29-30 there is a prohibition against eating the meat of animals; the story takes place in a period when there is only vegetarian diet. Here the verb *radah* means that human beings must be friendly to other living beings. As human beings they are the guardians, the leaders, the guides, the shepherds of all animals, and this is expressed in the ancient Eastern way by 'rule over'. They must act towards one another as God wills to act towards them, as friends. In other words, the Priestly tradition sees the initial state of creation as also a peaceful co-existence of human beings with animals. According to the story of this dangerous biblical recollection, what the great prophets had seen before the Priestly redaction as an eschatological state to come, in which the wolf lies down with the lamb and the child plays on the adder's hole (Isa.11.6,8), must be a daily concern for humankind.

In the second, Yahwistic, Genesis story (Gen.2.5-3.24) it is said: 'The Lord God took the man and put him in the garden of Eden to till (*abad*) it and keep (*shamar*) it' (Gen.2.15). Adam or humankind is here seen as a gardener or farmer who has to till or cultivate the *adamah* or rough ground (work on it in service). This second creation story is a creation story of an agricultural population. That in no way means that the Bible has a preference for agrarian life over industrial and technological life or nomadic life (although there was dispute and rivalry over this at one time among the Hebrews).

Here, too, what historically the prophets had foreseen as a vision of the future is projected back in the later creation story to the beginning of creation. After the chaos of the exile, when the agricultural land in Israel was like a wilderness because its inhabitants had been deported (cf. Lev.26.33), Ezekiel sees the time of salvation at the return as a period in which the devastated land is 'served' or worked (here, too, we also have *abad*, the same word as in Genesis): 'Then they shall say that this land which was a wilderness has become like the Garden of Eden' (Ezek.36.35). Work here is not a punishment for sin; in this view it is part of the normal condition of human happiness. By contrast, for the Bible 'work in the toil of your brow', i.e. servile and dehumanizing work, is a consequence of sinful human relations (Gen.3.17-19).

So here in a mythical story an answer is sought to real human problems. Human beings must not only cultivate the land but also keep (*shamar*) it; here we have the expression of something like a concern for the ecological environment. For it is already quite evident that through mismanagement and mistreatment of nature, human beings can turn their fertile oasis, their garden, the Garden of Eden, into a wilderness. We can in fact see this text as a charge to human beings not to allow their earthly environment to be threatened by chaotic, uncontrollable powers which they themselves call to life. So we read: 'Cursed is the *adamah* (the human environment) for your sake (for the sake of *adam*, humankind)' (Gen.3.17). It is not that God curses nature, but that nature – sound though it is – can be involved in the chaos of unwise human action. Sinful human behaviour (in the story, a cultivator) becomes visible in the disorganization of the land. Universal involvement in creation, not just co-humanity, is the task of human beings as creatures for whom God is concerned. Human beings must protect nature and guard it against the chaos which human beings can make of it through misbehaviour.

It is, moreover, striking how in the first Priestly creation story God first of all brings into being an ecological environment for all things: air as the environment of 'the birds of the air', the earth as the environment for animals, water as the environment for fishes. Without their own environment, there would no point in bringing birds, animals and fishes to life; their continued existence and their living conditions are dependent on this environment. And even before human beings appear on the scene, God saw that this order was good. But finally within these environments inhabited by many animate and inanimate things God creates human beings: beings who in peaceful fellow-creatureliness with all other existing beings nevertheless have a somewhat privileged position.

What, according to this mythical conception, is the real human environment? According to this view human beings may not touch the birds, the fish and animals (Gen.1.29-30); they must consume what grows from the earth, the work of the farmer's own hands. The story is thus constructed according to the theme of life and capacity for life

(Gen.1.9-12 corresponds to Gen.1.20-30), and this theme is crossed by a second theme, namely that of time: the theme of patient existence and survival. Therefore in this story first sun, moon and stars with their steady course in time are brought to life (Gen.1.14-18). The universe is firmly and unshakably fixed as the extreme condition for the survival and durability of all that fills the different environments with life and movement. When human beings then appear in this universe which has been made before them, God sees that it is very good: an appropriate environment for every living being.

So in the Bible the creation is presented to us as a cosmic community in solidarity. However much everything can turn into a chaos as a result of human misbehaviour, God's plan of creation is at least clear. He wills the life of the living and the survival of things. He creates its own environment for all that is created, an environment in which all the inhabitants of the earth can come into their own. Even then people were well aware of the essential connection betwen human beings and ecology. To be a creature is at the same time to be an 'ecological' being. Human beings thus need have no fear of demonic powers like sun, moon and stars. The only anxiety is that about the destructive chaos of sinful human action.

The first creation story, which knows no 'original sin' (but a growing human history of sinfulness and murder), nevertheless describes the primal history of humankind (after the mythical division of the earth among all peoples) as having been filled with human misbehaviour. In this tradition of religious experience God therefore takes offence at his creation. By a punitive flood he tries to begin it afresh with a new couple and with one pair each of all living animals (Gen.6.5-8.17).

All this is attractively summed up in the biblical conception that at creation human beings are created by God to be the 'image of God'. That is the image of himself which God placed in the world and its history: humankind! Where human beings live and emerge, it must become clear to each of them that God will rule, that here the kingdom of God begins, that here peace and justice are beginning to reign among human beings and peoples within a sound natural environment.

In and through human action it must become clear that God wills salvation through humankind for all his creation. For the Bible 'humankind' is God's representative on earth: for the salvation of human beings, of nature and of world history. And although human beings seem more often to fail than to succeed in their task of creation, this in fact opens up space for a truly human ethic governing our attitude to the world and nature.

The challenging call from God is thus: 'Come, my dear people, you are not alone.'

# Notes and Bibliography

In contrast to the first two parts of this trilogy, I have not put the most important literature for each chapter with the relevant text (which seems to have deterred some people), but here, just before the notes to each chapter. Some readers can therefore read the book without bothering about the bibliography and notes – and rightly so.

## A Guide to the Book

1. Denzinger-Schönmetzer, *Enchiridion*, no.1351; the text is inspired by Fulgentius, *Regula verae fidei ad Petrum* XXXV, 79, Migne, PL 65, 704. We find repetitions of it until very recently, see e.g. 'the holiest of all dogmas that no one can be saved outside the true, Catholic faith' (Gregory XVI in 1834, Mansi 51, 570); Pius IX in 1863 (Denzinger-Schönmetzer, no.2867); in the schema of the First Vatican Council, 28 November 1867 (Mansi 49, 624f.).
   2. Dogmatic Constitution *Lumen Gentium*, no.16.

## Chapter 1

### Bibliography

A.Auer, *Autonome Moral und christlicher Glaube*, Düsseldorf (1971), ²1980; E.Bochinger, *Distanz und Nähe*, Stuttgart 1968, 13-57; G.Baum, *Man Becoming: God in Secular Language*, New York 1970; Clodovis Boff, *Theology and Praxis. Epistemological Foundations*, Maryknoll 1987; C.Brémond, *Logique du récit*, Paris 1973; W.Dupré, *Einführung in die Religionsphilosophie*, Stuttgart 1985; C.Duquoc, *Messianisme de Jésus et discrétion de Dieu*, Geneva 1984; P.Eicher, *Offenbarung*, Munich 1977; H.-G.Gadamer, *Truth and Method*, London and New York ²1979, 235-73; C.Geertz, *The Interpretation of Cultures*, New York 1973; L.Goldmann, *Der christliche Bürger und die Aufklärung*, Neuwied 1968; H.J.Heering, *God ter sprake. Reflecties over de taal van de religie*, Meppel/Amsterdam 1984; E.Herms, *Theologie – eine Erfahrungswissenschaft*, Munich 1978; G.J.Hoenderdaal, 'Openbaring en ervaring', in *God ervaren?* (Jaarboek: Tenminste), Kampen 1981; W.James, *The Varieties of Religious Experience*, New York and London 1902; W.Kasper, *Glaube und Geschichte*, Mainz 1970, 120-43; R.Kellogg, *The Nature of Narrative*, New York and Oxford 1966; F.Kermode, *The Sense of an Ending: Studies in the Theory of Fiction*, London 1967; A.Kessler, A.Schöff and C.Wild, 'Erfahrung', in *Handbuch philosophischer Grundbegriffe* 2, Munich 1973, 373-86; H.M.Kuitert, *Wat heet geloven? Structuur en herkomst van de christelijke geloofsuit-*

*spraken*, Baarn 1977; id., 'Ervaring als toegang tot de godsdienstige werkelijk-heid', *Nederlands Theologisch Tijdschrift* 32, 1982, 177-96; id., *Philosophie van de theologie*, Serie Wetenschapstheorie, Leiden 1988; E.Leach, *Culture and Communi-cation*, Cambridge 1976; L.Luzbetak, *The Church and Cultures*, Divine Word Publications 1963; F.Maas, *God mee-maken in mensentaal. Over de draagkracht van ervaring in geloof en theologie*, two vols., Tilburg 1986; V.MacNamara, *Faith and Ethics. Recent Roman Catholicism*, Dublin and Washington 1985; J.B.Metz, *Faith in History and Society*, London and New York 1980; D.Mieth and F.Compagnioni (eds.), *Ethik im Kontext des Glaubens*, Fribourg 1976; D.Mieth, *Moral und Erfahrung*, Fribourg 1977; id., 'What is Experience?', *Concilium* 113, 1979, 40-53; id., *Gotteserfahrung und Welterfahrung*, Munich 1982; H.Müller, *Erfahrung und Gesch-ichte*, Munich 1970; W.Pannenberg, *Theology and the Philosophy of Science*, London and Philadelphia 1973, 156-224; L.Reinisch (ed.), *Vom Sinn der Tradition*, Munich 1970; J.P.Resweber, *La théologie face au défi herméneutique*, Brussels, Paris and Louvain nd; L.Richter, 'Erfahrung', *RGG³*, Tübingen 1958, 2, 550-2; P.Ricoeur, 'The Narrative Function', *Semeia* 13, 1973, 117-202; H.Rikhof, 'Narrative Theology', in *The Concept of Church*, London 1981, 129-48; H.Rombach, 'Erfah-rung', in *Lexikon für Pädagogik* 1, Freiburg ²1970; R.Schaeffler, *Religion und kritisches Bewusstsein*, Freiburg and Munich 1973; E.Schillebeeckx, *Christ*, London and New York 1980; *An Interim Report on the Books Jesus and Christ*, London and New York 1980; *Theologisch geloofsverstaan anno 1983* (Farewell Lecture), Baarn 1983; R.Schreiter, *Constructing Local Theologies*, Maryknoll and London 1985; E.Shils, *Tradition*, London and Boston 1981; J.Track, *Sprachkritische Untersuchungen zum christlichen Reden von Gott*, Göttingen 1976; A.Vergote, *Religie, geloof en ongeloof*, Antwerp and Amsterdam 1984; B. Wacker, *Narrative Theologie?*, Munich 1977; H.Wagner, 'Theologie und Wirklichkeitser-fahrung', *Theologische Quartalschrift* 157, 1977, 255-64.

*Notes*

NB: References to literature which is mentioned at the beginning of chapters are given in the notes in an abbreviated form.

1. *De dignitate hominis*, E.Garin, Florence 1942.

2. E.Wolf, *Europe and the People without History*, Berkeley and London 1982.

3. R.Schreiter (ed.), *The Schillebeeckx Reader*, New York and Edinburgh 1986, 78-81.

4. Kuitert, *Wat heet geloven*, 133-9; Schillebeeckx, *Christ*, 30-60.

5. Some talk in this connection of 'epoch-making shifts' in a horizon of experiences, cf. e.g. B.Welte, in H.Schlier et al., *Zur Frühgeschichte der Christologie*, Freiburg 1970, 103-5.

6. T.S.Kuhn, *The Structure of Scientific Revolutions*, Chicago ²1962; see N.Lash, *Change in Focus. A Study of Doctrinal Change and Continuity*, London 1973.

7. P.Ricoeur, *Finitude et culpabilité*, two vols., Paris 1960.

8. P.Berger and T.Luckman, *The Social Construction of Reality*, Harmondsworth 1977; P.Berger, B.Berger and H.Kellner, *The Homeless Mind*, New York 1974; A.C.Zijderveld, *De abstracte maatschappij; een cultuurkritische analyse van onze tijd*, Meppel 1971.

9. See W.Korff, *Norm und Sittlichkeit*, Mainz 1973, 131-42.

10. A.Paus, 'Zum Verhältnis vom Religion und Methode', in T.Michels (ed.), *Heuresis. FS A.Rohracker*, Salzburg 1969, 11-24.

11. Schillebeeckx, *Interim Report*, 56f.

12. A.Maslov, *Towards a Psychology of Being*, New York 1968.

13. *Interim Report*, 17-19.

14. R.L.Hart, *Unfinished Man and the Imagination*, New York 1968, 300-5.

15. H.Schelszky, *Auf der Suche nach Wirklichkeit*, Düsseldorf and Cologne, 250ff.

16. D.Mieth, *Moral und Erfahrung*, 120-34; 'What is Experience?', 40-53.

17. Gadamer, *Truth and Method*, 345ff.

18. Metz, *Faith in History and Society*, 65f., 154-68; Mieth, *Moral und Erfahrung*, 60-72.

19. *Interim Report*, 11f.

20. J.Track, *Sprachkritische Untersuchungen zum christlichen Reden von Gott*, Göttingen 1976; F.Mildenberger, *Theologie für die Zeit. Wider die religiöse Interpretation der Wirklichkeit in der modernen Theologie*, Stuttgart 1969, 157ff.; H.Zahrnt, 'Religiöse Aspekte gegenwärtiger Welt und Lebenserfahrung', *ZTK* 71, 1974, 94-122.

21. D.Tracy, *The Analogical Imagination*, above all the chapter on 'Interpreting the Christian Classic', 231-445.

22. This subtle distinction is almost classical in modern theology (though it follows an old theological tradition). Karl Rahner has developed it in his own way within his method of transcendental theology (summarized in *Foundations of Christian Faith*, London and New York 1978, 170-5). However, the distinction, which is difficult to describe, also remains in force outside this method. See e.g. P.Eicher, *Offenbarung*, 22-7, who in my view wrongly calls the first moment 'revelation as cypher' and the second, rightly, 'revelation as category'. In yet other terms, and from a quite different, Anglo-Saxon perspective, see R.Hart, *Unfinished Man and the Imagination*, New York 1968, 83-105.

23. Kasper, *Glaube und Geschichte*, 235; Schillebeeckx, *Christ*, 35.

24. Thomas, *Summa Theologiae* I-II, q.107, a.4.

25. J.B.Metz, above all 'The Future in the Memory of Suffering', *Concilium* 8.6, 1972, 9-25.

26. See W.Oelmüller, *Fortschritt wohin? Zum Problem der Normenfindung in der pluralen Gesellschaft*, Düsseldorf 1972, 99.

27. This is the problem already posed by G.Tyrrell, which certainly is not solved by Peter Berger, who discusses a similar problem in *The Heretical Imperative*, New York and London 1979.

28. L.Dupré, 'Ervaring en interpretatie. Een filosofische bezinning op de christologische studies van Edward Schillebeeckx', in *Tijdschrift voor Theologie* 22, 1982, 361-75 (substantially the article in *Theological Studies* 43, 1982, no.1, 30-51).

29. E.van Wolde, 'Semiotiek en haar betekenis voor de theologie', *Tijdschrift voor Theologie* 24, 1984, (138-67) 158ff.

30. Van Wolde has evidently allowed himself to be misled by the fact that in my Farewell Address I did in fact use the term 'substance of faith', where it wrongly has reminiscences of Aristotelianism or Scholasticism. In order to

avoid this misunderstanding I have therefore resumed my terminology from *Jesus* and *Interim Report*, namely 'offer of revelation', and have avoided the old familiar term 'substance of faith' (*substantia fidei*) which can (but need not) lead to misunderstanding.

## Chapter 2

*Bibliography*

P.Beauchamp, *Le Récit. La Lettre et le Corps*, Paris 1982; R.Bellah, *Beyond Belief*, New York 1970; id., *The Broken Covenant: American Civil Religion in Time of Trial*, New York 1985; id., *Habits of the Heart. Expressive Individualism*, San Francisco 1985; H.Berkhof, *Christian Faith*, Grand Rapids 1986; E.Bloch, *Atheismus im Christentum. Zur Religion des Exodus und des Reichs*, Frankfurt 1973; J.Bowker, *The Sense of God*, Oxford 1973; E.Cassirer, *An Essay on Man*, New Haven 1967; J.Cazeneuve, *Les Rites et la Condition humaine*, Paris 1985; A.Christian, *Meaning and Truth in Religion*, New Jersey 1964; D.Cupitt, *Taking Leave of God*, London 1980; H.Duméry, *Phenomenologie et Religion*, Paris 1958; id., *Philosophie de la Religion*, Paris 1957; L.Dupré, *The Other Dimension. A Search for the Meaning of Religious Attitudes*, New York 1972; M.Eliade, *The Myth of the Eternal Return*, London 1954; id., *The Sacred and the Profane*, New York 1961; M.Gauchet, *Le désenchantement du monde. Une histoire politique de la religion*, Paris 1985; C.Geertz, *The Interpretation of Cultures*, New York 1973; C.Geffré, 'La question de Dieu dans la théologie moderne', *Lettre* 320-1, Paris 1985, 5-13; E.Gellner, *Legitimation of Belief*, London 1974; L.Gilkey, 'Ervaring en interpretatie van de religieuze dimensie: een reactie', *Tijdschrift voor Theologie* 11, 1971, 293-302; C.Y.Glock and R.Start, *Religion and Society in Tension*, Chicago 1965; G.Gusdorf, *Mythe et métaphysique*, Paris 1953; W.D.Hudson, *Wittgenstein and Religious Belief*, London 1975; F.A.Isambert, *Le sens du sacré*, Paris 1982; W.James, *The Varieties of Religious Experience*, New York and London 1902; A.E.Jensen, *Mythos und Kultus bei Naturvölker*, Wiesbaden 1951; E.Jüngel, *God as the Mystery of the World*, Grand Rapids and Edinburgh 1983; G.Kaufman, *God. The Problem*, Cambridge, Mass. 1972; H.Küng, *Does God Exist?*, London and New York 1980; J.van der Lans, *Religieuze ervaring en meditatie*, Nijmegen 1978; V.Larock, *La pensée mythique*, Paris 1945; B.Lonergan, *Philosophy of God and Theology*, London 1973; H.Lübbe and H.M.Sass (eds.), *Atheismus in der Diskussion. Kontroversen um L.Feuerbach*, Munich 1975; T.Luckman, *The Invisible Religion*, London 1967; H.van Luyk, *Philosophie du fait chrétien*, Paris and Bruges 1964; B.Martin, *A Sociology of Contemporary Cultural Change*, Oxford 1981; M.Mauss, *Sociologie et Anthropologie*, Paris 1960; T.Munson, *Reflective Theology*, New Haven and London 1968; H.Richard Niebuhr, *Christ Against Culture*, New York 1951; W.A.de Pater, *Taalanalytische perspectieven op godsdienst en kunst*, Antwerp 1970, see *Analogy, Disclosures and Narrative Theology*, Louvain 1988; E.Paus, *Jesus Christus und die Religionen*, Graz 1980; J.Pohier, *God in Fragments*, London and New York 1985; J.Ratzinger (ed.), *Die Frage nach Gott*, Quaestiones Disputatae 56, Freiburg [4]1977; T.and Anthony D.Robbins (eds.), *In Gods we Trust. New Patterns of Religious Pluralism in America*, New York 1981; M.Scheler, *On the Eternal in Man*, London 1960; E.Schillebeckx (ed.), *J.B.Metz zu Ehren. Mystik und Politik*, Mainz 1988; H.R.Schlette, *Skeptische Religionsphilosophie*, Freiburg 1972; P.Schoonenberg, 'Denken naar God toe', *Tijdschrift voor Theologie* 17, 1977, 117-30, and *Auf Gott hin denken*, Vienna 1986; N.Schreurs, 'Naar de basis van ons spreken over God: de weg van Langdon Gilkey', *Tijdschrift voor Theologie* 11, 1971, 275-92; N.Smart, *The Phenomenology of Religion*, London 1973; id., *Reasons and Faith*, London 1958; W.Cantwell Smith, *The Meaning and End of Religion: A New Approach to the Religious Traditions of Mankind*, New York and London 1963; F.Sontag and M.Bryant, *God: The Contemporary Discussion*, New York 1982; H.Sunden, *Gott erfahren*, Gütersloh 1975; R.Towler, *The Need for Certainty. A Sociological Study of Conventional Religion*, London and Boston 1984; id., *Homo Religiosus*, London 1977; P.H.Vrijhof and J.Waardenburg (eds.), *Official and Popular Religion*, The Hague 1979; J.Waardenburg, *Reflections on the Study of Religion*, The Hague 1978; C.Waayman, *Betekenis van de naam Jahwe*, Kampen 1984; B.Welte, *Religionsphilosophie*, Freiburg 1978; A.N.Whitehead, *Religion in the Making*, New York 1926; J.R.Williams, *M.Heidegger's Philosophy of Religion*, Waterloo 1977; B.R.Wilson, *The Social Impact of New Religions*, London and New York 1981.

## Notes

1. N. Elias, *Über den Prozess der Zivilization*, Bern and Munich [2]1969, particularly the new introduction, pp. xliii-lxx; id., *Wat is sociologie?*, Utrecht 1971; A.Blok, *Wittgenstein en Elias. Een methodische richtlijn voor de antropologie* (inaugural lecture), Nijmegen; id., 'On the Comparative Understanding of Non-Modern Civilizations', *Daedalus* 1975, 153-72; id., *Homo Hierarchicus*, Paris 1967; H.Richter, *Der Gotteskomplex. Die Geburt und die Krise des Glaubens an die Allmacht des Menschen*, Hamburg 1979.

2. See e.g P.Berger, B.Berger and H.Kellner, *Homeless Mind*, New York 1974; P.Berger, *The Heretical Imperative*, New York and London 1980; L.Gilkey, *Reaping the Whirlwind*, New York 1977.

3. Berger, *Heretical Imperative* (n.2), 28.

4. Ibid., 95-124.

5. Above all Richter, *Gotteskomplex* (n.1), 155-62.

6. The word comes from Berger et al., *Homeless Mind* (n.2), 159-78.

7. G.Gutiérrez, *The Power of the Poor in History*, Maryknoll and London, 90-4; J.Sobrino, *Christology at the Crossroads: A Latin American Approach*, Maryknoll and London 1978, 7-37.

8. The 1980 Sao Paolo conference: *The Challenge of Basic Christian Communities*, ed S.Torres and J.Eagleson, Maryknoll 1981, 225-43.

9. H.Albert, *Das Elend der Theologie. Kritische Auseinandersetzung mit Hans Küng*, Hamburg 1979; Hans Küng, *Does God Exist?*, London and New York 1980.

10. See C.Hartshorne, *A Natural Theology for our Time*, La Salle, Illinois 1967, 3.

11. Ibid., 4f.

12. M.Horkheimer, *Eclipse of Reason*, New York 1974, 93.

13. In the next chapter we shall see that in the Jewish-Christian tradition the prohibition against making images of God is connected with the fact that God,

given his own nature, has reserved this privilege for himself. God himself made human beings 'in the image and likeness of God' (Gen.1.27), and finally he made the man Jesus 'the image of the invisible God' (Col.1.15).

14. Richter, *Gotteskomplex* (n.1), 29, 40f., 63.

15. Thus H.D.Lewis, quoted by J.J.Shepherd, *Experience, Inference, and God*, London 1975, 13.

16. Shepherd, *Experience* (n.15), 14-17; H.Kuitert, 'Ervaring als toegang tot de godsdienstige werkelijkheid', *Nederlands Tijdschrift voor Theologie* 32, 1982, 195. See Y.Labbé, *Humanisme et Theologie*, Paris 1975; J.Saward, 'Towards an Apophatic Theology', in *Irish Theological Quarterly* 41, 1974, 222-34; H.Waldenfels, *Absolutes Nichts*, Freiburg 1976; William S.Johnson, *The Search for Transcendence*, New York 1974.

17. As far as I can see, the phrase 'defenceless superior power' comes from H.Berkhof, *Christian Faith*, Grand Rapids 1988, section 22. See also P.Schoonenberg, 'Denken naar God toe', *Tijdschrift voor Theologie* 17, 1977, 118-30; H.Häring, 'Het kwaad als vraag naar Gods almacht en machteloosheid', ibid. 26, 1986, 351-72; N.Schreurs, *Die (in) alles voorziet? Gods voorziening handelen in de geschiedenis* (Inaugural Lecture), Tilburg 1985; E.Schillebeeckx, 'Doubt in God's Omnipotence: "When bad things happen to good people"', in *For the Sake of the Gospel*, London and New York 1989, 88-102.

18. Peter de Rosa, *The Best of All Possible Worlds*, Niles, Illinois 1976.

19. H.S.Kuschner, *When Bad Things Happen to Good People*, London and New York 1981.

20. D.Bonhoeffer, *Letters and Papers from Prison. The Enlarged Edition*, ed.E. Bethge, London and New York 1971, 361.

21. *A New Catechism. Catholic Faith for Adults*, London 1967, 495-502.

22. E.Levinas, *Totalité et Infini*, The Hague 1961, 201; cf. also *Autrement qu'être ou au-delà de l'essence*, The Hague 1974.

23. 'To welcome others is to put my freedom in question' (*Totalité*, 58).

24. 'An asymmetrical relation with the other who, infinite, opens up time and transcends and dominates subjectivity' (ibid., 210).

25. Ibid., 51.

26. Ibid., 53.

27. 'The self is not transcendent in relation to the other in the same sense that the other is transcendent in relation to me' (ibid., 201).

28. Ibid., 59.

29. Ibid.

30. Labbé, *Humanisme et Théologie* (n.16).

31. See the detailed analysis of this phenomenon in J.Pohier, *God in Fragments*, London and New York 1985, 261-314 (though here and there I feel that qualifications should be made).

32. C.Schmitt, *Politische Theologie. Vier Kapitel zur Lehre von der Souveränität*, Munich and Leipzig ²1934.

## Chapter 3

*Bibliography*

G.Anderson and T.Stransky (eds.), *Faith Meets Faith*, New York 1981; id., *Christ's Lordship and Religious Pluralism*, New York 1981: E.Benz, *Ideen zu einer Theologie der Religionsgeschichte*, Mainz 1961; H.Berkhof, *Christian Faith*, Grand Rapids 1986; J.Blank, *Vom Urchristentum zur Kirche*, Munich 1982; id., *Der Jesus des Evangeliums*, Munich 1981; J.Bowden, *Jesus: The Unanswered Questions*, London and Nashville 1988; H.Brück, *Möglichkeiten und Grenzen einer Theologie der Religionen*, Berlin 1979; H.Bürckle, *Einführung in die Theologie der Religionen*, Darmstadt 1977; R.Bureau, *Le Peril Blanc. Propos d'un ethnologue sur l'Occident*, Paris 1978; J.M. van Cangh (ed.), *Salut universel et regard pluraliste*, Collections Relais-Etude 1, Paris 1986; L.Caperan, *Le Problem du salut des infidèles*, Toulouse 1934; P.Clastres, *La société contre l'État*, Paris 1974; H.Küng and J.Moltmann (eds.), *Concilium* 183, 1986, *Christianity among the World Religions*; Y.Congar, *Diversity and Communion*, London 1984, and 'Die Weseneigenschaften der Kirche', in *Mysterium Salutis* IV.1, ed.J.Feiner and M.Löhrer, Einsiedeln 1972, 357-94; C.Davis, *Christ and the World Religions*, New York 1971; V.Drehsen, H.Häring, K.-J.Kuschel, H.Siemers and M.Baumotte (eds.), *Wörterbuch des Christentums*, Gütersloh and Zurich 1988; E.Drewermann, *Tiefenpsychologie und Exegese*, two vols, Olten 1984-5; T.F.Driver, *Christ in a Changing World*, New York and London 1981; C.Duquoc, *Dieu différent*, Paris 1977; id., *Libération et progressisme*, Paris 1987; J.-M.Ela, *Le cri de l'homme Africain*, Paris 1980; H.M.Enomiya-Lassalle, *Wohin geht der Mensch?*, Zurich, Einsiedeln and Cologne 1981; A.Geense, 'Der Dialog der Religionen und das Bekenntnis der Kirche', *Kerygma und Dogma* 26, 1980, 264-76; H.Häring, T.Schoof and A.Willems (eds), *Meedenken met E.Schillebeeckx*, Baarn 1983; A.Halder (ed.), *Sein und Schein der Religionen*, Düsseldorf 1983; B.Hebblethwaite, *The Incarnation*, Cambridge 1987; J.Hick, *God and the Universe of Faiths*, London 1973; id., *God has Many Names*, London 1980; id., and P.F.Knitter (eds.), *The Myth of Christian Uniqueness. Toward a Pluralistic Theology of Religions*, London 1987; A.Houtepen, *People of God*, London 1984; O.Karrer, *Das Religiöse in der Menschheit und das Christentum*, Frankfurt 1934; W.Kasper, *Absolutheit des Christentums*, Freiburg 1979; P.F.Knitter, *No Other Name? A Critical Survey of Christian Attitudes towards the World Religions*, Maryknoll and London 1985; H.Küng, *Christianity and the World Religions*, New York and London 1987; R.Lenze, *Die äusserchristlichen Religionen bei Hegel*, Göttingen 1975; A.T.van Leeuwen, *De macht van het kapitaal. Door het oerwoud van de economie naar de bronnen van de burgerlijke religie*, Nijmegen 1984; J.van Lin, *Jezus Christus en andersgelovigen in Nederland*, Kampen 1988; N.Lohfink, *Bibelauslegung im Wandel*, Frankfurt 1967, 107-28; G.Mensching, *Toleranz und Wahrheit in der Religion*, Heidelberg 1955; id., *Der offene Tempel. Die Weltreligionen in Gesprach miteinander*, Stuttgart 1974; W.Molinski (ed.), *Die vielen Wege um Heil. Heilsanspruch und Heilsbedeutung nichtchristlicher Religionen*, Munich 1969; J.Neuner (ed.), *Christian Revelation and World Religions*, London 1967; W.Oelmuller (ed.), *Wahrheitsansprüche der Religionen heute*, Paderborn 1986; C.van Ouwerkerk, A.Denaux, W.Logister and R.van Rossum, 'Jezus, der Enige', *Tijdschrift voor Theologie* 28, 1988, no.3; T.Ohm, *Die Liebe zu Gott in den nichtchristlichen Religionen*, Freiburg 1950;

R.Panikkar, *The Unknown Christ of Hinduism*, New York 1964; W.Pannenberg, *Basic Questions in Theology* (two vols), London and Philadelphia 1971, 1972; J.Pelikan, *Jesus Through the Centuries*, New Haven 1986; K.Rahner, 'Christianity and the Non-Christian Religions', in *Theological Investigations* 5, 1966, 115-34, see also 9, 1972, 145-64; 16, 1979, 199-226; 18, 1983, 288-95; summed up in *Foundations of Christian Faith*, New York and London 1978; T.Rendtorff (ed.), *Religion als Problem der Aufklärung*, Göttingen 1980; H.R.Schlette, *Die Religionen als Thema der Theologie. Überlegungen zu einer Theologie der Religionen*, Quaestiones Disputatae 22, Freiburg 1964; id., *Skeptische Religionsphilosophie*, Freiburg 1972; H.R.Schlette (ed.), *Aporie und Glaube*, Munich 1970; M.Seckler, 'Sind Religionen Heilswege?' in *Stimme der Zeit* 186, 1970, 187-94; id., 'Theologie der Religionen mit Fragezeichen', *Theologische Quartalschrift* 166, 1986, 164-84; R.Sesterhenn (ed.), *Das Schweigen der Religionen*, Munich 1983; N.Smart, *The Phenomenon of Christianity*, London 1979; W.C.Smith, in John Hick and Brian Hebblethwaite (eds.), *Christianity and Other Religions*, London and Philadelphia 1980, 87-107; id., *Towards a World Theology*, Philadelphia and London 1981; P.Steinacker, *Die Kennzeichen der Kirche*, 1982; A.Strobel, *Die Stunde der Wahrheit. Untersuchungen zu Strafverfahren gegen Jesus*, WUNT 21, Tübingen 1980,esp. 61-94; W.Strolz and H.Waldenfels (ed.), *Christliche Grundlagen des Dialogs mit den Weltreligionen*, Quaestiones Disputatae 98, Freiburg 1983; W.Strolz, *Heilswege der Weltreligionen*, two vols, Freiburg 1984-1986; G.Thils, *Propos et problèmes de la théologie des religions non-chrétiennes*, Tournai 1966; C.Thoma, *Christliche Theologie des Judentums*, Aschaffenburg 1978; D.Tracy, *Plurality and Ambiguity. Hermeneutics, Religion, Hope*, New York and London 1987; J.Verkuyl, *Zijn alle godsdiensten gelijk?*, Kampen 1984; H.Waldenfels, 'Der Absolutheitsanspruch des Christentums und die grossen Weltreligionen', *Hochland* 62, 1970, 202-17; id., *Absolutes Nichts. Zur Grundlegung des Dialogs zwischen Buddhismus und Christentum*, Freiburg im Breisgau ³1980; id., 'Ist der christliche Glaube der einzig wahre? Christentum und nichtchristlichen Religionen', *Stimmen der Zeit* 112, 1987, 463-75; id., *Kontextuelle Fundamentaltheologie*, Paderborn 1985, 193-9; id., *Der Gekreuzigte und die Weltreligionen*, Zurich 1983; id., 'Theologie der nichtchristlischen Religionen. Konsequenzen aus *Nostra Aetate*', in E.Klinger and K.Wittstadt (eds.), *Glaube im Prozess (FS K.Rahner)*, Freiburg 1984, 757-76; A.Willems, 'De absoluutheid en uitsluitendheid van het christendom', *Tijdschrift voor Theologie* 8, 1968, 125-39.

For the position of Vatican II, the decree *Nostra Aetate* on the non-Christian religions, see J.Oesterreicher, 'Das Zweite Vatikanische Konzil', *Lexikon für Theologie und Kirche* 2, 206-78 (prehistory and exegesis of the text); C.B.Papili, 'Christentum und Hinduismus', 2, 478-82; H.Dumoulin, 'Christentum und Buddhismus', 2, 482-5; G.C.Anawati, 'Christentum und Islam', 485-7.

*Notes*

1. Of the vast amount of exegetical literature see above all A.Stock, *Einheit des Neuen Testaments*, Zurich 1969; J.Blank, 'Jesus Christus/Christologie', in *Neues Handbuch theologischer Grundbegriffe*, Munich 1984, 2, 226-39; and my *Jesus*, passim.

2. See my *Jesus*, 62-76: expressed even more strongly in *God is New Each*

*Moment*, Edinburgh and New York 1983, 20-2; see *The Church with a Human Face*, London and New York 1985, 24-33.

3. *Jesus*, 44-6.

4. C.Duquoc, 'Enjeux théologiques d'un débat d'exégèse', *Lumière et Vie* no.175; id., *Histoire et vérité de Jésus Christ*, Paris 1986, 75-86. See already, but in a less evocative form, his *Dieu different*, Paris 1977.

5. In this sense Bultmann's position is in line with that of Karl Barth, who prizes not so much a positivism of revelation (though this is implicit in his theory) as a positivism of tradition which can be interpreted in a somewhat more favourable sense along the lines of the analysis by P.Berger, namely a new experience of the power of his own religious experiential tradition. P.Berger analysed this in *The Heretical Imperative*, 102-17.

6. Duquoc, 'Enjeux théologiques' (n.4), 81.

7. The same literature as in n.1.

8. M.E.Boring, *Sayings of the Risen Jesus. Christian Prophecy in the Synoptic Tradition*, Cambridge 1982; H.Kraft, *Die Enstehung des Christentums*, Darmstadt 1981; J.B.Gabus, *Critique du discours théologique*, Neuchâtel 1977; E.Schüssler Fiorenza, *In Memory of Her*, New York and London 1983.

9. For the distinctive image of God in the parables see W.G.Kümmel, *Heilsgeschehen und Geschichte. Gesammelte Aufsätze 1933-1964*, Marburg 1965; J.Dupont, *Études sur les Évangiles Synoptiques*, two vols., Louvain/Gembloux 1985; H.Merklein, *Die Gottesherrschaft als Handlungsprinzip. Untersuchung zur Ethik Jesu*, Forschung zur Bibel 34, Würzburg 1981; J.Zumstein, *La condition du croyant dans l'Évangile selon Mathieu*, Orbis Biblicus et Orientalis 16, Fribourg and Göttingen 1977, 407-16; H.Merklein and E.Zenger, 'Ich will euer Gott werden', *Beispiele biblischen Redens von Gott*, Bibelstudien 100, Stuttgart 1981, 152-76.

10. *Jesus*, above all 259-71, 637, 648, 652-69.

11. R.Brown, *Jesus. God and Man*, Milwaukee 1967, 23-38; see also J.Milet, *God or Christ? The Excesses of Christocentricity*, London and New York 1981; D.A.Lane, *The Reality of Jesus. An Essay in Christology*, New York 1975.

12. '*Defectus gratiae prima causa est ex nobis*', *Summa Theologiae* I-II, q.112, a.3.ad 2.

13. See e.g. H.Wolff, 'The Kerygma of the Jahwist', *Interpretation* 20, 1966, 131-58; R.Clements, *Abraham and David*, SBT II 5, London 1967; W.Brueggemann, 'David and his Theologian', *Catholic Biblical Quarterly* 39, 1968, 156-81; id., 'From Dust to Kingship', *Zeitschrift für die alttestamentliche Wissenschaft* 84, 1972, 1-18; B.Mazar, 'The Historical Background of the Book Genesis', *Journal of Near Eastern Studies* 28, 1969, 73-83. See further literature in my *Christ*, 882.

14. See *Jesus*, 172-9.

15. Some recent literature on the term *ekklesia* and on church theology (earlier literature is easily accessible through the bibliographies in these books): R.Banks, *Paul's Idea of Community. The Early House Churches in their Historical Setting*, Grand Rapids 1980; K.Berger, 'Volksversammlung und Gemeinde Gottes. Zu den Anfängen der christlichen Verwendung von *ekklesia*', *Zeitschrift für Theologie und Kirche* 73, 1976, 167-207; L.Boff, *Ecclesiogenesis: The Base Communities Reinvent the Church*, New York and London 1986; id., *Church, Charism*

256 *Church*

*and Power*, London and New York 1985; C.G.Brandis, 'Ekklesia', *PW* 5, 1905, 2163-200; R.E.Brown, 'New Testament Background for the Concept of the Local Church', *Proceedings of the CTSA* 36, 1981, 1-14; C.Duquoc, *Provisional Churches. An Essay in Ecumenical Ecclesiology*, London 1986; J.Hainz, *Ekklesia. Strukturen Paulinischer Gemeinde-Theologie und Gemeinde-Ordnung*, Regensburg 1972; A.Houtepen, *People of God*, London 1984; G.Lohfink, *Die Sammlung Israels. Eine Untersuchung zur Lukanischen Ekklesiologie*, STANT 39, Munich 1975; id., 'Hat Jesus seine Kirche gestiftet?', *Theologische Quartalschrift* 161, 1981, 81-97; id., *Jesus and Community. The Social Dimension of Christian Faith*, London and Philadelphia 1985; H.Merklein, 'Die Ekklesia Gottes. Der Kirchenbergriff bei Paulus und in Jerusalem', *BZ* 23, 1979, 480-70; W.Pannenberg, *Thesen zur Theologie der Kirche*, Munich 1970; H.Rikhof, *The Concept of Church*, London 1981; E.Schillebeeckx, *The Church with a Human Face*, London and New York 1985, 42ff.; R.Schnackenburg (ed.), *Die Kirche des Anfangs*, Leipzig 1977; W.Schrage, 'Ekklesia und Synagoge. Zum Ursprung des urchristlichen Kirchengbegriffs', *ZTK* 6, 1963, 178-202; F.Schüssler Fiorenza, *Foundational Theology. Jesus and the Church*, New York 1984; J.A.van der Ven (ed.), *Toekomst voor de kerk? Studies voor F.Haarsma*, Kampen 1985; id., *Jésus et l'Église*, BETL 77, Louvain 1987; id., *Tussen utopie en berusting. Over kerk-zijn vandaag*, Louvain and Amersfoort 1984.

16. Schrage, 'Ekklesia und Synagoge' (n.15).

17. Merklein, 'Ekklesia Gottes', and Schüssler Fiorenza, *Foundational Theology* (n.15).

18. The general literature on this theme is immeasurable. I have made a responsible selection, though it is perhaps not really representative: H.Ben Sasson (ed.), *Geschichte des jüdischen Volkes*, three vols, Munich 1978-80; W.Seifert, *Synagoge und Kirche im Mittelalter*, Munich 1964; J.Maier, *Geschichte der jüdischen Religion*, Berlin 1972; D.Goldschmidt and H.J.Kraus (eds.), *Der ungekündigte Bund*, Stuttgart 1962; S.Ben-Chorin, *Theologica Judaica*, Tübingen 1982; G.Mayer, *Ein Zaun um die Tora*, Studia Delitzschiana 15, Stuttgart 1973; C.Thoma, *Die theologischen Beziehungen zwischen Christentum und Judentum*, Darmstadt 1982; A.J.Peck, *Jews and Christians after the Holocaust*, Philadelphia 1982; P.von der Osten-Sacken, *Grundzüge einer Theologie im christlich-jüdischen Gespräch*, Munich 1982; J.Pawlikowski, *The Challenge of the Holocaust for Christian Theology*, New York 1978; A.T.Davies, *Anti-semitism and the Christian Mind*, New York 1969; E.P.Sanders, *Jesus and Judaism*, London and Philadelphia 1985.

19. S.Safrai and M.Stern (eds.), *The Jewish People in the First Century*, Vol.1, Assen 1974, 117-83.

20. P.Schäfer, *Geschichte der Juden in der Antike*, Neukirchen 1983, 145-55; P.Billerbeck, *Kommentar zum Neuen Testament aus Talmud und Midrasch*, IV.1, Munich 1928, 210; D.J.van der Sluis et al., *Elke morgen neu. Inleiding tot de Joodse gedachtenwereld aan de hand van een van de central Joodse gebeden. Sjemone Esre, het Achttiengebed*, Stichting voor Talmudica 1978, esp.293. See also three texts in the Fourth Gospel where the term *aposynagogos* refers to an exclusion from the synagogue (John 9.22; 12.42; 16.2).

21. See e.g. W.P.Eckert, N.P.Levinson and M.Stöhr (eds.), *Antijudaismus im Neuen Testament?*, Munich 1967.

22. Cf. above all Matt.22.1-14 par. 27.24-25; Mark 12.1-12; Luke 23.27-31; John 8.44; Acts 7.51-52; I Thess.2.15-16.

23. See the works by Ben-Sasson, Seifert, Maier, Goldschmidt and Kraus already cited.

24. See D.Zeller, *Juden und Heiden in der Mission des Paulus*, Stuttgart 1973; F.Hahn, *Mission in the New Testament*, SBT 47, London 1965; B.Mayer, *Unter Gottes Heilsratsbeschluss*, Würzburg 1974; F.Mussner, *Die Kraft der Wurzel*, Freiburg 1987; id., *Tractate on the Jews*, Philadelphia 1984; E.Graber, *Der Alte Bund im Neuen. Exegetische Studien zur Israelfrage im Neuen Testament*, WUNT 35, Tübingen 1975; E.Stegemann, 'Der Jude Paulus und seine antijüdische Auslegung', in R.Rendtorff and E.Stegemann, *Auschwitz: Krise der Christlichen Theologie*, Munich 1980, 117-39.

25. Here I prefer the last interpretation, which derives e.g. from F.Hahn, 'Paul and Paulinism', in *Essays in Honour of C.K.Barrett*, London 1982, 221-34.

26. See e.g. J.Baumgarten, *Paulus und die Apokalyptik*, Neukirchen-Vluyn 1975.

27. *Lumen Gentium* I.8.

28. H.Lübbe, 'Religion nach der Aufklärung', in H.Lübbe (ed.), *Philosophie nach der Aufklärung. Von der Notwendigkeit pragmatischer Vernunft*, Düsseldorf 1980, 59-86; id., *Religion nach der Aufklärung*, Graz and Cologne 1987.

29. In Germany it was above all O.Karrer, *Das Religiöse in der Menschheit und das Christentum*, who dealt extensively with this question as early as 1934. In France it was above all L.Caperan, *Le problème du salut des infidèles*, also in 1934! See also K.Adam, *The Spirit of Catholicism*, London 1928.

30. See the works by Rahner listed in the general bibliography.

31. H.Waldenfels, *Ist der christliche Glaube der einzig wahre?*, 470.

32. Seckler, *Theologie der Religionen mit Fragezeichen*, 178-81.

33. Schlette, *Die Religion als Thema der Theologie*, 66-112.

34. D.Barrett et al., *World Christian Encyclopedia. A Comparative Study of Churches and Religions in the Modern World, AD 1900-2000*, Nairobi and Oxford 1982.

35. Knitter, *No Other Name?*.

36. For monotheism as a political problem see E.Peterson, *Theologische Traktate*, Cologne 1951, esp.45-149.

37. See E.Wolf, *Europe and the People without History*, Berkeley and London 1982.

38. See e.g. J.-M.Van Cangh (ed.), *Salut universel et regard pluraliste*; also Mensching, *Toleranz und Wahrheit in der Religion*, 162-8.

39. This is also the view of Duquoc in his book *Dieu différent*, but see the following note.

40. In contrast to Duquoc, I do not refer to 'trinitarian symbolism' in order to provide a basis for this Christian view of other religions. I limit my argument to the uniqueness and at the same time historical contingency and thus limitedness of Jesus of Nazareth. Duquoc's position that the unity of the triune God is founded on a trinitarian multiplicity, through which the priority of pluralism over unity is said to be shown, seems to me to be philosophically and theologically unacceptable. For my view is that the oneness of the divine nature is the source and ground of the tri-'personality' of the one God, not that the

three persons form the basis of the unity of the divine nature. Moreover, how far can one call the three 'persons' a plurality in a monotheistic view of God? (In certain French theological tendencies the divine Trinity is in fact a kind of family.). Is there not a nonchalant switch here with the analogous character of categories like 'one' and 'many' as applied to God? And is not too little account taken here of a dialectical perichoresis – or mutual indwelling – in which unity and plurality hold each other in a mutual equilibrium? In that case for me pluralism in principle takes a different turn from the direction taken in Duquoc, for whom there seems to be no question of an implied but not thematized unity.

41. A.Pieris, 'Christentum und Buddhismus in Dialog aus der Mitte ihrer Traditionen', in A.Bsteh (ed.), *Dialog aus der Mitte christlicher Theologie*, Beiträge Religionstheologie 5, Vienna, Munich and Lucerne nd, 131-78, esp. 174-8. In the meantime two books by Pieris have appeared in the original English, *An Asian Theology of Liberation*, New York and London 1988, and *Love Meets Wisdom*, New York 1988.

42. Ibid., 177.

43. W.Pannenberg, *Theology and the Philosophy of Science*, London and New York 1974, 219.

44. Ibid., 219-20.

45. See my *Jesus*, 595-625, and for the question of universal meaning also *Christ*, 515-30.

46. H.Albert, *Der Positivismusstreit in der deutschen Soziologie*, Soziologische Texte 58, Neuwied and Berlin 1969, 193-324.

47. Pannenberg, *Theology and the Philosophy of Science*, 201.

48. J.B.Metz, *Faith in History and Society*, London and New York 1980, 60..

49. M.I.Lamb, 'The Theory-Praxis Relationship in Contempoary Christian Theologies', *Proceedings of the Catholic Theological Society of America, 31st Annual Convention*, Vol.31, Washington 1976, (149-78) 177.

50. See *Christ*, 728-30.

51. Pieris, *Asian Theology of Liberation* and *Love meets Wisdom* (n.41). See also the literature on mystical prayer in Chapter 2 and R.Lay, *Zukunft ohne Religion*, Olten 1970; Louis Dupré, *The Other Dimension*, New York 1972.

52. J.-M.Ela, *Le cri de l'homme Africain*, Paris 1980.

53. See also Vatican II, *Gaudium et spes* 53, and the amendments in *Expensio modorum* c.2.

## Chapter 4

### Bibliography

A.Acerbi, *Due Ecclesiologie. Ecclesiologia giuridica ed ecclesiologia di communione nella 'Lumen Gentium'*, Bologna 1967; P.Anderson, *Von der Antike zum Feudalismus. Spuren der Übergangsgesellschaften*, Frankfurt 1978, 219-53; H.Barth, *Wahrheit und Ideologie*, Zurich 1945; F.Borkenau, *Der Übergang vom feudalen zum bürgerlichen Weltbild*, Darmstadt ²1971; Y.Congar, *L'ecclésiologie au XIXᵉ siècle*, Paris 1960, esp.77-113; H.Dombois, *Hierarchie. Grund und Grenze einer umstrittener Struktur*, Freiburg 1971; H.Dumont, *Homo hierarchicus. Essai sur le système des castes*, Paris

1966; P.Eicher, *Offenbarung*, Munich 1977; also id., 'Priester und Laien – im Wesen verschieden?', in G.Denzler (ed.), *Priester für heute*, Munich 1980, 34-51; also id., 'Von den Schwierigkeiten bürgerlichen Theologie mit den katholischen Kirchenstrukturen', in K.Rahner and H.Fries (eds.), *Theologie in Freiheit und Verantwortung*, Munich 1981; J.Petuchowski and W.Strolz (eds.), *Offenbarung im jüdischen und christlichen Glaubensverständnis*, Freiburg 1981, 123-61; P.Eicher (ed.), 'Hierarchie', in *Neues Handbuch Theologischer Grundbegriffe* 2, Freiburg 1984, 177-96; I.Fetscher, *Herrschaft und Emanzipation. Zur politischen Philosophie des Bürgertums*, Munich 1975; B.Gladigow (ed.), *Staat und Religion*, Düsseldorf 1981; L.Goldmann, *Der christliche Bürger und die Aufklärung*, Neuwied and Darmstadt 1968; B.Groethuysen, *Die Entstehung der bürgerlichen Welt in Frankreich*, Frankfurt 1978; W.Jaeschke, *Die Suche nach den eschatologischen Wurzeln der Geschichtsphilosophie. Eine historische Kritik der Säkularisierungsthese*, Munich 1975; F.X.Kaufmann, *Kirche begreifen*, Freiburg, Basel and Vienna 1979: L.Kofler, *Zur Geschichte der bürgerlichen Gesellschaft*, Halle 1948, Darmstadt ⁷1979; H.Krings, *Freiheit als Chance – Kirche und Theologie unter den Anspruch der Neuzeit*. Munich 1972; id., 'System und Freiheit', in D.Henrich (ed.), *Ist systematische Theologie möglich?*, Bonn 1977, 35-51; J.B.Metz, *The Emergent Church. The Future of Christianity in a Postbourgeois World*, New York and London 1981; W.Näf, 'Frühformen des modernen Staates im Spätmittelalter', *Historische Zeitschrift* 171, 1951, 225-43; B.Nelson, *Der Ursprung der Moderne. Vergleichende Studien zum Zivilizationsprozess*, Frankfurt 1977; H.Pottmeyer, *Unfehlbarkeit und Souveränität*, Mainz 1975; T.Rendtorff, *Kirche und Theologie. Die systematische Funktion des Kirchenbegriffs in der neueren Theologie*, Gütersloh 1966; J.Ritter, *Hegel und die Französische Revolution*, Frankfurt 1956; D.Schellong, *Bürgertum und christliche Religion*, Munich 1975; W.Schneiders, *Die wahre Aufklärung*, Freiburg and Munich 1974; W.Schluchter, *Aspekte bürokratischer Herrschaft*, Munich 1972; M.Seckler, *Im Spannungsfeld von Wissenschaft und Kirche*, Freiburg 1980; N.Siegfried, *Actenstücke betreffend den preussischen Culturkampf*, Freiburg 1882; B.Wilmas, *Revolution und Protest oder Glanz und Elend de bürgerlichen Subjekts*, Stuttgart 1969; the issue is dealt with in *Christianity and the Bourgeoisie*, *Concilium* 125, 1979.

*Notes*

1. E.Herrmann, *Ecclesia in re publica. Die Entwicklung von pseudostaatlicher zu staatlich inkorporierter Existenz*, Frankfurt 1980.

2. *Schemata Constitutionum et Decretorum*, series secunda, Vatican City 1962, ch.1, nos.7, 12.

3. *Schema Constitutionis dogmaticae de Ecclesia*, pars prima, Vatican City 1963, ch.1, nos.2-4, 7-8.

4. Ibid., ch.1, nos.5, 9-10.

5. Ibid., ch.1, nos.7, 11.

6. Ibid.

7. *Relatio super caput primum textus emendati Schematis Constitutionis de Ecclesia*, Vatican City 1964, 3.

8. *Schema Constitutionis de Ecclesia*, Vatican City 1964, ch.1, nos.5, 9-10.

9. Ibid., ch.1., nos.7, 12-14.

10. *Relatio super caput primum* (n.7), 3.

11. Ibid., Ch.1, nos.8, 14-15.

12. *Schema Constitutionis de Ecclesia* (n.8), 15.

13. '*Loco* est *dicitur* subsistit in, *ut expressio melius concordet cum affirmatione de elementis ecclesialibus quae alibi adsunt*', in *Relationes de singulis numeris*, Relatio in no.8, 25.

14. *Relationes* (n.13), Relatio in no.8, 23.

15. Ibid.

16. Ibid.

17. Ibid., 23.

18. *Decretum de Oecumenismo*, Vatican City 1964, ch.1, no.4.

19. *Modi a Patribus conciliaribus propositi, a Commissione doctrinali examinati*, 1964, Chs.1,6. The commission did not want to go into this. On the other hand, the meaning of *subsistere in* is not to be rendered by a rather weak version as 'is actually found in' the Catholic Church. It is clearly meant by this council in a stronger sense: 'is *de iure* found in this church'. This is the wording of the draft of an amendment: '*Quod spectat ad additionem* iure divino *ex contextu paragraphi patet sermonem esse de institutione Christi*' (*Modi*, ibid., 6).

20. '*Alii... volunt apertiorem distinctionem inter Ecclesiam medium salutis et Ecclesiam fructum salutis. Quae distinctio iam satis videtur clara in textu*', in *Schema Constitutionis de Ecclesia*, 1964, relatio in no.8, p.24.

21. *Lumen Gentium*, ch.2, no.9.

22. *Lumen Gentium*, ch.1, no.8. See *Schema constitutionis de Ecclesia*, 1964, ch.1, no.8. The choice of the word *purificanda* above other suggested expressions is determined by the liturgical use of the formula *purificatio Ecclesiae* in the Roman Missal, e.g. on the first Quadragesima Sunday and the fifteenth Sunday after Pentecost. See *Schema Constitutionis de Ecclesia*, 1964, *Relationes de numeris*, in no.8, p.25. Of course many people here were influenced by a reluctance to take over directly the Reformation formula *Ecclesia semper reformanda*.

23. *Lumen Gentium*, ch.2, 9. It sounds over-pious and unctuous, remote from the prayer of most people, even Christians. If it is to be understandable and capable of being experienced, what is meant must be expressed in everyday language, even for Christians.

24. *Relationes de singulis numeris*, Relatio in no.8, p.23.

25. Ibid.

26. *Munus autem illud, quod Dominus pastoribus populi sui commisit verum est servitium quod in sacris libris diakonia seu ministerium significanter nuncupatur*, ibid., ch.3, no.24.

27. Ibid., ch.3, no.25.

28. Ibid., ch.3, no.25.

29. Ibid., ch.3, no.27.

30. Leo XII, encyclical *Annum sacrum*, ASS 31, 1898-99 (646-52) 647.

31. Pius IX, Apostolic Brief *Quanta Cura*, ASS 3, 1867-8 (160-7) 163.

32. *Syllabus*, ASS 3, 1867-68, 168-76.

33. Pius X, Encyclical *Pascendi*, ASS, 1907, (592-650) 613ff.

34. See N.Siegfried, *Actenstücke betreffend der preussischen Culturkampf*, Freiburg 1882, 99-100, quoted by Eicher in Rahner and Fries (ed.), *Theologie in Freiheit*, 122.

35. Siegfried, *Actenstücke* (n.35), 266. For the answer of the German bishops see ibid., 264-7. The pope approved the bishops' letter, ibid., 271.

36. Declaration of the German bishops at a celebration at the tomb of St Boniface, 20 September 1872, ibid., 133-50.

37. Denzinger-Schönmetzer, *Enchiridion*, 3074; see Mansi 52, (1330-1334) 1334.

38. Eicher, in Rahner/Fries, *Theologie in Freiheit*, 124.

39. *Syllabus* (n.32), 176.

40. Pius X, Decree of the Holy Office against any development in dogma, *Lamentabili*, ASS 40, 1907, 470-8.

41. Ibid., 477.

42. Ibid. The position is condemned that *Veritas non est immutabilis plus quam ipse homo, quippe quae cum ipso, in ipso et per ipsum evolvitur.*

43. Pius XII, Encyclical *Humani Generis*, AAS 42, 1950, (561-78) 566ff.

44. Pius X, Encyclical, *Pascendi* (n.33), 596.

45. Gregory XVI, encyclical *Mirari vos*, 1831, in ASS 4, 1868-69, (334-45) 341. Pius IX quotes this text later, in different circumstances. See Denzinger no.1690.

46. In the later editions of Denzinger this view of Pius IX (n.45), which is in fact worthless, is scrapped. These later editions adopt a church-political strategy: not damaging the 'image' of the church. Therefore historical documents are not mentioned!

47. '*Nuntius radiophonicus: Ai populi del mondo intero*', AAS 37, 1945, (10-23) 11-17.

48. See K.Walf, 'Die katholische Kirche – ein *Societas perfecta?*', *Theologische Quartalschrift* 157, 1977, 107-18; see also *Kirchenrecht*, Düsseldorf 1984.

49. J.H.Newman, *On Consulting the Faithful in Matters of Doctrine* (first appeared in *The Rambler*, July 1859, 198-230), ed. J.Coulson, London 1961.

50. See some literature (since Vatican II) on the church as mystery and communion: H.Küng, *The Church*, London and New York 1968; Y.Congar, 'Die Wesenseigenschaften der Kirche', in *Mysterium Salutis* IV.1, *Die Heilsgeschichte in der Gemeinde*, Einsiedeln 1972; J.Alberigo and F.Magistretti, *Constitutionis Dogmaticae Lumen Gentium Synopsis Historica*, Bologna 1975; O.Saier, *Communio in der Lehre des zweiten Vatikanischen Konzils. Eine rechtsbegriffliche Untersuchung*, Munich 1973; A.Houtepen, *People of God*. For the almost ideological use of the term 'mystery of the church' at the Synod of the Dutch Bishops (Rome, 14-31 January 1980) see the *Documenten* (edited by the secretariat of the Roman Catholic church province in the Netherlands, nd), 31-47; also the letter by Cardinal J.Willebrands in *Archief van de Kerken* 36, 1981, 477-82; H.Manders, 'Objectief en subjectief, norm en mondigheid. Een poging de besluiten van de Nederlandse Bischoppenconferentie te analyseren', in *Praktische Theologie* 7, 1980, 66f.; R.G.Ardelt, 'Anmerkungen zu antimodernistischen Ekklesiologie', in *Der Modernismus. Beiträge zu seiner Erforschung*, ed. E.Weinzierl, Graz, Vienna and Cologne 1974, 257-82; C.Duquoc, *La femme, le clerc et le laic*, Geneva 1989; H.Rikhof, *The Concept of Church. A Methodological Inquiry into the Use of Metaphors in Ecclesiology*, London 1981; also 'De kerk als "communio": een zinnige

uitspraak', in *Tijdschrift voor Theologie* 23, 1983, 39-59; and 'The Ecclesiologies of *Lumen Gentium*, the *Lex Ecclesiae Fundamentalis* and the Draft Code', *Concilium* 147, 1981, 54-63; H.J.Pottmeyer, 'Die zwiespältige Ekklesiologie des Zweiten Vatikanums – Ursache nachkonziliarer Konflikte', in *Trierer Theologische Zeitschrift* 92, 1983, 272-83.

51. See e.g. P.Berger and T.Luckman, *The Social Construction of Reality*, Harmondsworth 1977.

52. *Lumen Gentium*, ch.I no.8.

53. For 'church reception' see e.g. G.Gassmann, 'Rezeption in ökumenischen Kontext', *Oekumenische Rundschau* 26, 1977, 314-27; Y.Congar, 'La réception comme realité ecclésiologique', *Revue des Sciences Philosophique et Théologique* 56, 1972, 369-43; see also 'Reception as an Ecclesiological Reality', *Concilium* 1972, 7, 43-68; 'Norms of Christian Allegiance and Identity in the History of the Church', *Concilium* 1973, 9, 7-21; also 'Pour une histoire sémantique du terme "magisterium"', in *Revue des Sciences Philosophiques et Théologiques* 60, 1976, 85-98; P.Hegy, 'L'autorité dans le catholicisme contemporain', in *Du Syllabus à Vatican II*, Paris 1975; F.Wolfinger, 'Die Rezeption theologischer Einsichten und ihrer theologische und ökumenische Bedeutung', *Vox Cath* 31, 1977, 202-33; 'Rezeption – ein Zentralbegriff der ökumenischen Diskussion oder des Glaubensvollzugs', *Oekumenische Rundschau* 27, 1978, 14-21; P.Hojen, 'Wahrheit und Konsensus', in *Kerygma und Dogma* 23, 1977, 131-56; H.J.Sieben, *Die Konzilsidee der Alten Kirche*, Paderborn and Munich 1979; P.Lengsfeld and H.G.Strobe (eds.), *Theologischer Konsens und Kirchenspaltung*, Stuttgart, Berlin and Cologne 1981; M.Garijo, 'Der Begriff Rezeption und sein Ort im Kern der katholischen Theologie', ibid., 97-109; N.Afanasieff, 'L'Infaillibilité de l'Église du point de vue d'un théologien orthodoxe', in *L'Infaillibilité de l'Église*, Chevetogne 1962, 183-201; D.Dejaifve, '*Ex sese, non natum e consensu Ecclesiae*', in R.Baumer and H.Dolch (eds.), *Volk Gottes*, Freiburg 1967, 480-500; A.Houtepen, *Onfeilbaarheid en Hermeneutiek*, Bruges 1973.

54. See above all A.Faivre, *Naissance d'une hiérarchie. Les premiers étapes du cursus clérical*, Paris 1977; R.Hathaway, *Hierarchy and the Definition of Order in the Letters of Ps.-Dionysius*, The Hague 1969.

55. P.Berger, *The Heretical Imperative*, London and New York 1980, above all in connection with the case of F.Rosenzweig, 91-4.

56. '*Christi potestas et imperium in homines exercetur per veritatem, per iustitiam, maxime er caritatem*', in *In III Sent.*, d.13, q.2, see also *Summa Theologiae* III, q.8 and q.59, a.4.

57. See e.g. J.de Ghellinck, *Le mouvement théologique du XIIᵉ siècle, Museum Lessianum 10, Bruges and Paris* ²*1948*; M.D.Chenu, *La théologie au douxième siècle*, Paris ²1966; Y.Congar, 'Bref historique des formes du "magistère" et de ses rélations avec les docteurs', *Revue des Sciences Philosophiques et Théologiques*, 60, 1976, 99-112; id., 'Pour une histoire sémantique du terme magistère', in ibid. 60, 1976, 85-98; G.Posthumus Meyjes, Quasi stellae fulgebunt: *Plaats en functie van de theologische doctor in de middeleeuwse maatschappij en kerk*, Leiden 1979; J.van Laarhoven, 'Magisterium en theologie in de 12e eeuw: de processen te Soissons (1121), Sens (1140) en Reims (1148)', *Tijdschrift voor Theologie* 21, 1981, 109-31;

id., 'Kerk: Leerhuis of leerstoel? Naar een afweging van het magisterium van concilies', *Tijdschrift voor Theologie* 22, 1987, 277-9; G.Ackermans and J.van Laarhoven, 'Theologie tussen lof en blaam. De zaak Petrus Lombardus', *Tijdschrift voor Theologie* 29, 1989, 95-13; Report of the 1975 International Theological Commission: 'Thesen über das Verhältnis von kirchlichem Lehramt und Theologen zueinander', *Theologie und Philosophie* 52, 1977, 57-66; see also *Archief der Kerken* 31, 1976, 707-13; C.B.Daly, 'Magisterium and Theology', *Irish Theological Quarterly* 43, 1976, 225-46; R.Coffy, 'Magisterium and Theology', ibid., 247-59; P.Lengsfeld and H.G.Stobbe (eds.), *Theologischer Konsens und Kirchenspaltung*, Stuttgart 1981.

58. '*Docere sacram scripturam contingit dupliciter. Uno modo ex officio praelationis, sicut qui praedicat, docet. Alio modo ex officio magisterii, sicut magistri theologiae docent*' (Thomas, *In IV Sent.* d.19, q.2, a.2, qa 2, ad 4, see also *Quodlib*.III, q.4, a.1, ad.3).

59. See Chenu, *Théologie au 12ᵉ siècle, 323-65*.

60. *Corpus iuris canonici*, ed. A.Friedberg, 2, Leipzig 1879-1881, reprinted Graz 1955, 65.

## Chapter 5

### Notes

1. Since the study of the literature that I made in chapter 1 (where the mystical element in belief is mentioned), in this connection I can also refer to two new books: F.Maas, *Er is meer God dan we denken. Essays over spiritualiteit*, Averbode and Kampen 1989; J.Peters OCD, *Vlam. Meditaties om je an te warmen*, Hilversum 1988.

2. Martin Bogdahn (ed.), *Konzil des Friedens. Aufruf und Echo* (with a detailed explanation by C.F.Weizsäcker), Munich 1986, see C.F.von Weizsäcker, *Die Zeit drängt*, Munich 1986; J.Moltmann, *God in Creation. An Ecological Doctrine of Creation*, London and New York 1985; D.Sölle, *Lieben und Arbeiten. Eine Theologie der Schöpfung*, Stuttgart 1985.

3. E.g. A.Vögtle, *Das Evangelium und die Evangelien*, Düsseldorf 1971.

4. This is not a fashionable adaptation to later trends, which is what some individals have accused me of. I was already writing substantially the same thing in 1974 and even in 1960. See E.Schillebeeckx, 'Partnership tussen mens en natuur', in H.Bouma, *De aarde is er ook nog*, Wageningen 1974, 76-88, and at the opening of the Nijmegen University Animal Laboratory in 1960 I gave a lecture on 'The Animal in Man's World', see *Katholiek Artsenblad* 39, 1960, 58-63; later included in *World and Church*, London 1971, 256-68.

5. See e.g. O.H.Steck, *Der Schöpfungsbericht der Priesterschrift*, Göttingen 1975; N.Lohfink, *Unsere Grossen Wörter. Das Alte Testament zu Themen dieser Jahre*, Freiburg 1977.

# Index of Authors

In this index I have included only authors to whom direct reference has been made.

The Roman numerals refer to chapters of this book; the following numeral refers to the page in the text or that containing the most important literature which precedes the notes to each chapter. The indication n. (without page number) marks a reference to the notes to a particular chapter.

Acerbi, A., IV.258
Ackermans, G., IV n.57
Adam, K. III n.29
Afansieff, N., IV n.53
Alberigo, G., IV n.50
Albert, H., II.55, II n.9, III.174, III n.46
Altizer, T. J. J., II.87
Anderson, G., III.253
Anderson, P., IV.258
Ardelt, R. G., IV n.50
Auer, A., I.247

Bacon, F., I.2
Banks, R., III n.15
Barrett, D., III n.34
Barth, H., IV.258
Barth, K., III n.5
Baum, G., I.247
Baumer, R., IV n.53
Baumgarten, J., III n.26
Baumotte, M., III.253
Beauchamp, P., II.250
Bellah, R., II.250
Ben-Chorin, S., III n.18
Ben-Sasson, H., III n.18
Benz, E., III.253
Berger, B., I n.8, II n.2
Berger, P., I nn. 8, 27, II.46, 51, II nn.2, 3, 4, 6, III.136, III n.5, IV.219, IV nn.51, 55
Berkhof, H., II.250; II n.17; III.253
Billerbeck, P., III n.20
Bloch, E., II n.1
Bochinger, E., I.247
Boff, C., I.247
Boff, L., III n.15
Bogdahn, M., V n.3
Bonhoeffer, D., II.87, 89; II n.20
Boring, M. E., III n.8

Borkenau, F., IV.258
Bowden, J., III.253
Bowker, J., II.250
Brandis, C. G., III n.15
Bremond, C., I.247
Brown, R., III nn.11, 15
Brück, H., III.253
Brueggemann, W., III n.13
Bryant, M. D., II.251
Bsteh, A., III n.41
Buber, M., II.71
Bultmann, R., III.106, 127
Bureau, R., III.253
Bürckle, H., III.253
Butler, B. C., IV.191

Camus, A., II.95
Cangh, J. M. van, III.253, III n.38
Caperan, L., III.253, III n.29
Cassirer, E., II.250
Cazeneuve, J., II.250
Chenu, M.–D., IV nn.57, 59
Christian, A., II.250
Clastres, P., III.253
Clements, R., III n.13
Coffy, R., IV n.57
Compagnioni, F., I.248
Congar, Y., III.253, IV.258, IV nn.50, 53, 57
Coulson, J., IV n.49
Cupitt, D., II.250

Daly, C. B., IV n.57
Daniélou, J., III.161
Davies, A. T., III n.189
Davis, C., III.253
Dejaifve, D., IV n.53
Denaux, A., III.253
Denzler, G., IV.259